Introduction

What will Launch Your Android App cover?

Everything from installing Android Studio through deploying your Android app to the Google Play store.

Learn As You Read

Read the book and see every screenshot you'll encounter as you actually develop your app. Then, when you sit down to write your own app you will speed through development.

Focus On Running Apps

The main focus is on getting your App running. You will learn how to develop Android apps, but we will always focus on running your app on emulators and devices. Deploying code to devices and emulators requires a few tricks and this book will empower you to be able to deploy to those devices so you can see your app run everywhere.

Android Development Core Concepts

You will learn all of the core concepts that Android is built upon.

You'll learn layouts (User Interface design). Lot's of challenges.
You'll learn about Activities (the screens or forms) where your app code runs which make up your application.
How to start and use Intents (built-in functionality which enables you to retrieve web pages, make phone calls, vibrate the device and much more).

Why Learn Android Development?

There are numerous reasons to learn to create your own Android apps.

1. As an introduction to the programming world. Maybe you are interested in what programmers do and you would like to know if it is something you'd like to do. This book will make a great introduction for those who are starting out.
2. For personal pleasure - hopefully you are interested in seeing your own creations become real. You can write your own apps, run them on your phone and give them to all your Android-friends.
3. To create your own apps. Maybe you want to create a solution with an app that you can't find -- at least a reasonably good version that you trust.
4. To build a career (to make money) Android devices (phones, tv, wearables) are everywhere. Literally 100s of millions of devices out there. The person who knows how to create Android apps will likely have many opportunities to earn a living

How Will This Book Work?

No matter what level you are at, you will learn the essential skills and understand the code you need to create your first Android application while reading this book.
However, even if you're already a developer this book will help you.
Here's why this book can be read both by advanced developers and the very newest beginners.

As I said earlier, this book always targets the working / running app as the goal.

That means we will write applications that automate interesting activities and run.

The code will be explained as we go, so if you are an advanced user and you understand how the code works you won't be held back from skimming the code, building and running the app. You can focus on the parts you need more information about.

However, if you are a beginner and need more explanation, read the details that explain the more difficult parts so that you understand what the code does before moving on.

Beginner Help Extras

Instead of slowing down the more advanced developers with the extras which explain the small details, I will provide supplementary material that will provide extra examples and explanation for items which may overwhelm the newer programmer. These will be kept out of the way for advanced devs but easily accessible for beginners.

I will also do some organization work which will break the content into chapters that cover specific topics so that if a person understands the material in the chapter she can skip it and move directly to the material which better meets her needs.

Throughout the narrative, Launch Your Android App will always focus on writing code and building apps, because that is how you actually learn to program.

The Power of the Write, Build, Run Loop

You will learn to code when you write, build and run code.
Each of these steps offers it's own challenge.

Write Challenge

Can you type the code that will compile? Do you understand the syntax of the commands? Do you know how to instantiate an object in Java? Do you know how to access the library which contains the functionality you need?

Build Challenge

Does the code compile? Is the code valid? If not, what do you do? How do you understand what Android Studio is telling you to change? One of the most powerful abilities in the programming world is the ability to understand the errors you are seeing and knowing how to get the errors to go away. You will learn to do this here. Gradle (Java build system) is a huge part of Android Studio and may drive you crazy. We'll learn how to control it and what to do when it fights us.

Run Challenge

Can you deploy the app somewhere (emulator or device) to get it running. Android apps cannot run on your windows or linux box. You have to deploy them.
Does the program crash before you even see the main Activity (form)? Does it crash immediately after you click the only button on the form? Does your program crash for some unknown reason when you attempt to get data from the Internet? These are logic errors within your code that are probably based upon your lack of understanding about how the components and functions you have built upon work.

The point of all these three challenges is that you must write, build and run code to learn how the entire Android App ecosystem works. The more you go through those challenges the more you will become familiar with the errors that may occur. The more you become familiar with the errors that may occur the more likely it is that when you get stuck in an odd situation you will be able to figure out how to get your app written, building and running again.

Large Number of Android Apps In This Book
That's why we will focus on a large number of apps in this book. Many of those apps will be small to prove a point in code, but they will also test you through the three challenges we just mentioned (Write Code, Build, Run).

Complete Apps

We will also finish at least 5 fully developed applications and deploy them to the Google Play store.
This will take you through the complete development cycle of an Android app and provide you with validation that if you finish the book, you will be a professional app developer.

Blast Off!

I'm interested in writing code, building and running it so I'm not going to tell you the history of Android or Android Studio or anything else. Instead, I'm going to walk you through how to get Android Studio (Version 1.5.1 as of this writing), install it and generate your first program.

Let's go!

Chapter 1
Intro To Java SDK and Getting Started

The Dream: Button-click Installation

I wish I could let you click a button on a web page at my site and everything you need to develop Android apps would be installed on your computer. However, that is just a dream. Everyone's computer is different -- running various versions of each (Operating System) OS, etc. so it's just not possible.

However, the knowledge you gain even while simply installing Android Studio and the supporting tools is all part of your learning. In other words, simply installing the development environment is valuable to you as a developer. Keep that in mind as we move through these steps and I'll try to reveal some extras that you may not have noticed that will become important to you later when you're developing your apps.

Get Android Studio

Android Studio is free from Google and you can get it at:
http://developer.android.com/sdk/index.html

There are some hardware and Operating System requirements.
You have run it on a Mac, Windows or Linux system.
Since Android Studio consumes quite a few resources (memory and CPU) on your machine, the faster the machine you have and the more memory you have the better.

Emulator Eats Your Computer

Also, at times we will be running an Android emulator on our development computers. That emulator is basically the Android OS running inside your computer. That means it will be borrowing your CPU and memory also.

As of 2015-02-05 here are the basic requirements (straight from the Google site) so you will know what you need:

- Microsoft® Windows® 8/7/Vista (32- or 64-bit)

- 2 GB RAM minimum, 4 GB RAM recommended

- 400 MB hard disk space

- At least 1 GB for Android SDK, emulator system images, and caches

- 1280 x 800 minimum screen resolution

- Java Development Kit (JDK) 7

- Optional for accelerated emulator: Intel® processor with support for Intel® VT-x, Intel® EM64T (Intel® 64), and Execute Disable (XD) Bit functionality

+ Mine is at 1366x768 (below recommended width) and I don't experience any problems.
+ At least 1 GB - that's because for each version of Android OS you install (Jelly Bean 4.1.1, Jelly Bean 4.1.2) you are installing an entire OS again. It takes a lot of space and they're trying to warn you.
+ JDK 7 : Android code is written in a subset (and superset) of Java so you need the Java Development Kit. Notice that as of this writing, you still need the older version 7 (instead of the newer version 8) since Android doesn't support version 8 yet.

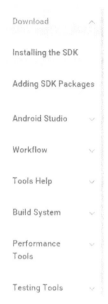

Download ∧

Installing the SDK

Adding SDK Packages

Android Studio ∨

Workflow ∨

Tools Help ∨

Build System ∨

Performance Tools ∨

Testing Tools ∨

- System Requirements

Download

Installing the SDK

Adding SDK Packages

Android Studio

Workflow

Tools Help

Build System

Performance Tools

Testing Tools

Support Library

Terms and Conditions

This is the Android Software Development Kit License Agreement

1. Introduction

1.1 The Android Software Development Kit (referred to in this License Agreeme including the Android system files, packaged APIs, and Google APIs add-ons) is of this License Agreement. This License Agreement forms a legally binding con relation to your use of the SDK.

1.2 "Android" means the Android software stack for devices, as made available Project, which is located at the following URL: http://source.android.com/, as u

☑ I have read and agree with the above terms and conditions

DOWNLOAD ANDROID STUDIO FOR WINDOWS

11

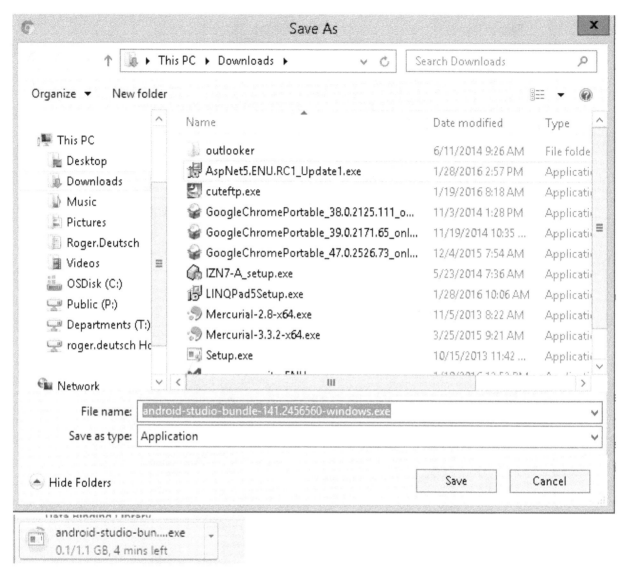

You can see that the download is 1.1GB so it might take a while, depending upon your Internet speed.

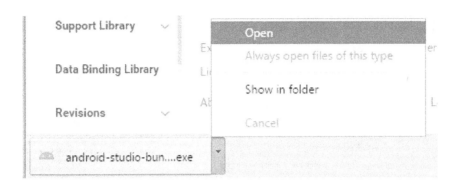

You can click "Open" or you can go to the folder where you downloaded the installation package and double-click it.

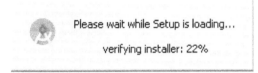

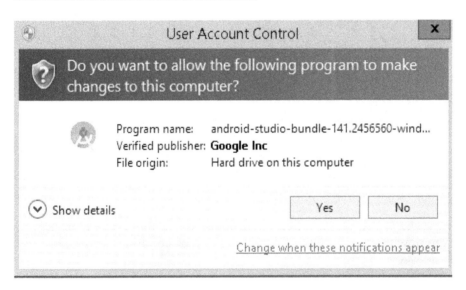

If you do not have a JDK (Java Development Kit) installed you will see a message like the following:

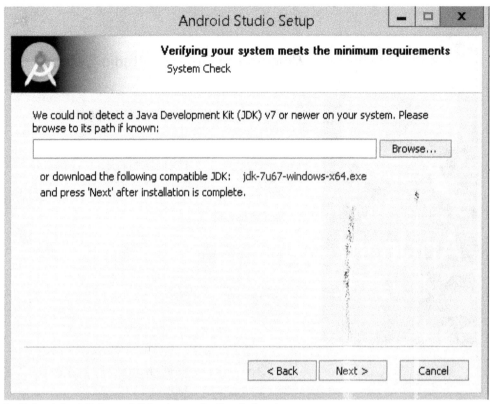

I clicked that link and it took me to the following page:

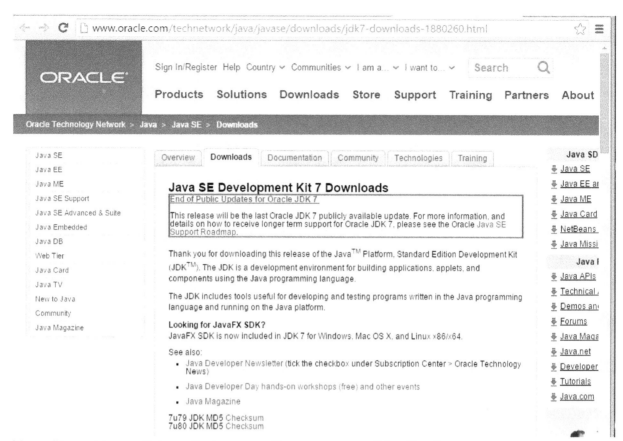

You will need to scroll down that page until you see something like the following:

Visit Java CPU and PSU Releases Explained for details.

Looking for JDK on ARM?
JDK 7 for ARM downloads have moved to the JDK 7 for ARM download page.

Java SE Development Kit 7u79

You must accept the Oracle Binary Code License Agreement for Java SE to download this software.

○ Accept License Agreement   ◉ Decline License Agreement

Product / File Description	File Size	Download
Linux x86	130.4 MB	jdk-7u79-linux-i586.rpm
Linux x86	147.6 MB	jdk-7u79-linux-i586.tar.gz
Linux x64	131.69 MB	jdk-7u79-linux-x64.rpm
Linux x64	146.4 MB	jdk-7u79-linux-x64.tar.gz
Mac OS X x64	196.89 MB	jdk-7u79-macosx-x64.dmg
Solaris x86 (SVR4 package)	140.79 MB	jdk-7u79-solaris-i586.tar.Z
Solaris x86	96.66 MB	jdk-7u79-solaris-i586.tar.gz
Solaris x64 (SVR4 package)	24.67 MB	jdk-7u79-solaris-x64.tar.Z
Solaris x64	16.38 MB	jdk-7u79-solaris-x64.tar.gz
Solaris SPARC (SVR4 package)	140 MB	jdk-7u79-solaris-sparc.tar.Z
Solaris SPARC	99.4 MB	jdk-7u79-solaris-sparc.tar.gz
Solaris SPARC 64-bit (SVR4 package)	24 MB	jdk-7u79-solaris-sparcv9.tar.Z
Solaris SPARC 64-bit	18.4 MB	jdk-7u79-solaris-sparcv9.tar.gz
Windows x86	138.31 MB	jdk-7u79-windows-i586.exe
Windows x64	140.06 MB	jdk-7u79-windows-x64.exe

Java SE Development Kit 7u79 Demos and Samples Downloads

You must accept the Oracle BSD License to download this software.

○ Accept License Agreement   ◉ Decline License Agreement

Product / File Description	File Size	Download
Linux x86	19.9 MB	jdk-7u79-linux-i586-demos.rpm
Linux x86	19.85 MB	jdk-7u79-linux-i586-demos.tar.gz
Linux x64	19.97 MB	jdk-7u79-linux-x64-demos.rpm
Linux x64	19.92 MB	jdk-7u79-linux-x64-demos.tar.gz
Mac OS X	18.5 MB	jdk-7u79-macosx-x86_64-demos.tar.gz
Solaris x86	23.04 MB	jdk-7u79-solaris-i586-demos.tar.Z
Solaris x86	16.06 MB	jdk-7u79-solaris-i586-demos.tar.gz
Solaris x64	1.24 MB	jdk-7u79-solaris-x64-demos.tar.Z

The first list with the heading, Java SE Development Kit 7u79, is the one we
want. Notice there is a radio button to "Accept License Agreement".
This isn't exactly the easiest web page to understand.
Click the "Accept License Agreement" radio button and choose:
Once you click that, the header will change so it looks like:

Java SE Development Kit 7u79

You must accept the Oracle Binary Code License Agreement for Java SE to download this software.
Thank you for accepting the Oracle Binary Code License Agreement for Java SE; you may now download this software.

Now you can click (way over on the right) the JDK for your OS.

Windows x86	138.31 MB	jdk-7u79-windows-i586.exe
Windows x64	140.06 MB	jdk-7u79-windows-x64.exe

I am running a 64-bit Windows 10 OS on an Intel 64 bit processor so I choose x64.

When you click it, Windows will help you so you can save the JDK download on your file system.

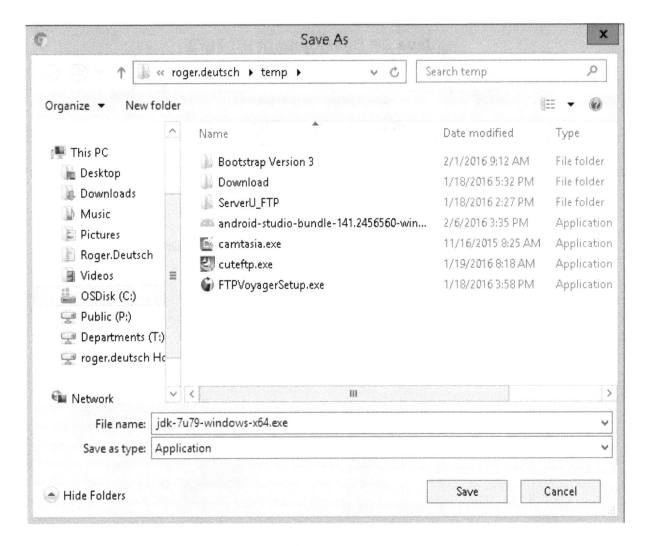

Remember the location, because we are going to have to start up the installation package after downloading it.

Again, in Chrome when you download the JDK it'll look something like the following at the bottom of the browser:

Once you open the installer UAC (User Account Control) is going to verify that you really want to allow the executable to run.

Click the [Yes] button.
You'll see something like the following:

And very quickly after that, you'll see:

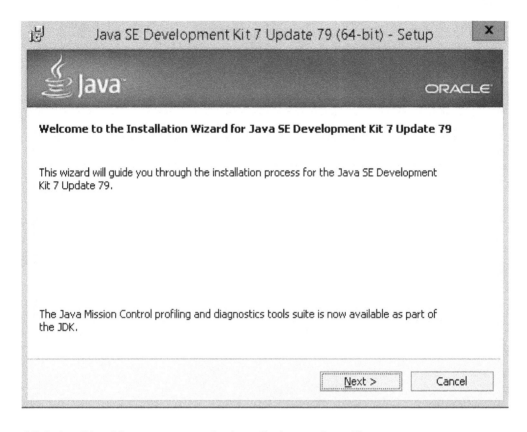

Click the [Next] button to start the installation and you'll see:

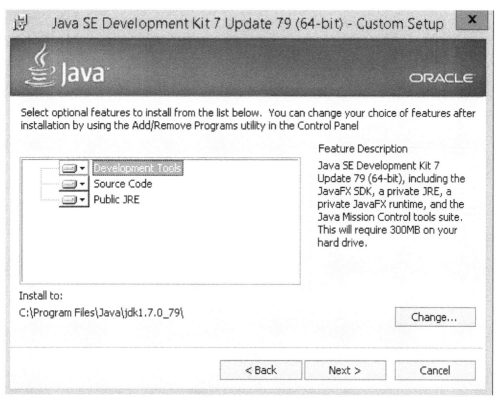

I'm just leaving everything to install in the default location. You can see it will go to c:\Program files\ which is the x64 Windows default.

Click the [Next] button.

You'll see something like the following:

And then, it'll ask you again if the default location is okay for the JRE (Java Runtime Environment).

The JRE is the Virtual Machine which Java apps actually run inside.

You can install the JRE without installing the JDK since the JRE allows Java apps to run. Many end-users only have the JRE because they only run programs, but never write Java applications. We are installing the JDK (Java Development Kit) because we are developing apps and need the tools it provides.

The default is fine. Click the [Next] button.

You will see something like the following:

Finally, it will complete and you will see something like:

You can just click the [Close] button.

Now, we need to make our way back to the Android Studio installation. It's still running, because it was waiting on us to install the JDK.
You should see an icon on your taskbar for Android Studio, which looks like:

Click the icon and the installation screen should come back up.

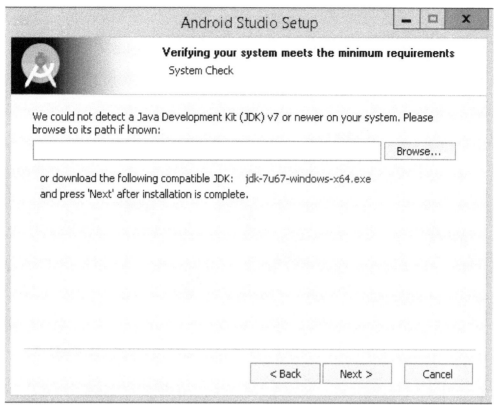

It says, we can just click the [Next] button (since we've installed the JDK) so let's try that.

You will then see the following:

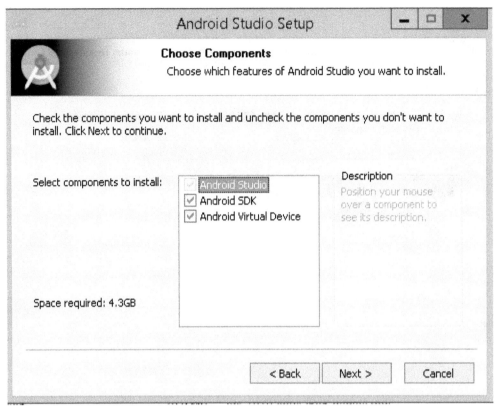

Take time to notice a couple of things on this dialog.

First of all it will intall three things on your computer:

1. Android Studio

2. Android SDK (software development kit) -- these represent the various versions of Android that have been released.

3. Android Virtual Device (AVD) -- this is the emulator and Android OS files for different versions of the Android OS so you can run the emulator as if your are running any version of Android on your computer. This is how we test our app on multiple Android devices.

Click the [Next] Button.

A license agreement will appear so you can read what you are agreeing to.

Click the [Agree] button so you can continue.

The location where Android Studio will be installed and separately where the Android SDK will be installed is shown.

Again, I'm accepting the defaults so click the [Next] button.

You will see the final dialog telling you about the shortcuts (icons) it will install so you can start Android Studio.

Again, I accept the defaults so click the [Install] button.

It will begin to install and display files it is adding:

If you click the [Show Details] button it will show you something like the following:

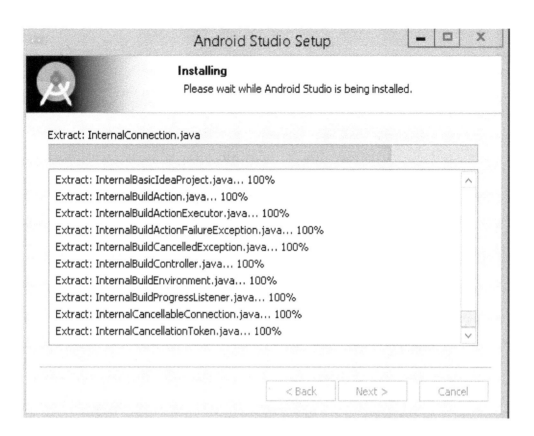

It was very fast but slowed down tremendously when it was doing the following:

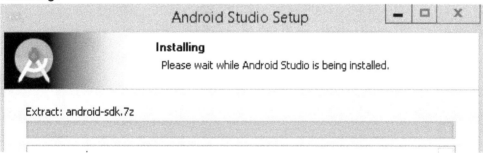

It was extracting the Android SDK
Then I could see that it was installing the Android SDK:

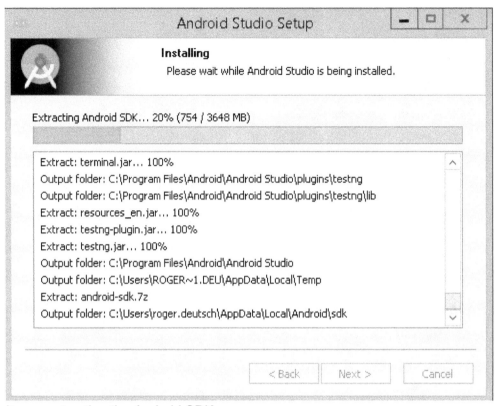

It was extracting the Android SDK

Then I could see that it was installing the Android SDK:

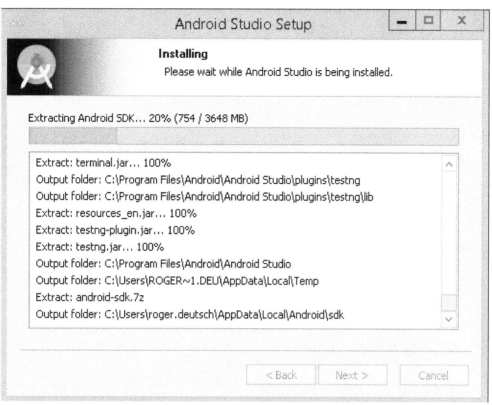

That's over 3.6GB of files extracting and so it took a while.

Finally, it completes and you will see the following :

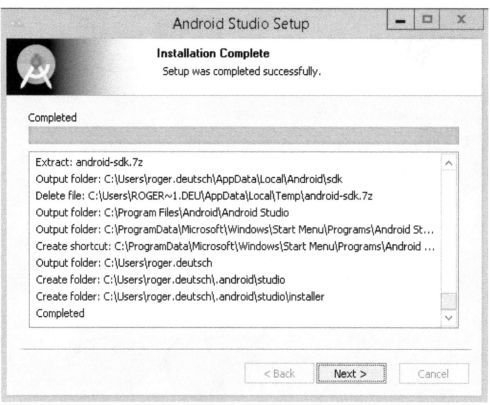

Click the [Next] button

Click the [Finish] button and we can finally start up Android Studio.
You will then be prompted about importing settings from a previous version of Android Studio.
I thought this was a bit odd since I didn't have any previous version installed.
Then I saw the last radio button choice and I selected it and clicked [OK].

The following splash screen showed up and that thin green line is actually a progress bar.

When the progress bar finally got to the far right of the splash screen a new window popped up.

Click the [Next] button to validate that your installation is correct.

The following window will display:

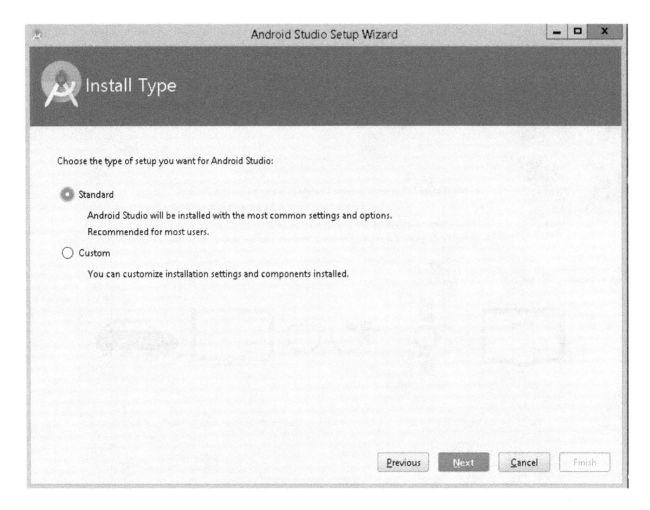

sidebar: You really have to wonder about the graphic / UI designers who created these installation screens. They are huge with so little information on them.

Click the [Next] button to accept the default settings for Android Studio. Since you are a new user you will need to learn more about the system before you have a good idea about how to customize Android Studio.

The next window provides an overview of the additional tools and SDKs it is going to download and install and the path where it will install them.

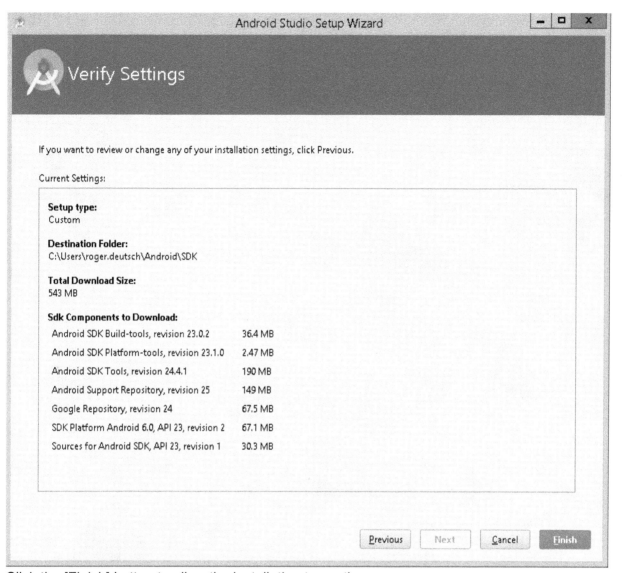

Click the [Finish] button to allow the installation to continue.

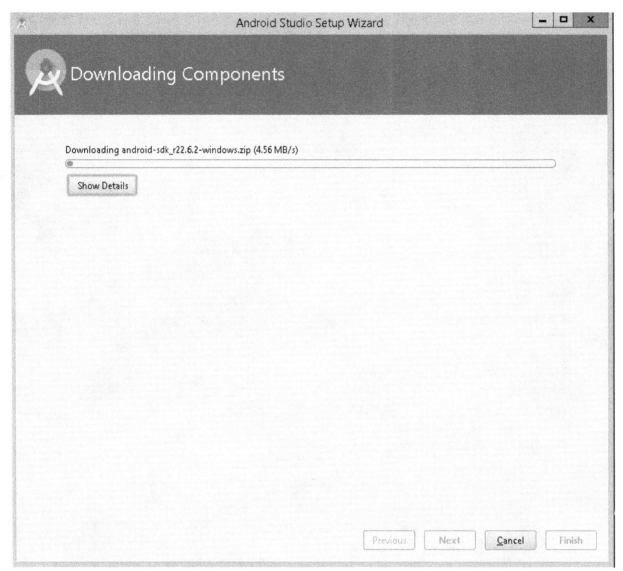

If you clicked the [Show Details] button, when it finally completes you will see
an entire list of everything it installed and the [Finish] button will be enabled
so you can click it.

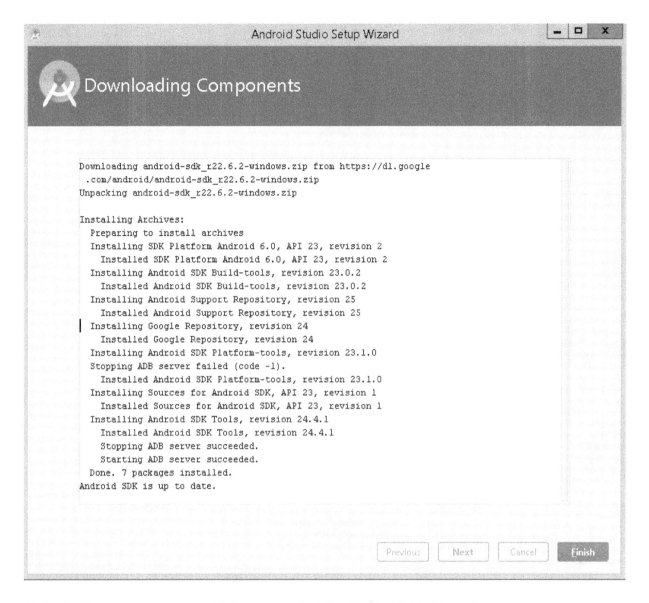

At the bottom you can see that informs you that the "Android SDK is up to date."
Click the [Finish] button.
Finally, Android Studio is actually ready to run.
You will now be able to choose to "Start a new Android Studio project".

Now we can go ahead and start a basic test project to make sure it all works. However, since this chapter has been extremely long with so many screenshots I'm going to move us to chapter two so that our first project is created separately to make it easier to skip this chapter on installation for those who've already done all that.

In chapter two, we'll start off, right where we stopped here.

See you there.

Chapter 2
Generate Your First Project

Click the "Start a new Android Studio project choice".

When you click the choice, a gigantic window will appear:

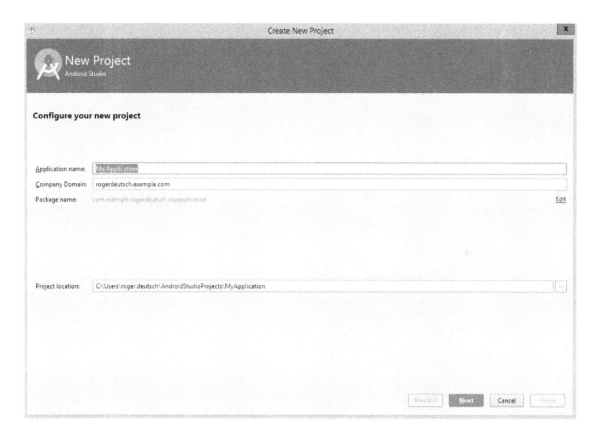

The Application name is highlighted and ready for you to type the name of your application.

Go ahead and type the word *test*, since that is what we are going to call this first app.

As soon as you type that word you will see that Android Studio gives you a hint about naming your app. (See red text in the next screenshot).

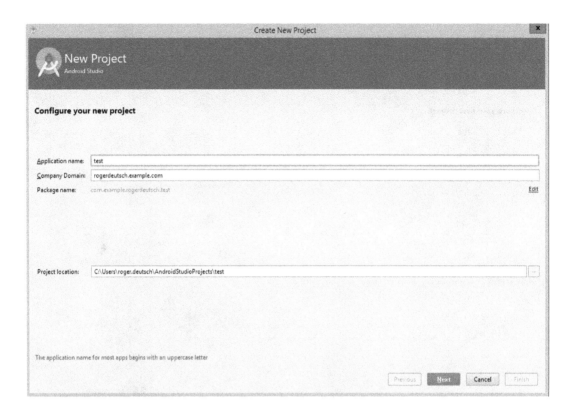

Go ahead and change the name to start with an uppercase T and tab to the next field (Company Domain).

I type the name of my web domain in that box (raddev.us) but you should not use my domain.

You should use your web site domain or if you don't have one, use your first name or first and last name or some other identifier.

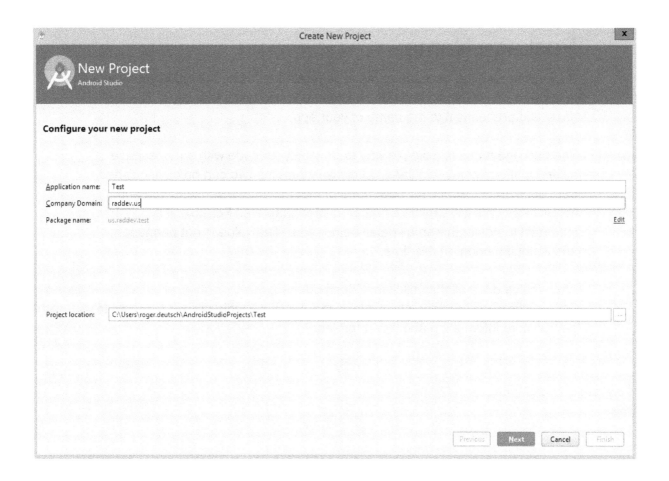

Company Domain Value

For now it doesn't matter much, but when you get ready to deploy your real app to the Google Play store you'll want something that identifies you more distinctly as the creator of your app.

Package Name

As you can see, the package name is generated by using the value you type in the Company Domain text box. Of course it also takes the value, flips the order and prepends it to the name of your app.

The package name is a simple way to provide your code with a namespace so that if others create similar Java classes then the two can be distinguished from each other. Again, for now, none of that may make sense to you and that is okay. We will explain it further in later chapters. For now, it is important to not let this small detail bother you. The value is not permanent and is not important at this time.

After you've done all that, click the [Next] button.
A new window will appear which allows the Android Studio project template to gather more information about your project.

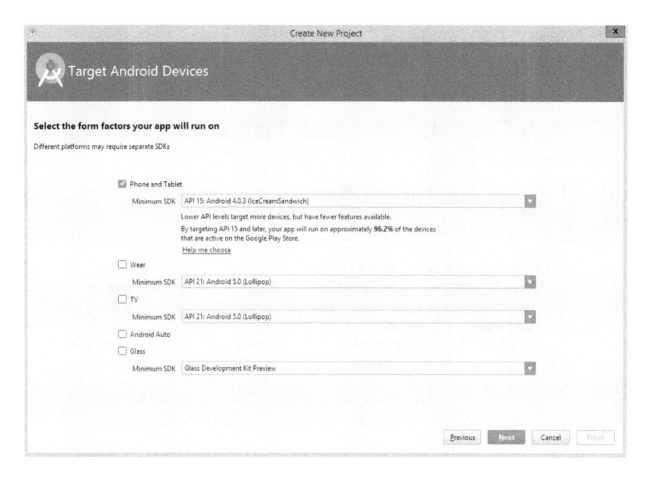

The first thing you'll notice is that the template automatically targets phone and tablet devices which are running API 15 (or newer). This is also known as the API level (API Level 15).

Every major version (1.x, 2.x, etc) of the Android OS is referred to by a code name which is the name of a dessert (or sugary snack). They did this in an attempt to make it easier for users to refer to the major version of the OS they are running. Users can say, "I'm running Ice Cream Sandwich." "I'm running Jelly Bean."

In our example, the template has targeted version 4, Ice Cream Sandwich. API 15 refers to the specific version (including minor revisions) of Android. API 15 is version 4.0.3 of Ice Cream Sandwich. This is important to Android developers because version 4.0 of Ice Cream Sandwich may not have certain functions which version 4.0.3 has so certain code may not work properly.

Why Does the Template Target This Older Version?

The template has chosen this slightly older version in an attempt to provide a balance between a large amount of functionality and the large number of users who can run your app.

If you target a newer platform, like Android 6.0 (Marshmallow, API Level 23) you will be targeting a smaller number of users because not as many devices have released that are running that version of the OS yet.
Statistical Data for OS Usage
You can see the current statistics for number of users running each version of the OS at:
http://developer.android.com/about/dashboards/index.html

Examining that data can help you choose the best version to target the greatest number of users so that your app will have a larger market.

The template has automatically chosen API Level 15 because it knows it currently provides a strong balance between functionality and market size. At the time of this writing, if you choose API Level 15 then over 98% of the devices in use will be able to run your app.

Other Platform Types

You can also see that the project template allows you to create an app which runs on wearables (watches, etc), TV and even Android Auto and Android Glass.

For now, we are going to accept the default and run as a phone or tablet app so go ahead and click the [Next] button.

When I clicked that button another installation occurred which looked like the following:

Android Studio determined that I needed some build tools so I could build the app.

Here are the details I saw:

```
Installing Android SDK Build-tools, revision 19.1.0
   Installed Android SDK Build-tools, revision 19.1.0
Done. 1 package installed.
```

Finally the [Next] button was enabled so go ahead and click [Next] now and you will see the following:

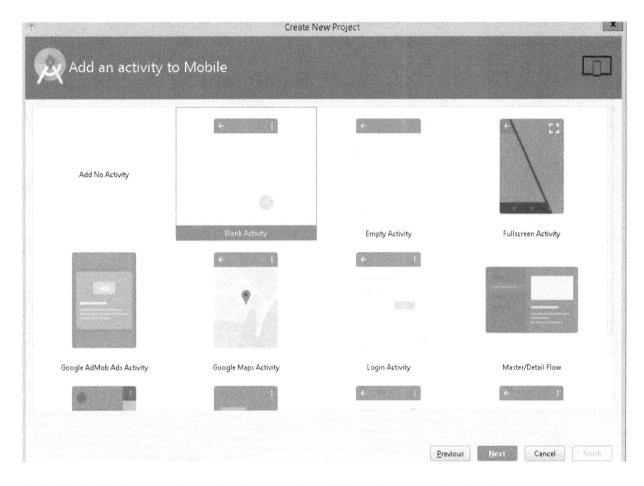

Android Studio is prompting us to choose a Layout type for our application's Activity.

An Android Activity is the User Interface which allows the user to interact with your application. Each Activity should focus on allowing the user to do one thing.

For now, we are going to select the default Activity called Blank Activity. Notice that it is not the Empty Activity -- which is an Activity with nothing on it. Instead this just provides an Activity which will have a few UI elements on it, but which are not filled out in any way.

It will make more sense once we build the application.

Click the [Next] button.

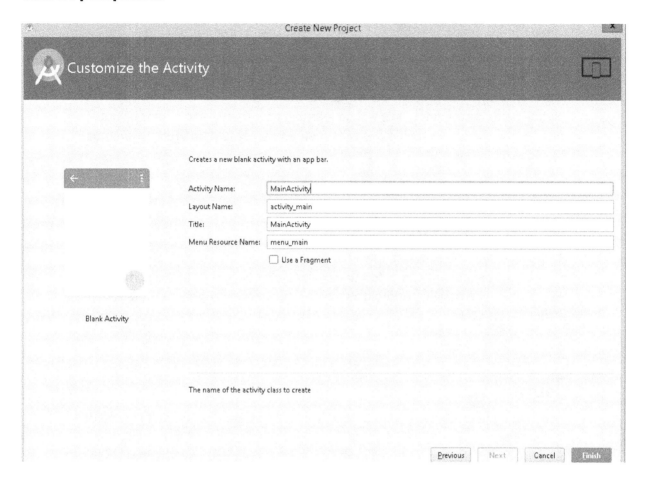

Activity Name

Android Studio wants you to name your Activity so you can refer to it in code. It suggests the name of MainActivity since this will be the Activity the user sees when the application starts. That is a good name and the name I always like to use in my projects as a developer convention to remind me which Activity is the first one the user sees.

Layout Name

The Layout Name is generated according to the name you type in the Activity name edit box. The layout name is the name of the XML (eXtensible Markup Language) file which is generated by Android Studio. The layout file represents all of the graphic elements that the user sees on the Activity (buttons, edit boxes, etc). We will be learning how to edit and create layout files so that our apps provide a way for users to enter text and run commands by clicking buttons.

Graphic Layout Editor

Android Studio also provides a way to drag and drop User Interface elements like edit boxes and buttons onto our Activities. When you drop these new elements on the Activity, Android Studio will automatically generate the XML layout file for you.

Title

The Title edit box allows you to enter a Title that will be displayed at the top of the Activity.
Go ahead and change that value to "First App" just so you can see that when we build and run the app.

It'll look like the following:

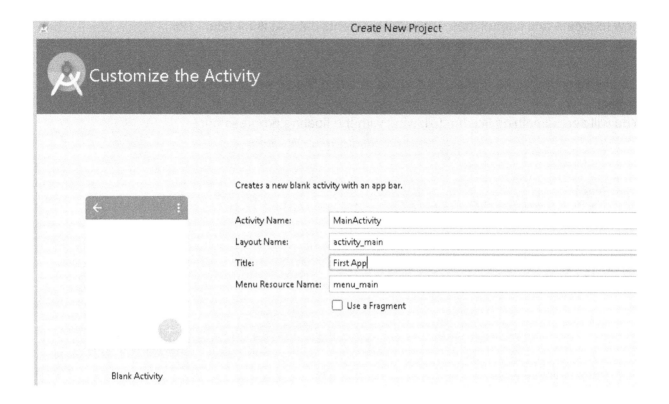

Customize the Activity

Creates a new blank activity with an app bar.

Activity Name:	MainActivity
Layout Name:	activity_main
Title:	First App
Menu Resource Name:	menu_main
	☐ Use a Fragment

Blank Activity

Menu Resource Name

The Menu Resource Name allows you to name the menu which appears at the top of the Activity so you can refer to it in code. That's the menu which appears when you click the vertical line of three dots in the upper right corner of the app.
For now, menu_main is fine and again will allow us to remember that it is the main menu for our main Activity.

Fragment Checkbox

For now, we will not use a layout Fragment, but we will learn about using them later. Layout fragments are a powerful way to reuse Activities simply by reloading a fragment of the UI into the currently loaded Activity. We will learn how to create and control these powerful elements but that is for later. For now, leave the checkbox unchecked.

Go ahead and click the [Finish] button and Android Studio will create the project.
You will see something like the following with the floating progress bar.

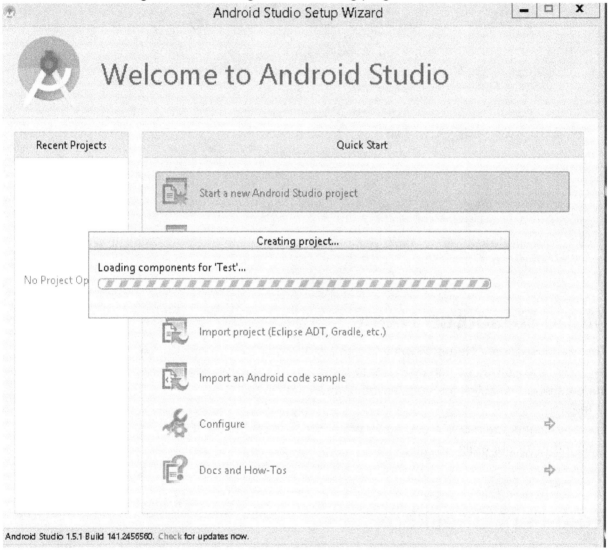

Android Studio is getting everything ready so you can begin to develop your application.

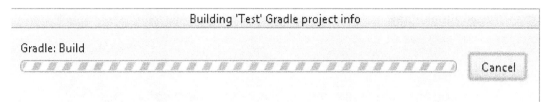

The build system known as Gradle is doing a lot of work preparing your app for development.

Finally, you will see the main Android Studio Window.

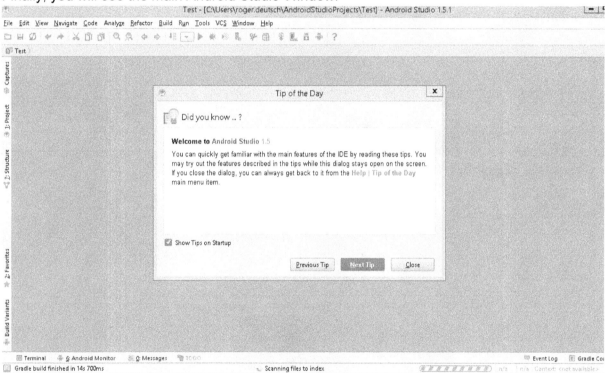

Tips

Studio also attempts to provide tips to help you learn more about the system each time you start it up. Of course, you can turn these off if they bother you, however, it's trying to provide these while other work is going on.

Gradle Is Still At Work

Even though the Android Studio main window is now visible, there is still some work going on. You can see at the bottom of the window there is a status bar which will indicate some work that Gradle (the build system) is trying to do in the background.

It is indexing files (to help you find code later). It is building your project so that it can run the first time and it does other tasks in an attempt to use background processing power while you are not doing much.

Finally, if you wait long enough, then Android Studio will open a few files for you and it will look similar to the following.

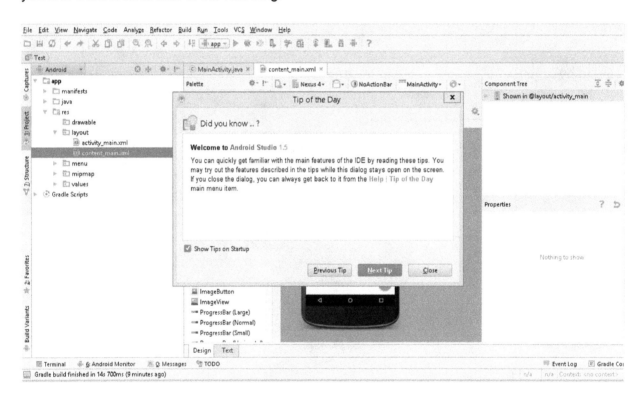

You can see a bit behind the tips dialog.

I'll click the [Close] button on the tips and show you the main Android Studio window again.

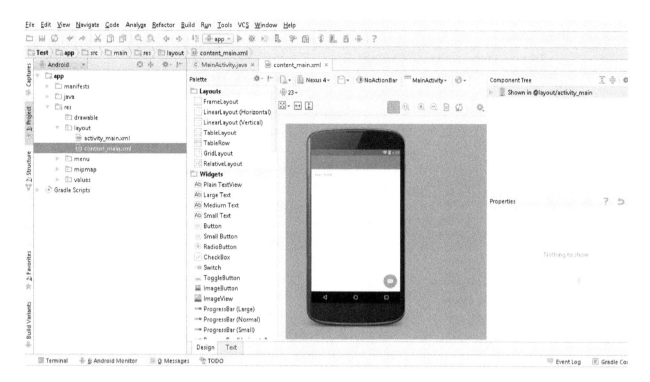

You can see the main Activity as it will appear on an Android phone. If you look closely enough you will see that in the top left corner of the Activity, the words, "Hello, world" show up.

Understanding Where We Are In the Project

A lot of code has been generated and there are a lot of things going on in the Android Studio User Interface. It's quite overwhelming for a first look at a project. Let's take a look at a few key areas in Android Studio which will clear this up.

Project Navigator

First of all, take a look at the far left side of Android Studio which looks like the following:

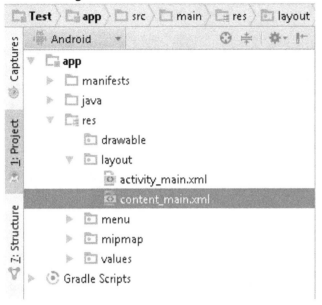

Project TreeView Similar To File Explorer

This is similar to a File Explorer type of treeview, but a bit different.
Notice that the blue highlight indicates the file that is currently being viewed on the right side.
The blue highlight is showing us that the file named content_main.xml, which is found under the layout folder is currently open. That's the XML layout file I mentioned when we were creating the project.

Vertical Project Bar

Take a look at the vertical bar, a bit further to the left and notice that there are three words on that bar. They are:

1. Structure
2. Project
3. Captions

The important thing to note for now is that Project is currently selected. If you click one of the others your view will change. For now, the others won't do much of anything except slightly change the view in this navigation bar. But later they will have some meaning. The important thing to note for now is that you are on the Project choice and it displays the treeview which allows you to examine the files in the project.

Two XML Files

You will also notice that there are two XML files in the layout folder, even though we only talked about one earlier. The two files are named:
1. activity_main.xml
2. content_main.xml

That is simply because the project has split these two XML files up to help you better manage the User Interface elements. We will see more about this in a moment.

Project Structure

The next thing to help you get familiar with the files in the project is to take a look at the folders that the files are contained in.

Again, notice that these XML files which represent the UI are under the folder named layout.

And, then notice that the layout folder is inside a folder named res.

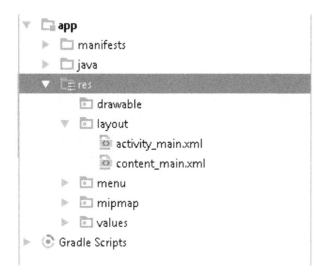

Conventional Organization

res is an abbreviation for resource. All of the files found under this folder are resources that you project will use. Things like images, icons and other user interface elements. You can see there are other folders such as menu, mipmap and values also under the res folder. We will learn more about those later.

This is all a conventional way of keeping things organized. You could change the way things are organized, but the Android Studio developers have provided you with a structure and understanding it will help you understand what you are doing as you develop your app.

Dude, Where's My Code?

So far, however, we haven't seen any of the Java code.
If you take a look all the way at the top of the project tree you'll see that the top node (folder) is named app.
That folder contains the one we've been look at (res) but it also contains one named manifests and another named java.

Again, this is all for organization.

Android Manifest File

The manifests folder has only one file and it is named (surprise) AndroidManifest.xml. More XML. This is a configuration file which provides information to the OS and even to the Google Play store about your application. We will see what this file does as we develop our apps.

For now, though let's take a look at what is in the java folder.
If you'll click the triangle-arrow next to the java folder you will see that the folder will expand.

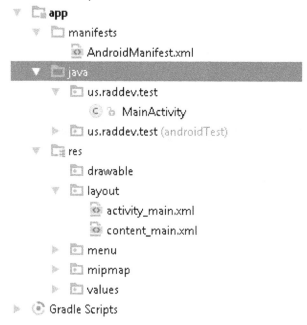

Then, if you'll expand the one that says us.raddev.test that one will expand also and you'll see an item with an icon and the label MainActivity.

This is the java code that represents our MainActivity.

Note, you will also see a folder named us.raddev.test(androidTest) but that code represents some code that we can use later to test our application. For now, we'll ignore that.

Open MainActivity Code

To open (and view) the code, go ahead and double-click the MainActivity item now.

When you do that, the file will be displayed on the right side like the following:

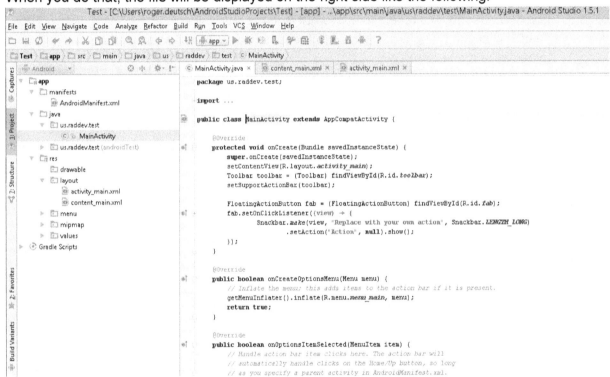

Important Clues to Understanding What You're Looking At

There are a few important clues to understanding what you're looking at.

1. The title bar (light blue) has changed to show you the complete path to the file you are viewing on the right.
2. The project navigation tree on the left shows MainActivity highlighted.
3. The tab above the content on the right displays the name of the file MainActivity.java.

Collapsed Sections of Code

However, you still aren't seeing all of the code.

The Android Studio editor collapses sections of code, places a [+] symbol next to them and displays ellipses (...) and arrows where it has collapsed code.

Here's the first example at the top of MainActivity.java, where the imports section is located:

```
package us.raddev.test;

+import ...

public class MainActivity extends AppCompatActivity {
```

Click the [+] button to expand the code and you will see:

```
package us.raddev.test;

import android.os.Bundle;
import android.support.design.widget.FloatingActionButton;
import android.support.design.widget.Snackbar;
import android.support.v7.app.AppCompatActivity;
import android.support.v7.widget.Toolbar;
import android.view.View;
import android.view.Menu;
import android.view.MenuItem;

public class MainActivity extends AppCompatActivity {
```

A little further down there is some more collapsed code which looks like the following (I highlighted the section)

```
public class MainActivity extends AppCompatActivity {

    @Override
    protected void onCreate(Bundle savedInstanceState) {
        super.onCreate(savedInstanceState);
        setContentView(R.layout.activity_main);
        Toolbar toolbar = (Toolbar) findViewById(R.id.toolbar);
        setSupportActionBar(toolbar);

        FloatingActionButton fab = (FloatingActionButton) findViewById(R.id.fab);
        fab.setOnClickListener((view) → {
                Snackbar.make(view, "Replace with your own action", Snackbar.LENGTH_LONG)
                        .setAction("Action", null).show();
        });
    }
```

See the small arrow within the code (after the word (view))?
That is a collapsed section of code. To see all of the code, click the [+]
button on the left again.
It'll look like:

```
        FloatingActionButton fab = (FloatingActionButton) findViewById(R.id.fab);
        fab.setOnClickListener(new View.OnClickListener() {
            @Override
            public void onClick(View view) {
                Snackbar.make(view, "Replace with your own action", Snackbar.LENGTH_LONG)
                        .setAction("Action", null).show();
            }
        });
    }
```

You can see that the code is actually doing something with the Snackbar
which shows some kind of message like, "Replace with your own action."

Now that you know how to create a new project and how to navigate around
in Android Studio a bit, we are ready to go ahead and build and run the app.
Building the app is quite easy. It's just a simple matter of executing a
command in Android Studio. However, running the app contains a few
challenges since we will have to run the app on an Android emulator.

Emulator Challenge

If all goes well, the emulator will start up and run perfectly on your computer. There are quite a few steps to successfully get through to get it running though.

Again, since this chapter has had a lot of basics in it and because building and running the app is going to take quite a lot of screenshots and explanation we will do that work in chapter 3.

This chapter has attempted to provide a good walkthrough of the experience of using Android Studio to generate your first project. If you've followed along you've come a long way and it hasn't taken long.

As we build and run the application on a emulator you'll gain a lot of knowledge about how the system works.

We will dive into running the emulator and executing our app immediately in Chapter 3.

Chapter 3

Run Device Emulator and Debug Code

At the top of Android Studio in the main menu, we want to click and expand the Run menu

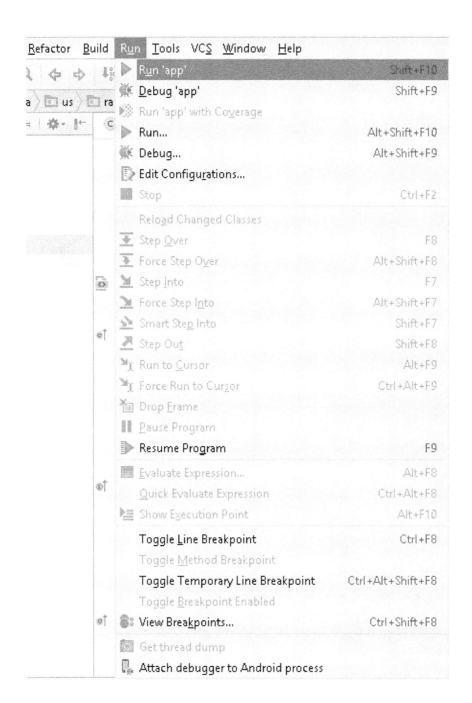

When it expands, we want to choose the Run app choice.

When you click that menu item a dialog box will appear which looks like the following:

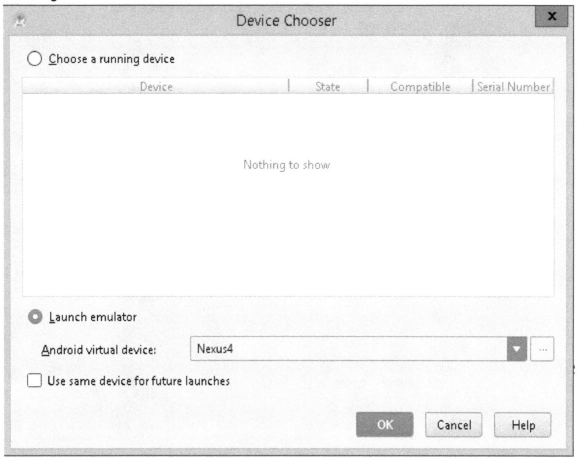

The bottom portion of that dialog is the part that is important to us. You can see that Android Studio has auto-selected the Launch emulator radio button for us, because it knows that there is no emulator running yet.

You can also see that the Android virtual device (AVD) that it is suggesting we run is named Nexus4.
Go ahead and click the [OK] button now.

###
##

##
##

Note: When I attempted to start the Virtual Device nothing happened and I went through a number of steps to attempt to figure it out. I'll add all of the things I ended up trying as a sidebar in case you have issues. Otherwise, this chapter will proceed as if you had no problems starting the emulator.

##
##

##
##

Eventually*, you should see something like the following:

*Depending upon your hardware it may take a long time for the Android Virtual Device (emulator) to finally start up.

At this point the app looks fairly close to what we saw in the preview within Android Studio.

However, for some reason the preview doesn't show the word, Test, in the title bar as the emulator version does.

Clicking Emulator to Touch Screen

Also, you can click on the interface using your mouse and the app will react as it would if you ran it on a real device and touched the screen.

The Freebies

You get a few items for free in the application, simply because we chose the layout template that was provided by Android Studio.

First of all, click the vertical ellipsis (menu at top right of app) and you'll see that it displays one menu item : Settings.

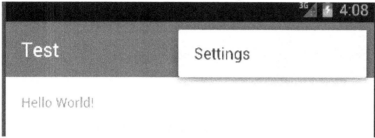

However, clicking the Settings menu which appears will not do anything, because we haven't written any code for it yet.

Now, let's go ahead and click the round pink button with the envelope on it. Clicking it will not do much, but it will active the "snackbar".
Try it now.
The UI will adjust and a small message will appear.

Before we begin to delve into the code, let's make sure we know how to use our tools fairly well. In the long run it will pay off.

We'll look at the following list of items to finish out this chapter and then next chapter we will start writing some code and actually doing some things to alter the app.

Of course, if you are confident with skipping these items because you already understand them, then feel free to do so.

We'll look at:
1. Android Monitor with Logcat
2. Adding code in our app to write lines to logcat
3. Run (output) window
4. Messages window : look a little closer at output when app fails to build properly
5. ADB (Android Debug Bridge) from the command line

After we work through these items you will be quite familiar with Android Studio and it will be much easier to move around Studio and easier to understand the code we are working on.

Close A Running Android App

The first thing we want to do is close the app that we just ran on the emulator. There is an easy way to do that. Go back to the emulator and click on the "back" button.
It is the curved arrow button shown on the left in the following image.

We will learn more about this later, but when you touch that button in an Android app, it actually suspends and closes the app.

Go ahead and do that now on your emulator.
The app should disappear and you'll probably see the Android "desktop" again.

Now, switch back over to Android Studio and make sure you choose the Android Monitor button at the bottom of the window. That will cause the Android Monitor to display so we can look at it.

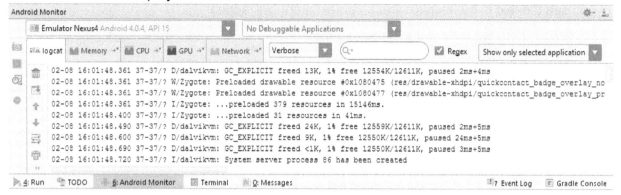

If you will slowly move over the top border of that window your cursor will change to a double updown arrow so you can resize the window to see more if you like.

Notice that you can tell that this window has focus because its title bar says "Android Monitor". Also notice that the tab that is highlighted on the left says logcat.

Right now, this window is showing us the Android log which is constantly being written while to while Android runs.

Overwhelming Amount of Information

At times the amount of information that is written to this window can be overwhelming because every event which occurs in the system is being written here, but we will learn how to filter this down so we can see only events we are interested in and which are helpful to us when debugging our app.

Clearing the Android Monitor

First of all, let's clear the Android Monitor. To do so, simply right-click where you see the text in the monitor and a context menu will appear.

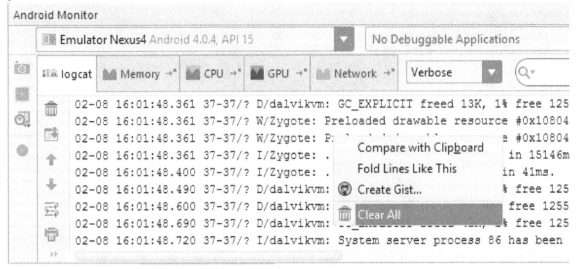

Choose the Clear All menu item and all of the text in the window will disappear.

This will help us see the events which are written when we start our app.

Start the App Again

Let's start our application again, but this time, we are going to view the output which occurs in this window.

To do that, click the green triangle arrow near the top of Android Studio, below the main menu.

It's the green arrow pointing to the right in the following image:

Once you click that, you'll see the Device Chooser window.

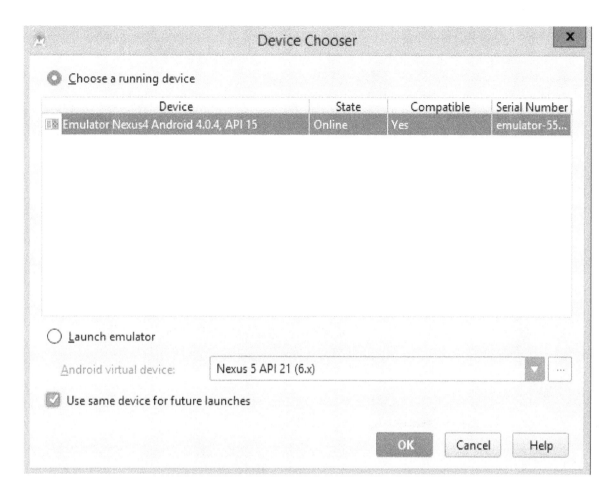

That window will appear every time even though your emulator is still running. However, you can check the "User same device for future launches" choice so it will always use your running device so it won't bother you with this window any more. Don't worry, there is still a way to switch it using another menu option later if something happens.

Click the [OK] button to allow the app to start.

When you do, keep your eye on the Android Monitor logcat window, because a lot of messages are going to be written there as the application starts.

I copied out the text that was written and it is more than 4,600 lines. At 50 lines per page that would be over 92 pages if you printed it out.

Here are a few of the interesting lines from the output with notes (marked with note) and bold is my emphasis:

```
02-08 16:01:48.361 37-37/? D/dalvikvm: GC_EXPLICIT freed 13K, 1% free
12554K/12611K, paused 2ms+4ms
```
Note: dalvikvm is the Virtual Machine that all Android programs ran in under Android versions 4.4 (KitKat) and before. This is the Java Run Time which runs the applications on all Android devices (version 4.4 and before) not just within the emulator.
```
02-08 16:01:48.361 37-37/? W/Zygote: Preloaded drawable resource
#0x1080475 (res/drawable-
xhdpi/quickcontact_badge_overlay_normal_light.9.png) that varies with
configuration!!
02-08 16:01:49.070 86-100/? I/SystemServer: Entropy Service
02-08 16:01:49.130 86-100/? I/SystemServer: Power Manager
02-08 16:01:49.141 86-100/? I/SystemServer: Activity Manager
02-08 16:01:49.170 86-101/? I/ActivityManager: Memory class: 64
02-08 16:01:49.291 86-101/? A/BatteryStatsImpl: problem reading
network stats
```

```
java.lang.IllegalStateException: problem parsing idx 1
                                        at
com.android.internal.net.NetworkStatsFactory.readNetworkStatsDetail(N
etworkStatsFactory.java:300)
                                        at
com.android.internal.net.NetworkStatsFactory.readNetworkStatsDetail(N
etworkStatsFactory.java:250)
```
Note: You can see that exceptions (errors) occur within the system that are unrelated to our application.

```
02-08 16:08:29.517 86-93/? I/dalvikvm: Jit: resizing JitTable from
4096 to 8192
02-08 16:08:29.737 86-104/? I/PackageManager: Removing non-system
package:us.raddev.test
02-08 16:08:29.737 86-101/? I/ActivityManager: Force stopping package
us.raddev.test uid=10040
```
Note: These lines indicate that the previous version of our app are being removed from the device and stopped from running.

```
02-08 16:08:37.737 86-100/? D/BackupManagerService: Received
broadcast Intent { act=android.intent.action.PACKAGE_ADDED
dat=package:us.raddev.test flg=0x10000010 (has extras) }
```
Note: Here the newly built version of our app is being deployed to the device.
```
2-08 16:08:42.007 622-622/? D/dalvikvm: Not late-enabling CheckJNI
(already on)
02-08 16:08:42.037 86-233/? I/ActivityManager: Start proc
us.raddev.test for activity us.raddev.test/.MainActivity: pid=622
uid=10040 gids={}
```
Note: Here the app is being started.
```
02-08 16:08:44.647 86-114/? I/ActivityManager: Displayed
us.raddev.test/.MainActivity: +2s716ms
```
Note: Finally, the MainActivity is being displayed on the screen.

Hopefully, that provides you with a bit of insight into the logging and that you
can actually get some information about what your app is doing even when it
hasn't yet been drawn on the screen.

However, that is way too much information to dig through. That's why you
can add some code to the application and turn on a filter so only the
information you want to see is shown in the logcat window.

Alter MainActivity.java

Let's go ahead and make some changes to our Java code to add our logging
functionality.
We'll make the application log when the user clicks the Settings menu item.

Go back to Android Studio and open up the MainActivity.java class in the
editor. Double-click the file on the left side in the project tree view if
necessary and the file should open up for you on the right in an editor
window.

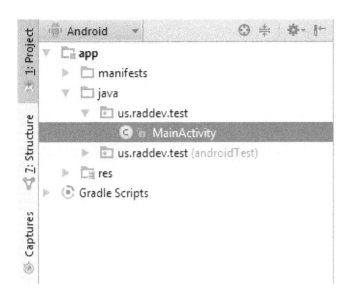

Scroll down to the bottom of the MainActivity.java file and you'll see a function named onOptionsSelected. It looks like:

```java
    @Override
    public boolean onOptionsItemSelected(MenuItem item) {
        // Handle action bar item clicks here. The action bar will
        // automatically handle clicks on the Home/Up button, so long
        // as you specify a parent activity in AndroidManifest.xml.
        int id = item.getItemId();

        //noinspection SimplifiableIfStatement
        if (id == R.id.action_settings) {
            return true;
        }

        return super.onOptionsItemSelected(item);
    }
}
```

We are going to type some code in the if statement shown, right after the opening curly brace.
That code currently looks like:
if (id == R.id.action_settings) {

```
            return true;
    }
```
Now, let's change it (add the bolded line shown in the following code snippet.
```
if (id == R.id.action_settings) {
```
Log.d("test","User clicked the Settings menu item.");
```
            return true;
    }
```


When you get as far as the d in that line Android Studio is going to offer some help.

```
        if (id == R.id.action_settings) {
            Log.d
 m      Log.d (String tag, String msg) (android.util)                    int
 m    Log.d (String tag, String msg, Throwable tr) (android.util)   int
     Log.DEBUG (android.util)                                        int  π
        return super.onOptionsItemSelected(item);

    }
```


It's just trying to let you know that there is a function it knows about named Log.d and there are a couple of function overloads (function takes varying number and types of parameters).

We are going to use the first one shown, but you can just type an opening parenthesis (.

When you do, Android Studio will automatically type the closing parenthesis and will offer you more help:

```
? android.util.Log? Alt+Enter  SimplifiableIfStatement
        if (id == R.id.action_settings) {
            Log.d()
            return true;
        }

        return super.onOptionsItemSelected(item);
    }
}
```

It is telling you that the function you are looking for exists in a specific package (library - android.util.Log) which you haven't included a reference to yet. To add the package simply press Alt and the Enter key combination.

When you do that Android Studio adds the following line at the top of MainActivity.java:
import android.util.Log;

That causes the Java compiler to include the package when it builds the code. That makes the Log.d function, which was written by the original Android Devs, available to you for calling.

Now, however, we still need to add the two strings to the Log.d function or the code will not compile.
Go ahead and make sure you line looks complete now.

```
      Log.d("test","User clicked the Settings menu item.");
```
When it is correct, it will look like the following:

```
          if (id == R.id.action_settings) {
              Log.d("test", "User clicked the Settings menu item.");
              return true;
          }
```

Notice that Android Studio code editor colorizes the strings to green for some contrast.

What Does the Code Do?
This code allows us to write the Android log and the Android log will display this code when we have our logging set to the debug level. That's why the function is named d().
If we had wanted to output a Warning we would've called the function named w() with two strings.
We can also call the e() function to indicate an error.

If you want to investigate more of the functions you can allow Android Studio to help you by opening up another line where we typed the first line of code and typing:
Log. (that's Log with a period following). When you do that the built in Android Studio help with offer suggestions of function and property names of the Log class.

Our Function Call

In our function call, we create a filter named "test" and we are writing a log entry line which will say, "User clicked the Settings menu item."

Filter Not Used Yet

For now, the filter name isn't used. We'll use more of them later because they are very helpful so we can filter out other messages.

```
if (id == R.id.action_settings) {
    Log.d("test", "User clicked the Settings menu item.");
    Log.|
}

ret
```

m	d (String tag, String msg)	int
m b	d (String tag, String msg, Throwable tr)	int
m b	e (String tag, String msg)	int
m b	e (String tag, String msg, Throwable tr)	int
m b	getStackTraceString (Throwable tr)	String
m b	i (String tag, String msg)	int
m b	i (String tag, String msg, Throwable tr)	int
m b	isLoggable (String s, int i)	boolean
m b	println (int priority, String tag, String msg)	int
m b	v (String tag, String msg)	int
m b	v (String tag, String msg, Throwable tr)	int

You can see there are so many suggestions that there is even a scrollbar provided so you can see them all.

Build and Run To See Output

Let's go ahead and build and run to see the output. Make sure you delete the unfinished line if necessary and go ahead and run the application (it will automatically build and deploy to your running emulator).

Keep an eye on the Android Monitor Logcat window.
When you do and the app finally starts you will probably notice that there is still tons of output.
We need to make a small change to filter the output.

There is a droplist that is currently set to Verbose in the Android Monitor window.
We want to change that value to Debug, since we are writing a Debug line by calling Log.d.

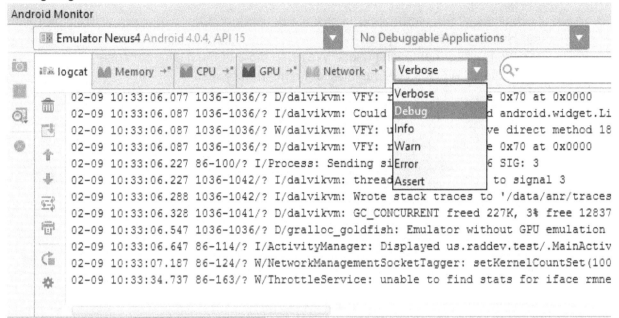

Make that selection now.
Then, make sure you grab the scrollbar on the far right side of the Android Monitor window and scroll all the way to the bottom of the window so that when new output is written you are sure to see it.

Switch over to your emulator which should be displaying your test app.
Click the vertical ellipsis menu in the upper right corner.
Next, click the Settings menu item which appears and keep an eye on the Android Monitor Logcat window.

When you click that Settings menu item.
You will see a line in your Logcat window which looks like the following (I highlighted it to emphasize the one to look at):

That's the text that we put in our Log.d function call.

You can also see the filter name (test) just before the message text.

Of course, we will use Logging all through the book and you will use it all through your Android development so we will continue to see much more of this as we go. Now, let's move on to the other smaller items I promised to cover.

Run Window
When you click the Run button at the bottom of Android Studio you can see a bit more information about your running program.

The first line gives you the target device. This can be important if you have more than one device attached. At times you may have an emulator running and a physical device attached so it helps to know where Studio deployed the app.

APK (Android Package Kit)
The second line is extremely interesting, because it is the APK file which android uses to deploy your app. The full path to the file which was created when Android Studio built the app is provided.

```
Installing APK:
C:\Users\roger.deutsch\AndroidStudioProjects\Test\app\build\ou
tputs\apk\app-debug.apk
```

Also notice that it names the file generically as app-debug.apk. We'll talk more about that later since it will become important when deploying our app to real users.

Moving File to Android Emulator (Device)
The third line shows where the APK file gets renamed and moved for deployment to the emulator.
Uploading file to: /data/local/tmp/us.raddev.test

You can see it renames the file and places our app in a directory named /data/local/tmp.
Next, Studio runs a command to install the APK onto the emulator.

```
DEVICE SHELL COMMAND: pm install -r
"/data/local/tmp/us.raddev.test"
```

Finally, you can see where the app is launched and the command that Studio fires to do that:

```
Launching application:
us.raddev.test/us.raddev.test.MainActivity.
DEVICE SHELL COMMAND: am start  -n
"us.raddev.test/us.raddev.test.MainActivity" -a
android.intent.action.MAIN -c android.intent.category.LAUNCHER
```

The additionally interesting thing is that you can run those commands yourself from a command line to manually do this work. We will see how this works later, but it is good to know what Android Studio is doing on your behalf. Knowing these things are what will make you excel as an Android Developer.

Let's wrap this chapter up so that (next chapter) we can start writing our first app.

However, I still need to cover the Messages window since it is important when something goes wrong.
First of all, go ahead and click the Messages button at the bottom of Android Studio.

You can see that the top is now labeled : Messages: Gradle build.

Now, go back to MainActivity.java and type a single letter inside our if statement that we previously worked on. I'm trying to cause an error when we build and run.
It'll look something like:

```java
//noinspection SimplifiableIfStatement
if (id == R.id.action_settings) {k
    Log.d("test", "User clicked the Settings menu item.");
    return true;
}

return super.onOptionsItemSelected(item);
```
}

See the red letter k?

Android Studio already knows it is a problem and is trying to warn me.

However, I am going to run anyways. I am a stubborn programmer.

Click the Run button again to start the build.

Auto-Collapse of Messages

When you do that Studio automatically collapses the Messages window, so make sure you click the Messages button again so you can see what gets output there.

When the build finishes (fails) you will see something like the following:

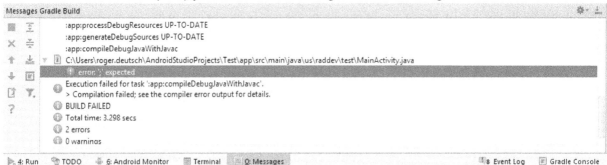

It is warning us that we have an error in MainActivity.java.

Right now, it just thinks we are missing a line-ending semicolon.

The last error line indicates that we can "see compiler error output for details."

To do that you need to open the main menu, File...Settings...

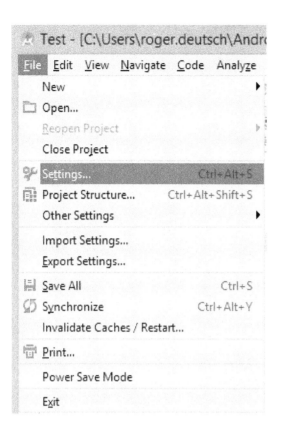

When you choose that, a large window will open.

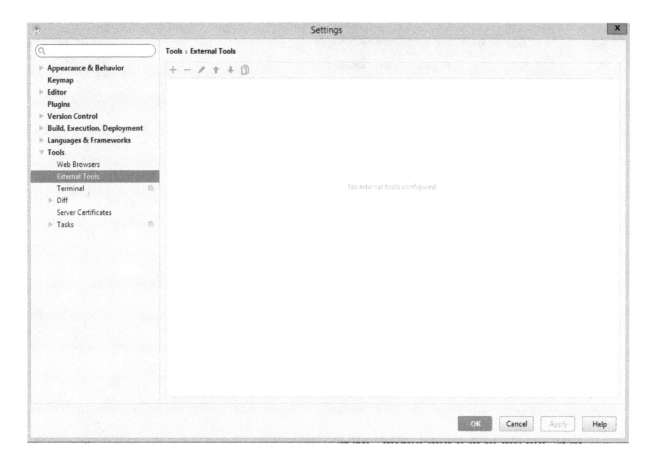

You can move up to the Build, Execution, Deployment item and expand it by clicking the down arrow.

Next, choose the Compiler item and you can add a couple of string values which will be provided to the build system (Gradle) when the app builds.

The two strings are:

--stracktrace --info

Those options tell the build system to provide more output information. You could also add --debug, but that creates a vast amount of output and makes the app build very slowly.

Click the [OK] button to save your settings.

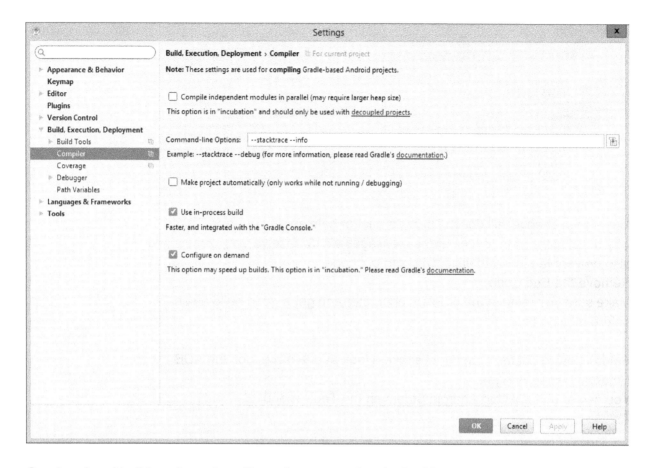

Go ahead and build again and you'll see far more output in the Messages window.

Slow Build?

Keep in mind that if at any time you perceive that your builds are slow, you will want to alter the Compiler Command-line options and remove those two strings we added.   They generate a lot of output.

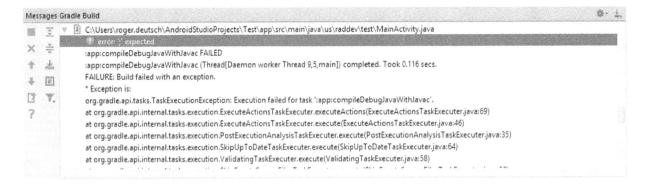

Making the change still doesn't provide a lot of help about our error. That's why developers have to look at the messages we do receive very closely and also be very familiar with valid syntax in our code.

Remove the Bad Code

Make sure you remove the problem character and get a good build again, before moving on.

Before closing out the chapter let's take a look at one more tool, the ADB (Android Debug Bridge).

You can enable it within Android Studio on the Tools menu.

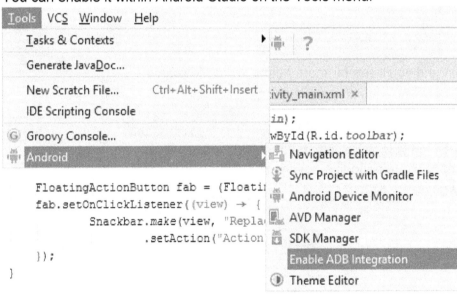

Once you do that you can run a Debug version of your code.

Go to the Run menu and select the Debug app option.

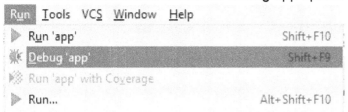

When you do that a special debug version of your app will be built and deployed to your emulator.

When the app is started a new window will appear at the bottom of Android Studio.

It is letting you know it is connected to your emulator and is ready.
Move to your emulator and you should see your app running normally. Click the two different action items available in your app. You will not see any difference at this point.

Set a Breakpoint
Move back to Android Studio and click to the left of the if statement we've been examining.
If you do that in the little tray next to the editor then a red dot will appear.
That is a breakpoint.

```
    //noinspection SimplifiableIfStatement
    if (id == R.id.action_settings) {
        Log.d("test", "User clicked the Settings menu item.");
        return true;
    }

    return super.onOptionsItemSelected(item);
}
```

Now, when you run the code that hits that line, the execution will break at this location and you will be able to control the execution.

Go to the Run menu and choose Debug app.

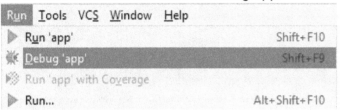

The app will start in debug mode.

Go back to your app running in your emulator and once again, click the ellipsis menu and then the Settings menu item. When you do that Android Studio will jump to the top window again and the code will stop and highlight the line it stopped on in blue.

```
    //noinspection SimplifiableIfStatement
    if (id == R.id.action_settings)
        Log.d("test", "User clicked the Settings menu item.");
        return true;
    }

    return super.onOptionsItemSelected(item);
}
```

You can see a small check on top of the breakpoint now. The execution has stopped on that line.

Press your F8 button and the code will advance one line, into the the first statement within the

You can also float over variables with your cursor to find out what value they are currently set to. Try this with the id value, even though it isn't meaningful to us yet -- we'll learn about it in later chapters.

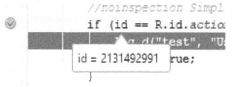

You can see that the id is equal to 2131492991.

You can also see values of variables at the bottom of Android Studio.

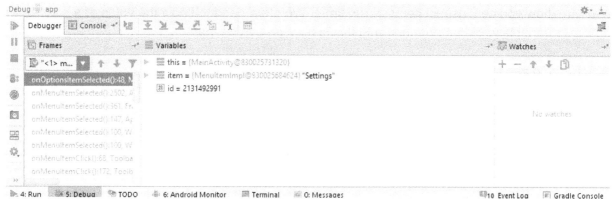

Again, you can see the value of the id variable.

You can inspect objects in the window also. For example our Activity object which we named MainActivity is the first item showing in the list. Click the down arrow next to it to expand it and you can see all of it's member variables and more.

At this point we don't know what all of that means, but it is important to know how you can inspect items at run time. We often need to know the value of a variable to debug our code and this is how we can do that.

Go ahead and stop the debugging so we can end ;the chapter.
Go to the Run menu again and click the Stop menu item.

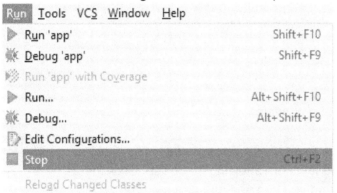

Once you do that the debug connection will stop.
However, your app will still be running in the emulator.

Warning and Crashes

Very often switching between debug and running a normal copy of the app crashes the system running in the emulator. If this happens the app will become unresponsive and then you'll probably see the boot up screen again in the emulator. You'll just have to wait for the OS (Operating System) to start again.

Chapter Summary

This chapter has brought you a long way toward building a solid foundation for you as a professional Android app developer.
You built an application that is based upon a template. That may not feel like much, but you are much further along because you've conquered one of the most difficult barriers to Android development: getting the emulator running.

We've not only got your app running and deployed to the emulator, but we've also successfully altered a small bit of code and learned various ways to know what is going on via logging and debugging.

These points of knowledge will serve you well over your Android development career as they grow more solid.

Building a Real App : Next Chapter

But none of this information matters until we build a real application. That's why in chapter 4 we will:

1. build a complete app which will allow you to write and save notes on your device.
2. run it on the emulator
3. show you how to sideload the app to a real device -- sideloading allows you to deploy to a device without deploying it to the Google Play store.

While building this app we will :

1. design a User Interface (UI) using XML and learning about layouts.
2. write Java code to save files, display note lists and more
3. learn a bit about the app manifest (AndroidManifest.xml) and app permissions
4. learn more about how apps are structured.

Now, let's go write some real code!

Chapter 4
Stenotes App Part 1

Now that we've been all through using Android Studio to create a new project, I can tell you very quickly what to do and you will know how to do it.

A Good Project Name, Worth It's Weight In Gold
We want to start a new project named, Stenotes. This is a portmanteau using an abbreviation for stenography (art of writing in short-hand) and the word notes. But wait, there's more. If you put the word into Google Translate you will see it is a Greek word meaning narrowness or thin.

That is fitting since this will be a somewhat thin app. It's simply going to allow users to create short notes that they can save to their device. It will also provide a way to view the list of notes that they've saved so they can open them for viewing and editing at a later time. We'll also have to provide a way to delete notes.

Get the Complete App Right Now
You can get the complete app right now, simply by pointing a browser at:
http://raddev.us/LYAA/Downloads/stenotes.apk

Create New Project
Go ahead and open up Android Studio and name the app: Stenotes.
Build for phone and tablet and keep API Level 15.
Choose the Blank Activity as the Layout for the project, just like we did in our first project.
Name the default Activity as MainActivity, just as we did in our first app.

Finally, click the [Finish] button and Android Studio will generate the basic
app project framework for you.

Android Studio and Gradle Build

As soon as you click the [Finish] button you will see something like the
following:

Notice that right beneath the image of the Android device there is a message
that states: Rendering Problems.

At this point, Android Studio is attempting to display the basic User Interface (UI) that it has created for your project. However, it cannot do so yet, because it needs to compile (build) the Layout XML (eXtensible Markup Language) to turn it into the UI you will see in the preview device.
As you can see at the bottom of the previous screenshot, Gradle is working on doing this, but hasn't completed. This process can take a while depending upon your hardware, but eventually when Gradle completes the build, you should see a preview of the basic UI.

These are the types of things that new Android devs see and they can be confusing so I try to mention them.

Android Studio Preview
You will also find that the Android Studio UI preview is far from perfect. There's already one obvious item missing from the Preview and that is the app's Title bar text. If you run the app, you'll see that text is actually set but in the Studio preview it is blank.
A Plan for the Layout & Functionality

My idea for the design is the following.
1. We need a way to add a new note so we will use the pink + (plus) button on what is called the Snackbar to run the code that adds a new note.
2. Adding a new message means the user needs a place to type his note. To do that, we'll add a new Activity (Window or Form) that will hold the text (we'll call it NoteActivity) that is typed into the note.
3. The MainActivity will be a list of all saved notes with some kind of indication of what is in the note. We'll change MainActivity to look that way.
   a. This means that when a user touches (taps) one of the items, it should open the NoteActivity and load the message from the device storage.
4. We need to provide a way to delete any specific note and we'll do that by activating some functionality upon long-hold of any item in the list displayed on the MainActivity. Long-hold is when the user touches and holds a UI item rather than just taps it.

First Step : Add New Activity

Let's add the new Activity first and then we can learn how to load that Activity to make it visible to the user.

We will make the Activity load when the user clicks the pink + (plus) button.

Screen Real Estate

First of all, there isn't a lot space on the screen to see everything, so let's collapse the UI preview for now.

On the right portion of Android Studio where the preview is shown, take a look at the very bottom and you should see two small tabs. One is labeled Design and the other is labeled Text.

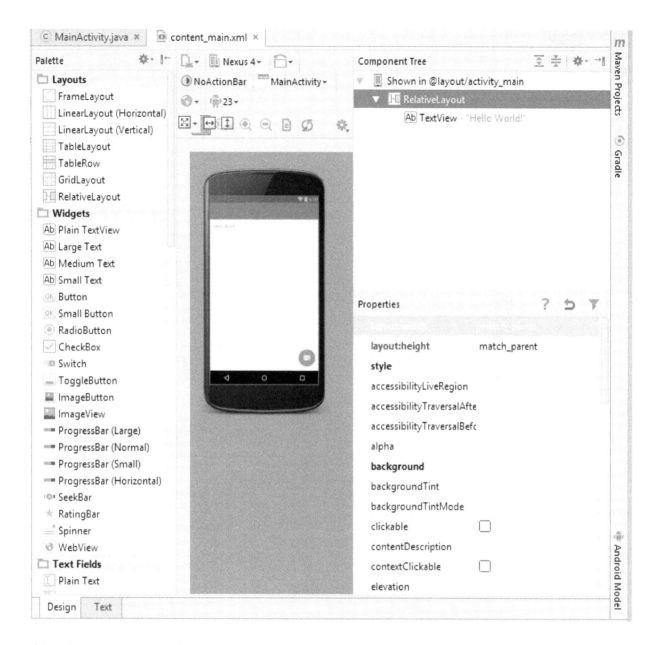

Click the one that says Text and the UI preview will be replaced with the Text (XML) editor view of the Layout.

It'll then look something like:

The Text on the left is the XML Layout code which creates the MainActivity
view that the user will see and which is represented in the (now) smaller
window on the right.

For now, I want to make it so I have plenty of space to write the XML without distraction so go ahead and click the vertical menu item which says Preview at the top far right side of Studio.

When you do that, the Preview window will collapse and hide itself. If you want it back, simply click that vertical menu again and it'll appear again.

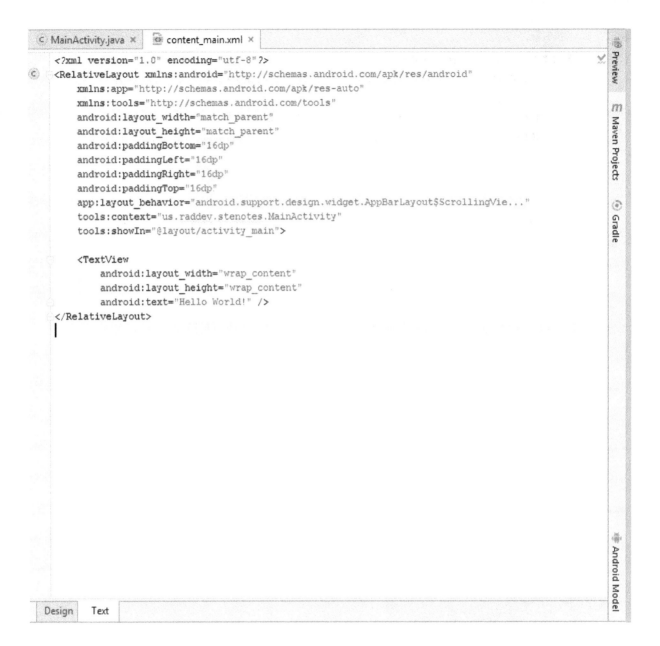

```xml
<?xml version="1.0" encoding="utf-8"?>
<RelativeLayout xmlns:android="http://schemas.android.com/apk/res/android"
    xmlns:app="http://schemas.android.com/apk/res-auto"
    xmlns:tools="http://schemas.android.com/tools"
    android:layout_width="match_parent"
    android:layout_height="match_parent"
    android:paddingBottom="16dp"
    android:paddingLeft="16dp"
    android:paddingRight="16dp"
    android:paddingTop="16dp"
    app:layout_behavior="android.support.design.widget.AppBarLayout$ScrollingVie..."
    tools:context="us.raddev.stenotes.MainActivity"
    tools:showIn="@layout/activity_main">

    <TextView
        android:layout_width="wrap_content"
        android:layout_height="wrap_content"
        android:text="Hello World!" />
</RelativeLayout>
```

Now we want to focus on adding a new Activity to our project. To do this, we want to add it in the same location where our MainActivity has been created. To find that location, we need to use the Project explorer to find it. The project explorer is on the left side and provides a tree structure that we can navigate through to find the files in our solution.

Yours might be collapsed right now.

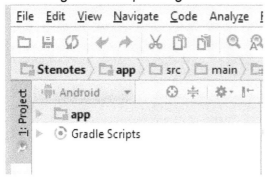

If it is, then focus on the app folder and expand it (click it).

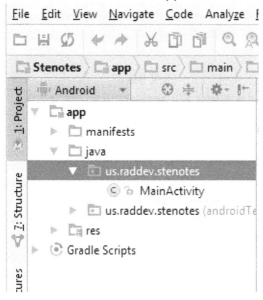

Under the app folder you'll find a java folder. Expand that one. Finally, you'll find the us.raddev.stenotes folder. Expand that one too and notice that the MainActivity class is listed in that one. That's what the little blue 'c' means : class. The MainActivity class is found in the MainActivity.java file so if you double-click the MainActivity class on in the project explorer then the file will open in the editor on the right.

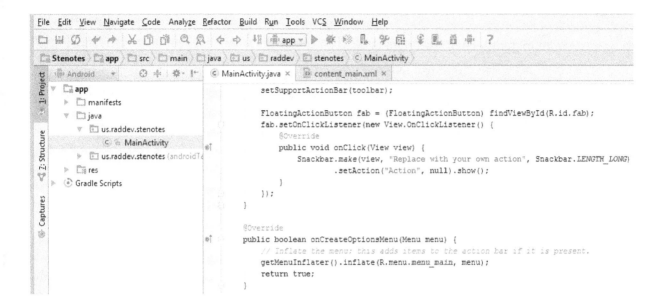

```
                              setSupportActionBar(toolbar);

                              FloatingActionButton fab = (FloatingActionButton) findViewById(R.id.fab);
                              fab.setOnClickListener(new View.OnClickListener() {
                                  @Override
                                  public void onClick(View view) {
                                      Snackbar.make(view, "Replace with your own action", Snackbar.LENGTH_LONG)
                                              .setAction("Action", null).show();
                                  }
                              });
                          }

                          @Override
                          public boolean onCreateOptionsMenu(Menu menu) {
                              // Inflate the menu; this adds items to the action bar if it is present.
                              getMenuInflater().inflate(R.menu.menu_main, menu);
                              return true;
                          }
```

Add the New Activity

What we want to do is add a new Activity. To do that, right-click the us.raddev.stenotes folder in project explorer and a menu will appear.

When that menu appears, hover your mouse over the New menu item and it will expand.

Keep hovering down over the Activity menu item and the menu will expand again.

Finally, hover down over the Empty menu item and click it.

It will look like the following:

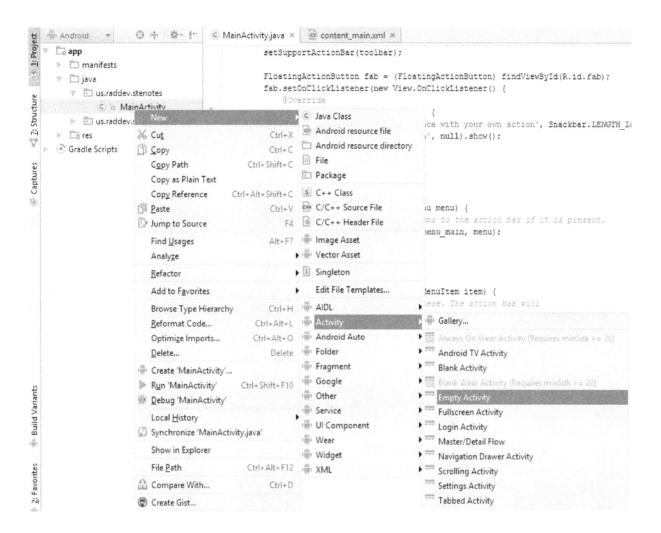

Keep in mind, this is not the Blank Activity template we used for the MainActivity. This is the Empty Activity.

When you click that menu item, Android Studio will present you with a configuration window so you can set up the new Activity.

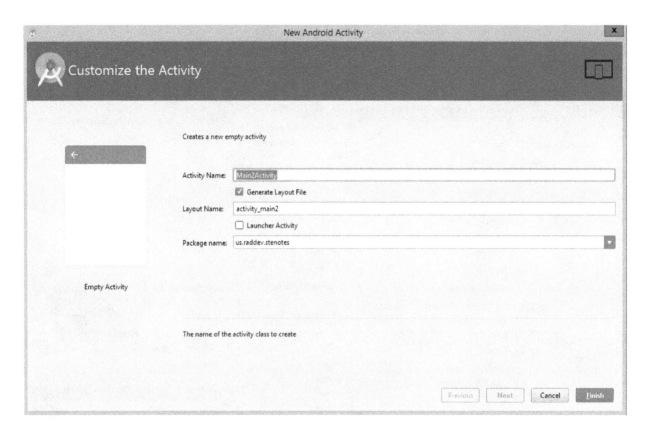

Studio offers a default name, but we want to name ours NoteActivity so type that in your Activity Name text box.

When you do, Studio will automatically update the values in Layout Name and title.

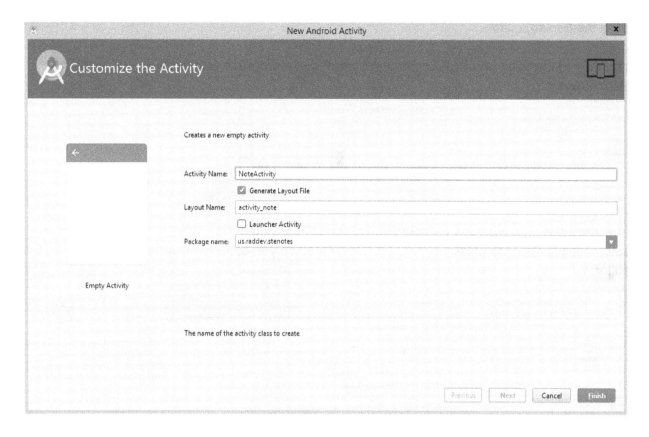

By typing the Activity name you are indicating the name of the Activity class for the programmable object in your code. And, you are also indicating that the java file will be named NoteActivity.java.

Layout Naming Convention
The convention for naming the layout that is used for the Activity is to simply flip the name you provide around and separate each capitalized word with underscores. You can name your layout anything you want. This is simply the convention that is suggested by Google and makes it easier to match up the layout file (XML) with the Activity file (java).

Notice that if you do not want Studio to create a layout file for you for use with this Activity, you can uncheck the "Generate Layout File" choice. Of course, we do want the layout file generated so we will leave it checked.

Click the [Finish] button.

You may (depending upon your computer speed) see a progress window like the following:

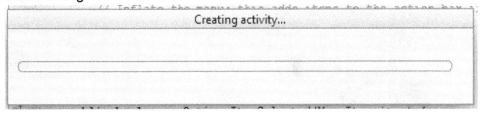

At some point, that progress window will disappear and Studio will automatically open the class file that you just created so you can view it in the editor.

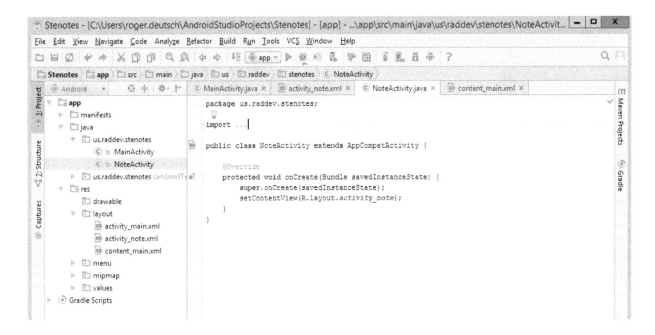

Notice that the file is highlighted in the project explorer on the left and it is displayed in the text editor on the right. You can see the file name at the top of the tab.

Notice also, that Studio has also created a new file in the re\layout\ directory named activity_note.xml.

Android Studio has also taken the liberty of opening that file already too. If you look closely on the right side you will see a tab with the file name (activity_note.xml) at the top.

Go ahead and click the activity_note.xml tab or double-click the activity_note.xml file on the left in project explorer so that the file will become active in the editor.

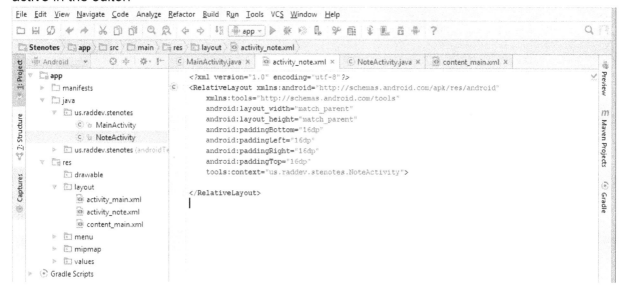

You can see that the activity_note.xml contains very little code in it. Let's go ahead and preview it. Click the vertical Preview button on far right side of Android Studio.

When I clicked that button I saw the following:

It looks like some class cannot be instantiated and I guess the previewer needs it to do its work.

My guess is that the layout is depending upon something in the Activity class (NoteActivity.java) and that class hasn't been compiled yet.

Go to the main menu Build...Rebuild Project... and click it to rebuild.

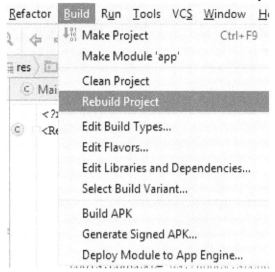

When you do that and the build completes, the errors will go away and the preview will look correct.

Go ahead and collapse the preview window again, by clicking the vertical Preview button on the far right. Now we can focus on the Layout XML so we can alter it to allow the user to type her note.

The auto-generated layout looks like the following:
```
<?xml version="1.0" encoding="utf-8"?>
<RelativeLayout
xmlns:android="http://schemas.android.com/apk/res/android"
    xmlns:tools="http://schemas.android.com/tools"
    android:layout_width="match_parent"
    android:layout_height="match_parent"
    android:paddingBottom="@dimen/activity_vertical_margin"
    android:paddingLeft="@dimen/activity_horizontal_margin"
    android:paddingRight="@dimen/activity_horizontal_margin"
    android:paddingTop="@dimen/activity_vertical_margin"
    tools:context="us.raddev.stenotes.NoteActivity">
```

```
</RelativeLayout>
```

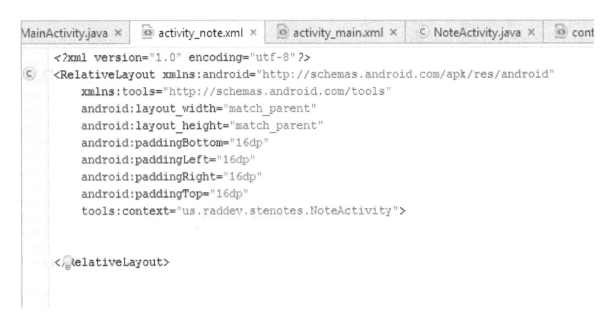

```xml
<?xml version="1.0" encoding="utf-8"?>
<RelativeLayout xmlns:android="http://schemas.android.com/apk/res/android"
    xmlns:tools="http://schemas.android.com/tools"
    android:layout_width="match_parent"
    android:layout_height="match_parent"
    android:paddingBottom="16dp"
    android:paddingLeft="16dp"
    android:paddingRight="16dp"
    android:paddingTop="16dp"
    tools:context="us.raddev.stenotes.NoteActivity">


</RelativeLayout>
```

Layout XML : Basic Explanation
The first line is simply a document definition so that anything that parses this document can know that we are trying to let it know that we believe what follows is valid and well-formed XML.

Since we've stated that, anything that parses it will try to let us know when things we add don't look like valid or well-formed XML. This includes the Android Studio editor.

Quick XML Overview
XML is simply a data structure described by text. Each structure or tag in a an XML document is called an element. An element will take the form of a pair of one opening tag and one closing tag (in most cases).
One XML element will look like the following:
Generally, data for the tag is typed between the two tags something like the following:
<elementName>sample data</elementName>

Each element may also contain one or more attributes which describe the element.

<elementName attributeName1=value1 attributeName2=value2>sample data</elementName>

Each attribute is what is called a name-value pair. That means each one has a name and a value.

As you can see, the name comes first then an equal sign (=) and then the value. It's that simple.

Name-value pairs are used everywhere in the programming world.

Now that you understand these basics. Examine the Layout xml in activity_note.xml again and I believe you'll notice that there is actually only one element in the entire document: <RelativeLayout>

That is the root element.

However, this one element contains numerous attributes:

```
xmlns:android="http://schemas.android.com/apk/res/android"
xmlns:tools="http://schemas.android.com/tools"
android:layout_width="match_parent"
android:layout_height="match_parent"
android:paddingBottom="@dimen/activity_vertical_margin"
android:paddingLeft="@dimen/activity_horizontal_margin"
android:paddingRight="@dimen/activity_horizontal_margin"
android:paddingTop="@dimen/activity_vertical_margin"
tools:context="us.raddev.stenotes.NoteActivity"
```

All of those attributes describe the RelativeLayout.

Let's take a look at each one so you can understand exactly what the XML code is doing.

Again, understanding these things will make your life far easier as an Android developer and will help you understand problems you run into when something renders improperly because you will understand where the code comes from.

XML Namespaces
We touched upon namespaces with Java code and packages in an earlier chapter.

What is the purpose of a namespace?

It is simply to keep things separated.

It is possible that some other library you use could use a variable or function with the same name. That would cause the system to fail to build and not run since it cannot differentiate between them.

Namespaces provide a simple way to provide more qualifiers to the name of your things.

It's like placing everything in a box with your label on it. That way the compiler can know which box to go to when it needs a particular variable. This keeps code from clashing with each other.

I know that was a long explanation, but now it becomes important while we look at the layout XML.

The very first attribute of the RelativeLayout element defines an xml namespace and it looks like the following:

xmlns:android="http://schemas.android.com/apk/res/android"

That is saying to use a an XML NameSpace (xmlns) with the name android for this element.

The second attribute creates a namespace named tools like this:

xmlns:tools="http://schemas.android.com/tools"

All of the Other Attributes

Now, as you look at all the other attributes and you see the word android followed by a colon you can know that it is referencing the android namespace.

The following six attributes of the RelativeLayout element all use that namespace and they look like:

```
android:layout_width="match_parent"
android:layout_height="match_parent"
android:paddingBottom="16dp"
android:paddingLeft="16dp"
android:paddingRight="16dp"
android:paddingTop="16dp"
```

Now that you know what that first part is, you can basically ignore it.

The last RelativeLayout attribute has the tools namespace and looks like:

```
tools:context="us.raddev.stenotes.NoteActivity"
```

Name-Value Pairs

Now you can see if you ignore the namespace portion that each attribute is a name-value pair just as we previously learned.

Now this mess of code is beginning to make a bit more sense.

The name-value pairs are the attributes and they are the things that are going to change the style of our elements. The first two we see are:

layout_width="match_parent"

layout_height="match_parent"

These two attributes insure that the RelativeLayout element width and height are going to match the parent (container).

Since the RelativeLayout is the outermost element, what would the parent container be?

In this case, it is the basic window frame that is automatically added. That means these values set the RelativeLayout to expand to the entire window height and width.

Editable Text Box

We are going to need some kind of editable text box. The editable text box which will allow a user to type text is called a EditText control. Let's go ahead and add one to our Layout.

Go to the activity_note.xml file in the editor and move down a line or two after the last attribute of the RelativeLayout tag and type the following:

<EditText and press the ENTER key.

When you press the ENTER key Android Studio is going to pop up some help.

It requires you set the layout_width so it immediately allows you to choose a value for this new control.

As soon as you choose (or type) the match_parent value for layout_width
then Android Studio will jump to the android:layout_height="" value and
suggest a value for that one too.

You can't see it entirely in the next snapshot, but it is there.

We want both of these to be match_parent, because we want the EditText
control to take up the entire view for now.

When you are done typing / adding the match_parent values your code
should look like the following:

```xml
<?xml version="1.0" encoding="utf-8"?>
<RelativeLayout xmlns:android="http://schemas.android.com/apk/res/android"
    xmlns:tools="http://schemas.android.com/tools"
    android:layout_width="match_parent"
    android:layout_height="match_parent"
    android:paddingBottom="16dp"
    android:paddingLeft="16dp"
    android:paddingRight="16dp"
    android:paddingTop="16dp"
    tools:context="us.raddev.stenotes.NoteActivity">

    <EditText
        android:layout_width="match_parent"
        android:layout_height="match_parent" />

</RelativeLayout>
```

Add Code to Display Activity

Let's go add some code so we can display this new Activity to the user and let him type some text.

Open up the MainActivity.java file and move to the place in the code where there is a line that has the text which starts with...

    Snackbar.make(view,

Open up a line before the Snackbar.make(... line so it looks like the following:

```java
        FloatingActionButton fab = (FloatingActionButton) findViewById(R.id.fab);
        fab.setOnClickListener(new View.OnClickListener() {
            @Override
            public void onClick(View view) {
                |
                Snackbar.make(view, "Replace with your own action", Snackbar.LENGTH_LONG)
                        .setAction("Action", null).show();
            }
        });
    }
```

You can see the cursor on the line where we want to be.

That code is actually inside a function named onClick(). That is the function that is called when the FloatingActionBar is clicked. That FloatingActionBar only contains one element which is the circular button with the envelope on it. We are going to use that button to load and show our Note Activity, since the button is there for us to use.

We want to type the following two lines of code and then comment out the lines of code which are already in the onClick() function since we don't want those lines to run any more.

```java
Intent i = new Intent(MainActivity.this, NoteActivity.class);
startActivity(i);
```

Code Comments

Java (and most programming languages) allow developers to add comments to the source code so developers can place notes and information about the code inline with the code. This can help us remember something important about the code later.

In Java, the way to make a line a comment is by placing two slash characters before the text you want to be commented.

// this is a comment

This causes the Java compiler to simply ignore the lines so they are not compiled. Since, in most cases the notes would not be valid Java code, this allows the notes to be in the source code fiile but not affect the program..

We can also comment out lines in an effort to keep those lines from being recognized by the compiler and built into our program. That is what I am doing with the original lines of code found in the onClick method. That way I don't lose those lines, in case I want them later. However, since the compiler will ignore them now, those lines will not be built into our final program.

You can see that the Android Studio editor grays out commented lines to indicate that they are not compiled into the program.

The final code will look something like the following:

```
FloatingActionButton fab = (FloatingActionButton) findViewById(R.id.fab);
fab.setOnClickListener(new View.OnClickListener() {
    @Override
    public void onClick(View view) {
        Intent i = new Intent(MainActivity.this, NoteActivity.class);
        startActivity(i);
        //Snackbar.make(view, "Replace with your own action", Snackbar.LENGTH_LONG)
                //.setAction("Action", null).show();
    }
});
}
```

Build and Run
Let's build this and run it and type some text into the EditText control.

Once you build and run you'll see the MainActivity and it'll display the round
pink button with the envelope on it. Once that displays, go ahead and click it.
When you do, the NoteActivity will be loaded and displayed. There's not
much to it, but you can type some text in the EditText control.
Here's a snapshot of it after I typed some text.

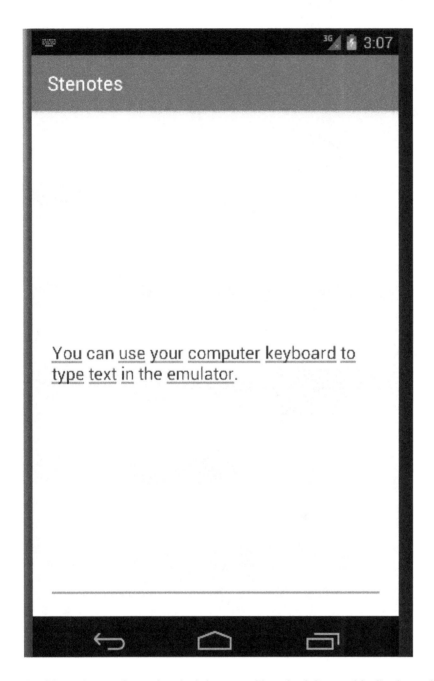

You can use your computer keyboard to type text in the emulator.

At this point we have loaded the new NoteActivity and it displays the EditText for us, but otherwise the app doesn't do much. The text isn't saved and the

EditText box takes up the entire screen and centers the text vertically which seems a little odd.

We will fix all of these things of course, but first let's talk about an Activity's lifetime.

Activity Lifetime
Each Activity has a certain lifecycle and specific events associated with the lifecycle.
Understanding the lifecycle and the associated events helps us to understand what we can do while working within the Activity.

To learn more about the lifecycle of the Activity we are going to use our knowledge of logging to help us look at how the NoteActivity object is constructed and determine when each lifecycle event fires.

Let's look more closely at the code we added to our onClick event and talk about exactly what they do.

The first line:
```
Intent i = new Intent(MainActivity.this, NoteActivity.class);
```

That line creates a new Intent object. An Intent is simply a description of the functionality that you want Android to start for you. In this case we want Android to load a new Activity for us. This constructor for the Intent object takes two parameters. The first parameter is a Context which the new Activity will be loaded within. In other words, what is the context in which the NoteActivity is loaded? The answer is the context of the MainActivity. It's as if you are telling the Intent constructor who owns the NoteActivity. In our case it is the activity which is loading the new NoteActivity.

After we instantiate the new Intent object, we make a call to the startActivity method which takes the Intent object we just created as a parameter. That call looks like:
```
startActivity(i);
```

That method is a part of our MainActivity. We have gotten this method for free since we derived MainActivity from AppCompatActivity.

If you look at the definition of our MainActivity you can see where it is derived from that class:

```
public class MainActivity extends AppCompatActivity {
```

Extends Keyword and Inheritance

The Java keyword extends allows us to inherit all of the abilities of the AppCompatActivity class in our MainActivity class. The reason we may not have noticed this code is because the Android Studio project template wrote it for us when we created our new app.

What Is AppCompatActivity?

That leads us to the next obvious question: what is AppCompatActivity?
It is a built-in class that the android libraries make available.
If you look at the top of the file in the import statements you will see a line which looks like the following:

```
import android.support.v7.app.AppCompatActivity;
```

You can see the project template went ahead and imported that library and derived our main Activity from it. That's because there have been some changes to the Activity class and those have been moved into a specific library to make them compatible on newer devices. That way when you create your app you can use code that makes your app look the same on various devices running different versions of Android.

For Less Experienced Developers

If you want more details on understanding Java classes, see my notes at:

The reason we examined each of these items was simply to determine where the startActivity() method came from and now we know that it is part of the base Activity class (and the AppCompatActivity class). Now that we know where it came from, let's continue our talk about our code.

Add Logging : Watch Event Order

First of all, let's alter our onClick() method in MainActivity.java and add two lines which will log some information we can watch as the app runs. You'll need to add the lines which are bolded in the code snippet which follows. It's the three lines which call the Log.d() method. Note, I also deleted the lines that we had previously commented out so you can do that also, if you like.

```
    public void onClick(View view) {
        Log.d("MainActivity", "in onClick...");
        Intent i = new Intent(MainActivity.this, NoteActivity.class);
        Log.d("MainActivity", "after new Intent()...");
        startActivity(i);
        Log.d("MainActivity", "after startActivity");
    }
});
```

With that code you'll see some output when you click the action button. We also want to alter the NoteActivity class and add some logging to it so we will see the order of all the events.

This will help us understand what is happening.

Alter the NoteActivity.java class so it now contains the following code. The bolded lines are the ones you'll need to add. You can see that we've added a constructor method. That is the method that is named exactly the same as the class (public NoteActivity()). That method will run when the NoteActivity class is instantiated. We do that so we can log the moment when the NoteActivity class is loaded into memory.

```
public class NoteActivity extends AppCompatActivity {

    public NoteActivity ()
    {
        Log.d("NoteActivity", "Inside NoteActivity constructor..." );
    }


    @Override
```

```java
    protected void onCreate(Bundle savedInstanceState) {
        Log.d("NoteActivity", "In NoteActivity.onCreate()...");
        super.onCreate(savedInstanceState);
        setContentView(R.layout.activity_note);
        setTitle("Note - new");
    }
}
```

| C MainActivity.java × | C NoteActivity.java × | ◇ activity_note.xml × | ◇ activity_main.xml × |

```java
+ import ...

public class NoteActivity extends AppCompatActivity {

    public NoteActivity ()
    {
        Log.d("NoteActivity", "Inside NoteActivity constructor..." );
    }

    @Override
    protected void onCreate(Bundle savedInstanceState) {
        Log.d("NoteActivity", "In NoteActivity.onCreate()...");
        super.onCreate(savedInstanceState);
        setContentView(R.layout.activity_note);
        setTitle("Note - new");
    }
}
```

Next, we've added a Log.d() call in the onCreate so we can see when that code actually runs.

Finally, you can see that I've also added a new method call on the last line of the onCreate() method which is called setTitle(). This method simply allows me to put a new string into the title area at the top of our NoteActivity. This is a nice way to indicate to the user that our new NoteActivity has loaded because the text at the top will change from Stenotes to "Note - new".

Set Up Logcat

Before we run the code, let's set up logcat so it'll only show us the lines from the Log.d() method.

To do that, you :

1. Open Android Monitor
2. Click the Filters droplist
3. Choose Edit Filter Configuration item

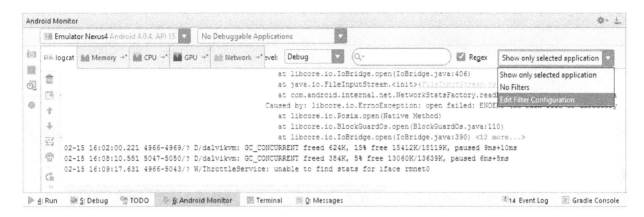

When you make that choice a dialog box will appear.

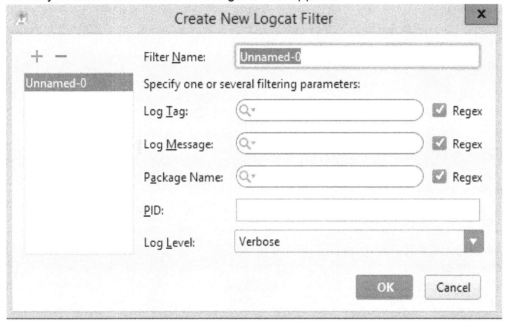

It attempts to name the filter for you as Unamed-0.

Type Main since this will be our Main filter.

Then, move to the Log Tag edit box and type the filter as follows (no spaces):

MainActivity|NoteActivity

That's the name of the two tags that we are using in our Log.d() statements as the first parameter.

They are separated by the pipe character | -- shift and backslash keys get a pipe.

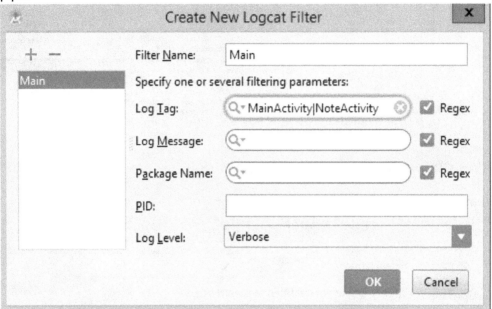

Once everything looks like that, go ahead and click the [OK] button.
Once you click the [OK] button, your logcat window should get much cleaner if you've already ran the app.

Build and Run, Watch Logcat
Go ahead and make the changes to the code and build and run the app.

Get the Code
If you have any problems building or running the app you can get the project download that matches this code at : stenotes_v2.zip

When you run the app, you won't see anything in the logcat window.
But when you click the envelope button the app will write five lines to the window.

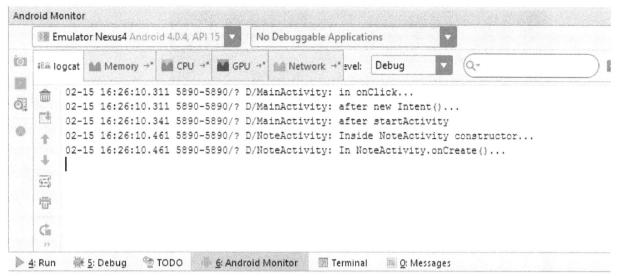

The first three lines come from our onClick method.

The first one is right after the onClick() is called.

Then, the new Intent() object is created and finally, the startActivity() method is called.

What this shows us, is that the startActivity actually creates our NoteActivity object , because after startActivity is called, you see the first line from NoteActivity where the constructor is called.

Once the constructor is finished, the object is loaded in memory and ready for use by the program.

Finally, we see that the NoteActivity.onCreate is called. Remember, we added a line of code to the onCreate() method to change the text at the top of the Activity.

You can see that it did work:

We went through all of that so we can understand how to Log events so we can know exactly how our program runs.

Now, we're going to talk about other events that occur on the Activity object and how to override those events so our code gets called when those events happen.

Activity Has Six LifeCycle Events

We've already seen the onCreate() lifecycle event but now we are going to add five more to our NoteActivity class.

Here's the code we are going to add to NoteActivity:

```java
@Override
public void onStart()
{
    super.onStart();
    Log.d("NoteActivity", "onStart()...");
}


@Override
public void onPause()
{
    super.onPause();
    Log.d("NoteActivity", "onPause()...");
}


@Override
public void onResume()
{
    super.onResume();
    Log.d("NoteActivity", "onResume()...");
}


@Override
public void onStop()
{
    super.onStop();
    Log.d("NoteActivity", "onStop()...");
}


@Override
public void onDestroy()
{
    super.onDestroy();
```

```
        Log.d("NoteActivity", "onDestroy()...");
}
```

You want to add that code right after the onCreate() function.

The code will now look like the following:

```java
        @Override
        protected void onCreate(Bundle savedInstanceState) {
            Log.d("NoteActivity", "In NoteActivity.onCreate()...");
            super.onCreate(savedInstanceState);
            setContentView(R.layout.activity_note);
            setTitle("Note - new");
        }

        @Override
        public void onStart()
        {
            super.onStart();
            Log.d("NoteActivity", "onStart()...");
        }

        @Override
        public void onPause()
        {
            super.onPause();
            Log.d("NoteActivity", "onPause()...");
        }

        @Override
        public void onResume()
        {
            super.onResume();
            Log.d("NoteActivity", "onResume()...");
        }

        @Override
        public void onStop()
        {
            super.onStop();
            Log.d("NoteActivity", "onStop()...");
        }

        @Override
        public void onDestroy()
        {
            super.onDestroy();
            Log.d("NoteActivity", "onDestroy()...");
        }
    }
```

Here we've simply added five new methods (onStart, onPause,
onResume,onStop, onDestroy)

136

These five methods are already implemented by the base class (AppCompatActivity) which we know our NoteActivity class is derived from. That means those methods are available to us.
In this case, we override those methods so that our method is called when those events are fired by the OS.

We want to learn when those events are fired, because we need to manage the data in our app.

Make the previous code changes or download this version of the code, build and run it.

Get the Code
Get stenotes_v3.zip.

Once the app is running go ahead and click the Envelope button and you'll see some additional Log messages in Logcat.

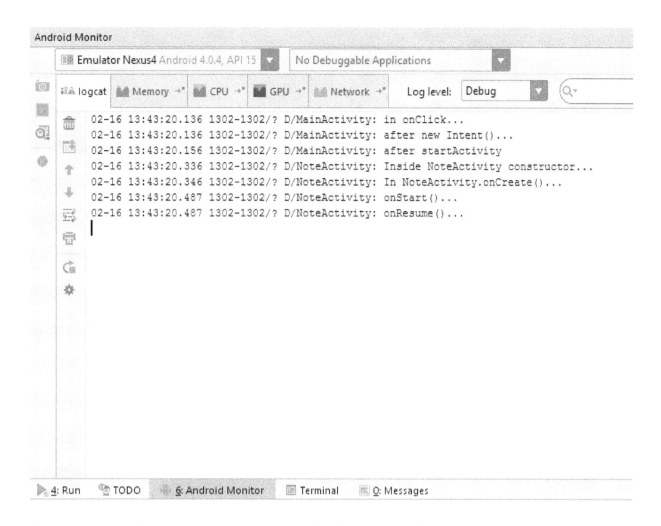

Now we can see that some other events are fired in the app also, when you click the Envelope button.

Now, you can see that note only is the onCreate() event called but the onStart() and onResume() events are also called (last two lines in the logcat output above).

Those events were called even when we weren't overriding them, but since we didn't override them and implement some functionality we weren't aware of them running.

Activity LifeCycle

So, when a new Activity is instantiated then the constructor runs, then onCreate(), onStart() and onResume() runs.

Now, we know that we can be alerted within our code when those run and we can run our custom code to do something.

Device Rotation : Causes Activity To Unload

Now, we're going to show you that device rotation actually causes the foremost Activity - the one the user can see on her screen to go through the lifecycle events. When a user has device rotation enabled and she rotates the device, the app attempts to redraw the current (displayed) Activity. When that happens, the entire Activity is destroyed and rebuilt.

We can see that by watching the series of LifeCycle events that are fired when we rotate the app.

Rotating the Emulator Device

But, how do we simulate app device rotation on the emulator?

You simply do a CTRL-F12 combination and the emulator device will redraw in the opposite rotation style.

Go to your emulator and try it now.

When you do the rotate you are going to see that logcat has a number of new entries:

02-16 13:54:30.366 1302-1302/? D/NoteActivity: onPause()...

02-16 13:54:30.376 1302-1302/? D/NoteActivity: onStop()...

02-16 13:54:30.376 1302-1302/? D/NoteActivity: onDestroy()...

02-16 13:54:30.526 1302-1302/? D/NoteActivity: Inside NoteActivity constructor...

02-16 13:54:30.536 1302-1302/? D/NoteActivity: In NoteActivity.onCreate()...

02-16 13:54:30.756 1302-1302/? D/NoteActivity: onStart()...

02-16 13:54:30.776 1302-1302/? D/NoteActivity: onResume()...

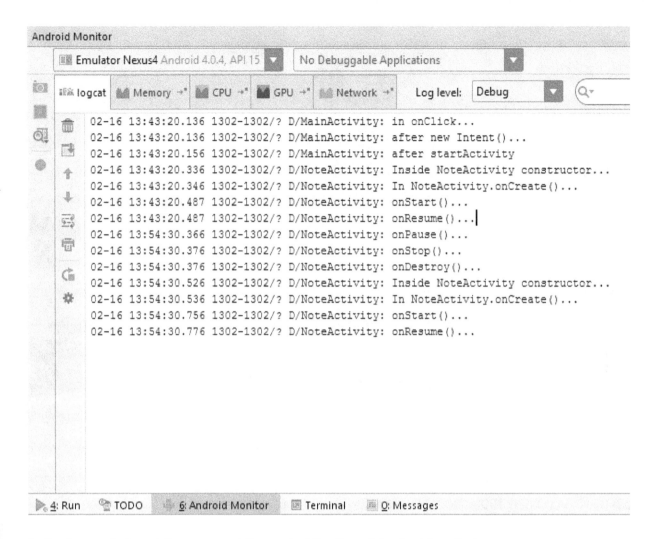

In the image I placed the cursor at the end of the line of the last line that was already in the logcat window.

onPause : Keep In Memory, No Display

You can see that the first new entry is the onPause(). The onPause() lifecycle event is an attempt to keep the Activity in memory but remove it from the display.

onStop : Stop the Activity

Next, the OS determines that the Activity needs to be stopped so send fires the onStop() event.

It has decided that the Activity is being completely redrawn in another configuration (in our case landscape) so the OS knows it should stop the Activity and sends out the event to us so we can do something if we need to.

onDestroy : Unloading the Activity From Memory

Finally, the OS has decided that it needs to unload the Activity object from memory and it sends us our final event as a warning that the object is going away.

Build Activity Again

However, since our app is simply changing the aspect view of our Activity, it knows that it needs to display the Activity again. That's when we see the NoteActivity being built again and the constructor is called along with the onCreate(), onStart() and onResume() events. That puts us right back in the same place in our app, except now in landscape view.

Similar Events Occur When Using Back Button

Similar events occur when you use the back button. Go ahead and switch back to the portrait view (CTRL-F12).

Now, type some text in the EditText box. Mine looks like the following:

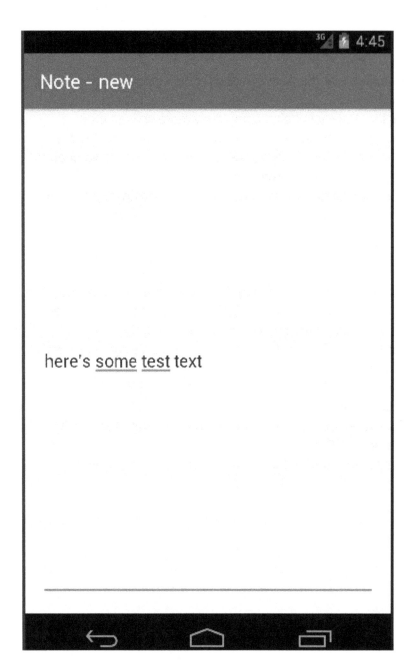

Go ahead and click the back button to return to the MainActivity.

When you click that button, some LifeCycle events for NoteActivity are going to fire.

They are going to be Pause, Stop, and Destroy.

That's because the NoteActivity is unloaded from memory.

EditText Data Is Gone

Go ahead and load the NoteActivity again (click the Envelope button).

Notice that you've lost your text that you had previously entered.

That's because the application knows that you unloaded the NoteActivity and decided it wasn't important to keep that information around.

We've learned quite a lot about the app's lifecycle so let's finish this app up and move to our next one.

Requirements We Still Need to Fulfill

We need the MainActivity to list the notes that we've previously saved.

It should display any notes upon opening the app.

We need to be able to save or cancel the NoteActivity changes we make.

Implementing the Data Save Functionality

First thing we want to do is add a ListView to our MainActivity.

Adding a ListView isn't entirely trivial but I will show you everything you need to do so and explain the code so you know exactly what is going on. However, it's going to take some pages to walk you through it so let's start that work in chapter 5. Again, I won't waste time with introductions, we will jump right into the code to get our app going, but this will provide you with a break to absorb what you've learned.

Chapter 5
Stenotes App Part 2

First thing we want to do is change the MainActivity's view from a RelativeLayout to a ListView.
It's very easy to do and only requires a couple of changes to the content_main.xml.

Two XML Files Represent One Activity
However, you may have noticed that our NoteActivity is represented by only one XML file (activity_note.xml) while the MainActivity is actually made up of two XML files.

The Android Studio template simply broke up the MainActivity XML (layout files) into two so we could handle the two sections of the view more easily.
If you look closely at the activity_main.xml you will see that it contains the shell of the view and a reference to the main content of the Activity (the large white-space in the middle).

In this case I am calling it the shell because the activity_main.xml contains the XML which represents the top Settings menu and the bottom FloatingActionButton.

```
<?xml version="1.0" encoding="utf-8"?>
<android.support.design.widget.CoordinatorLayout
xmlns:android="http://schemas.android.com/apk/res/android"
    xmlns:app="http://schemas.android.com/apk/res-auto"
    xmlns:tools="http://schemas.android.com/tools"
    android:layout_width="match_parent"
    android:layout_height="match_parent"
```

```xml
    android:fitsSystemWindows="true"
    tools:context="us.raddev.stenotes.MainActivity">

    <android.support.design.widget.AppBarLayout
        android:layout_width="match_parent"
        android:layout_height="wrap_content"
        android:theme="@style/AppTheme.AppBarOverlay">

        <android.support.v7.widget.Toolbar
            android:id="@+id/toolbar"
            android:layout_width="match_parent"
            android:layout_height="?attr/actionBarSize"
            android:background="?attr/colorPrimary"
            app:popupTheme="@style/AppTheme.PopupOverlay" />

    </android.support.design.widget.AppBarLayout>

    <include layout="@layout/content_main" />

    <android.support.design.widget.FloatingActionButton
        android:id="@+id/fab"
        android:layout_width="wrap_content"
        android:layout_height="wrap_content"
        android:layout_gravity="bottom|end"
        android:layout_margin="@dimen/fab_margin"
        android:src="@android:drawable/ic_dialog_email" />

</android.support.design.widget.CoordinatorLayout>
```

```xml
<?xml version="1.0" encoding="utf-8"?>
<android.support.design.widget.CoordinatorLayout xmlns:android="http://schemas.android.com/apk/res/android"
    xmlns:app="http://schemas.android.com/apk/res-auto"
    xmlns:tools="http://schemas.android.com/tools"
    android:layout_width="match_parent"
    android:layout_height="match_parent"
    android:fitsSystemWindows="true"
    tools:context="us.raddev.stenotes.MainActivity">

    <android.support.design.widget.AppBarLayout
        android:layout_width="match_parent"
        android:layout_height="wrap_content"
        android:theme="@style/AppTheme.AppBarOverlay">

        <android.support.v7.widget.Toolbar
            android:id="@+id/toolbar"
            android:layout_width="match_parent"
            android:layout_height="?attr/actionBarSize"
            android:background="?attr/colorPrimary"
            app:popupTheme="@style/AppTheme.PopupOverlay" />

    </android.support.design.widget.AppBarLayout>

    <include layout="@layout/content_main" />

    <android.support.design.widget.FloatingActionButton
        android:id="@+id/fab"
        android:layout_width="wrap_content"
        android:layout_height="wrap_content"
        android:layout_gravity="bottom|end"
        android:layout_margin="16dp"
        android:src="@android:drawable/ic_dialog_email" />

</android.support.design.widget.CoordinatorLayout>
```

However, you can see in the bolded line that there is an included layout file named content_main.

This is a reference to the broken out content_main.xml file which represents the main content or view area of the Activity. This is the part that is currently represented by a RelativeLayout and which we are going to convert to a ListView.

Ignore activity_main.xml For Now
The point is that you can ignore activity_main.xml for now. It contains the outer menu framework and we don't want to change those right now.

Open up content_main.xml and change it so it looks like:

```xml
<?xml version="1.0" encoding="utf-8"?>
<ListView xmlns:android="http://schemas.android.com/apk/res/android"
    xmlns:app="http://schemas.android.com/apk/res-auto"
    xmlns:tools="http://schemas.android.com/tools"
    android:layout_width="match_parent"
    android:layout_height="match_parent"
    android:paddingBottom="@dimen/activity_vertical_margin"
    android:paddingLeft="@dimen/activity_horizontal_margin"
    android:paddingRight="@dimen/activity_horizontal_margin"
    android:paddingTop="@dimen/activity_vertical_margin"
    android:id="@+id/mainListView"
    app:layout_behavior="@string/appbar_scrolling_view_behavior"
    tools:context="us.raddev.stenotes.MainActivity"
    tools:showIn="@layout/activity_main">

</ListView>
```

You only have to make two changes to the file:
1. Alter the tag from RelativeLayout to ListView
   a. When you change the top tag in the file, AndroidStudio will alter the closing tag at the bottom of the file automatically.
2. Add the bolded line of xml to your file.

New Resource ID
The second line adds a new resource id which can be used to reference this ListView from your code. We will see how you can do that when we alter the MainActivity.java file.

The Android build system will create an integer which is unique throughout your app, which it will then use to reference this specific ListView. It's as if the system is naming it after a unique integer value. To make it easier for you to remember the ListView's name for use in your code, we have added a text name (mainListView). Again, we will see how this is referenced in code in the java file.

Now that you've made that change, if you were to switch over to Design mode you will see that the main content now has a preview which looks like a list of items.

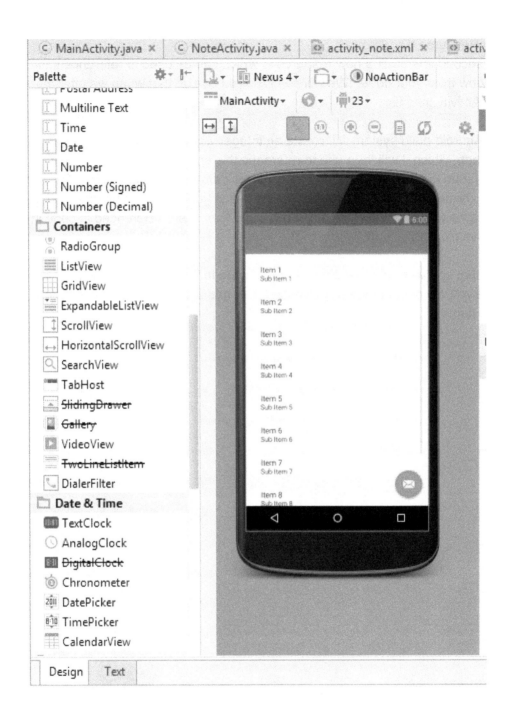

However, if you run the application right now, you won't see any list items yet, since the application isn't adding any.

Adding List Items

Let's switch over to the MainActivity.java file in Android Studio and alter it to add some test items.

To manipulate the ListView (add items programmatically) we need to have a reference to the object which represents the item on screen. To do that, we need to first create an empty ListView object and name it.

It's one easy line of code like the following:

```
private ListView listView;
```

That adds the ListView object, but we still can't use it, since we haven't tied it to anything.

To tie that object to our screen element, we call a helper method provided to us by the Activity named findViewById().

The id that we will use is the one we created for the ListView. Again, you can look back at the content_main.xml file and examine the bold line.

Next, we'll add the line which calls findViewById() and loads our ListView object reference.

Again, it's just one line of code which looks like:

```
listView = (ListView)findViewById(R.id.mainListView);
```

The code inside MainActivity now looks like the following:

```java
public class MainActivity extends AppCompatActivity {

    private ListView listView;

    @Override
    protected void onCreate(Bundle savedInstanceState) {
        super.onCreate(savedInstanceState);
        setContentView(R.layout.activity_main);
        listView = (ListView) findViewById(R.id.mainListView);
```

Where We've Added Each Line Matters
You can see we've added the first line inside the MainActivity class, but outside of any other method (function) call.
However, we placed our findViewById() function call inside the onCreate method.

The onCreate() method runs only once when the activity is instantiated so that is a good place to initialize our member variable listView.

Once, the listView object reference is set to our screen element we can use the object to make things happen in our app.

However, there is a specific way of making a ListView work and it requires the creation of an ArrayAdapter which we'll attach it to our ListView.

So now, let's add two more member variables like the following, after our ListView.

```java
private ArrayList<String> listViewItems = new ArrayList<String>();
private ArrayAdapter<String> adapter;
```

```
public class MainActivity extends AppCompatActivity {

    private ListView listView;
    private ArrayList<String> listViewItems = new ArrayList<String>();
    private ArrayAdapter<String> adapter;

    @Override
    protected void onCreate(Bundle savedInstanceState) {
```

The first new variable we added is simply a list of strings which will represent the items we will add to the list.
The second item is our reference to the ArrayAdapter which we will use to actually add the items to the ArrayList.

We still need to initialize the adapter however so let's add that code in the onCreate() after the initialization of the listView object.
We want it to look like the following:

```
adapter = new ArrayAdapter<String>(
this, android.R.layout.simple_list_item_1, listViewItems);
```

The following image shows all of the code we are going to add now, but I will continue explaining each line as we go.

```
    @Override
    protected void onCreate(Bundle savedInstanceState) {
        super.onCreate(savedInstanceState);
        setContentView(R.layout.activity_main);
        listView = (ListView)findViewById(R.id.mainListView);

        adapter = new ArrayAdapter<String>( this, android.R.layout.simple_list_item_1, listViewItems);
        listView.setAdapter(adapter);
        adapter.add("thing 1");
        adapter.add("thing 2");
        adapter.add("thing 3");
        adapter.notifyDataSetChanged();
```

To initialize the ArrayAdapter we have to send in three things in the function:
1. a reference to the Context it is associated with
2. a style which will be used to render the items.
3. the actual ArrayList which contains the items (in this case they are strings).

154

First Parameter : this Variable
The this variable is difficult to talk about because of its name, but otherwise it is a simple concept.
The this variable represents the object which is currently instantiated and running the code. Of course in our case, that means the this variable is referencing our MainActivity. Providing this as the first parameter to the ArrayAdapter provides it with a context in which the ArrayAdapter will function.

Second Parameter : Resource ID of Layout
The second parameter is a resource ID but this time it's not one we created (such as in the case of the R.id.mainListView. Instead, this is a template layout provided to us by the Android development libraries. This item defines the styles used to render our ListView on screen. It is an XML file which contains one item.

Android Studio : Go To Declaration
If you would like to see how this item is defined you can do so easily by using Android Studio's
Go To=>Declaration functionality.
To do this simply right-click the simple_list_item_1 text in the MainActivity.java file and a menu will appear. Go down to the Go To menu item and another menu will pop out. Next, select the Declaration menu item and Android Studio will open up that layout (XML) file for you.

```
oter<String>( this,android.R.layout.simple_list_item_1, listViewItems);
apter);
:
:
:
nanged();

lbar) findViewById(R.id.toolbar);
olbar);

ab = (FloatingActionButton) findViewBy
(new View.OnClickListener() {

<(View view) {
ivity", "in onClick...");
ev Intent(MainActivity.this, NoteActiv
ivity", "after new Intent()...");
/(:-'
iv:
```

Jump to Navigation Bar	Alt+Home	
Declaration	Ctrl+B	
Implementation(s)	Ctrl+Alt+B	
Type Declaration	Ctrl+Shift+B	
Super Method	Ctrl+U	
Test	Ctrl+Shift+T	

✂ Cut	Ctrl+X	
▢ Copy	Ctrl+C	
Copy as Plain Text		
Copy Reference	Ctrl+Alt+Shift+C	
▢ Paste	Ctrl+V	
Paste from History...	Ctrl+Shift+V	
Paste Simple	Ctrl+Alt+Shift+V	
Column Selection Mode	Alt+Shift+Insert	
Find Usages	Alt+F7	
Analyze	▶	
Refactor	▶	
Folding	▶	
Search with Google		
Go To	▶	
Generate...	Alt+Insert	
Save 'MainActivity'		
Run 'MainActivity'	Ctrl+Shift+F10	
Debug 'MainActivity'		

Studio may open the simple_list_item_1.xml file in Design mode. If it does, the preview will be blank because this is a very simple layout. Click the Text tab and take a look at what is in the file.

```xml
<?xml version="1.0" encoding="utf-8"?>
<!-- Copyright (C) 2006 The Android Open Source Project

     Licensed under the Apache License, Version 2.0 (the "License");
     you may not use this file except in compliance with the License.
     You may obtain a copy of the License at

          http://www.apache.org/licenses/LICENSE-2.0

     Unless required by applicable law or agreed to in writing, software
     distributed under the License is distributed on an "AS IS" BASIS,
     WITHOUT WARRANTIES OR CONDITIONS OF ANY KIND, either express or implied.
     See the License for the specific language governing permissions and
     limitations under the License.
-->

<TextView xmlns:android="http://schemas.android.com/apk/res/android"
     android:id="@android:id/text1"
     android:layout_width="match_parent"
     android:layout_height="wrap_content"
     android:textAppearance="?android:attr/textAppearanceListItemSmall"
     android:gravity="center_vertical"
     android:paddingStart="?android:attr/listPreferredItemPaddingStart"
     android:paddingEnd="?android:attr/listPreferredItemPaddingEnd"
     android:minHeight="?android:attr/listPreferredItemHeightSmall" />
```

You can see there are some obvious styles in there like textAppearance and minHeight.
This is the basic style for a simple list view so it is good to use.
You can close the file now and go back to MainActivity.java.

Back to our discussion of parameters sent in to the ArrayAdapter.

Parameter Three: Object List to Represent
Finally, the last item sent in is the list of objects that will be represented (line items drawn for each) in the ListView.
Notice that I call these *objects*. That's because they do not have to be strings.
In our case we are simplifying by using strings.

In the snapshot of the code you could see the additional lines we are adding, let's go over the rest of those lines now and then we can build and get a basic view of the app with our limited functionality ListView.

After we initialize the adapter to be associated with the proper context, style and list of items, we want to associate it with our listView object. It just takes one line of code.

```
listView.setAdapter(adapter);
```

The ListView provides this function named setAdapter() since the original developers know we are going to want to connect the adapter with our ListView.

This now means that changes we make to our associated adapter (add or remove items) will be displayed in our ListView.

Let's go ahead and add a few items to our ListView, which we do by adding the items to the adapter.

The lines to add three items look like the following:

```
adapter.add("thing 1");
adapter.add("thing 2");
adapter.add("thing 3");
```

Those three items add three new list items to our ListView and the associated strings will appear in our ListView when it renders on the screen.

However, there is one more function call we have to make to insure the adapter is updated and forces the ListView to redraw itself so the items actually show up on the screen.

```
adapter.notifyDataSetChanged();
```

Now, we have all the code which will allow us to run the app and see some test items in our MainActivity.

Go ahead and build and run the app.

If you haven't typed in the code you can get it with the changes up to this point at:

Stenotes_v4.zip

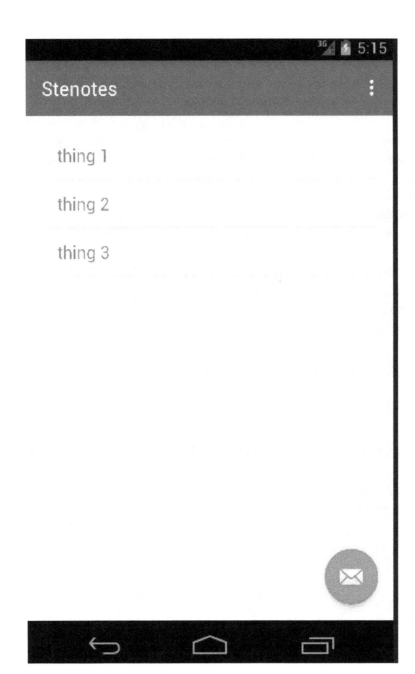

Each of the items in the list is clickable. If you click any of the items right now, you will see each of them flash to a different style when clicked, but the click won't start any other action.
We'll add that code in a moment. For now, let's create a first step in adding a new item to the list.

Add A New Item
We are going to use the FloatingActionButton's onClick method to add new items to our ListView. I'm doing that simply so we don't have to add another button anywhere. We'll comment out the code that launches the NoteActivity for now, but we'll replace that after we do the test code which will allow us to learn how to easily add items to the ListView.

Go ahead and move back to the Android Studio editor and make sure you have MainActivity.java open again. If it's not already open, remember you just go to the project navigator and double-click the MainActivity.java and it'll open again.

Move down in the file to the place where the onClick() function is implemented.

```java
FloatingActionButton fab = (FloatingActionButton) findViewById(R.id.fab);
fab.setOnClickListener(new View.OnClickListener() {
    @Override
    public void onClick(View view) {
        Log.d("MainActivity", "in onClick...");
        Intent i = new Intent(MainActivity.this, NoteActivity.class);
        Log.d("MainActivity", "after new Intent()...");
        startActivity(i);
        Log.d("MainActivity", "after startActivity");
    }
});
}
```

Let's go ahead and comment out all of the lines in there except the first one. That way we'll still see in the Logcat that we are in the onClick.
We can quickly comment those lines by highlighting them all and then choosing the main Code...menu (at the top of Android Studio) and then choosing the Comment with Line Comment menu item.

Note: Instead of using the menu item you can highlight the lines and then type Ctrl+Slash and the lines will switch to comments. If you do Ctrl+Slash on any commented line, Android Studio will uncomment the line. The command simply toggles between the two.

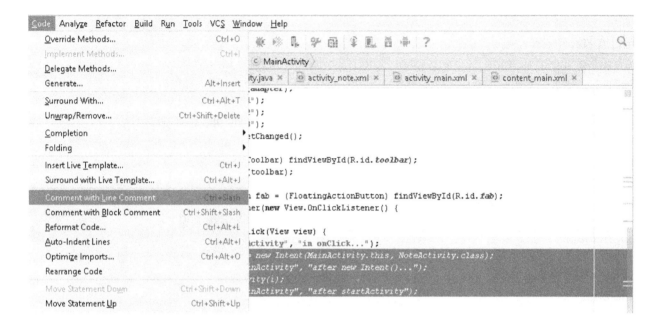

Once you make that choice those four lines will include the // comment marks and will no longer compile into the code.

```
        FloatingActionButton fab = (FloatingActionButton) findViewById(R.id.fab);
        fab.setOnClickListener(new View.OnClickListener() {
            @Override
            public void onClick(View view) {
                Log.d("MainActivity", "in onClick...");
//              Intent i = new Intent(MainActivity.this, NoteActivity.class);
//              Log.d("MainActivity", "after new Intent()...");
//              startActivity(i);
//              Log.d("MainActivity", "after startActivity");

            }
        });
    }
```

Once you comment out those lines, move to the line right past those commented lines so we can begin adding our code to add new ListView items. You can see the bar cursor in the previous image which shows you where we'll type our code.

Date, Time & Formatting

In an effort to add items with unique string values in them, I'm going to use the Java Date object and some formatting methods. It'll take a couple of lines of code simply to generate our item string so don't let it get you too confused on that.

Here's the first line we want to add:

```
SimpleDateFormat sdf = new SimpleDateFormat("yyyyMMdd_HHmmss");
```

When we add that line we've simply added a formatter that will make our time string look a little better. You can see that we are telling it to use a 4-digit year followed by 2-digit month and 2-digit day, then an underscore and 2-digits for each of the remaining elements (hour, minute, second).

When you add that line, Android Studio is going to try to help you add the appropriate package which contains the function and you'll need to hit Alt+Enter to do so.

```
        FloatingActionButton fab = (FloatingActionButton) findViewById(R.id.fab);
        fab.setOnClickListener(new View.OnClickListener() {
            @Override
            public void onClick(View view) {
                Log.d("MainActivity", "in onClick...");
//              Intent i = new Intent(MainActivity.this, NoteActivity.class);
//              Log.d("MainActivity", "after new Intent()...");
  ? java.text.SimpleDateFormat? Alt+Enter });
//              Log.d("MainActivity", "after startActivity");
                SimpleDateFormat sdf = new SimpleDateFormat("yyyyMMdd_HHmmss");
            }
        });
    }
```

Next we'll add one line of code which will get the current DateTime from the system and use the formatter to create a string.

```
String outItem = sdf.format(Calendar.getInstance().getTime());
```

Again, Android Studio will offer to add the import upon pressing Alt+Enter.
Go ahead and make sure you do that.

```java
FloatingActionButton fab = (FloatingActionButton) findViewById(R.id.fab);
fab.setOnClickListener(new View.OnClickListener() {
    @Override
    public void onClick(View view) {
        Log.d("MainActivity", "in onClick...");
        Intent i = new Intent(MainActivity.this, NoteActivity.class);
        Log.d("MainActivity", "after new Intent()...");
        startActivity(i);
        Log.d("MainAc       ? java.util.Calendar? Alt+Enter   ity");
        SimpleDateFormat sdf = new SimpleDateFormat("yyyyMMdd_HHmmss");
        String outItem = sdf.format(Calendar.getInstance().getTime());


    }
});
}
```

Order of Operations on Method Calls

This line of code actually calls three methods : getInstance(), getTime() and
format(). The order of operations on multiple method calls on one line follows
the rules of standard math. Items within parenthesis would be called first and
then after that, you just go left to right in order. In this case, we see that the
first method call is:

```java
Calendar.getInstance()
```

That retrieves an instance of the provided Calendar object. Which is returned
"in-place" and then the next method is called:

```java
getTime()
```

This returns the current date and time object.

Finally the SimpleDateFormat method is called to format the object's output
as a string

```java
sdf.format(Calendar.getInstance().getTime())
```

We then store the what is returned from the format() method in our string variable we have named outputItem.

Now, all we need to do is add the item to our adapter and notify the adapter that we have updated the data. This code is just like the code where we add the "thing 1", "thing 2" & "thing 3" items.

```
adapter.add(outItem);
adapter.notifyDataSetChanged();
```

Finally, our complete code which is ready to run looks like the following:

```
            FloatingActionButton fab = (FloatingActionButton) findViewById(R.id.fab);
            fab.setOnClickListener(new View.OnClickListener() {
                @Override
                public void onClick(View view) {
                    Log.d("MainActivity", "in onClick...");
//                  Intent i = new Intent(MainActivity.this, NoteActivity.class);
//                  Log.d("MainActivity", "after new Intent()...");
//                  startActivity(i);
//                  Log.d("MainActivity", "after startActivity");
                    SimpleDateFormat sdf = new SimpleDateFormat("yyyyMMdd_HHmmss");
                    String outItem = sdf.format(Calendar.getInstance().getTime());
                    adapter.add(outItem);
                    adapter.notifyDataSetChanged();
                }
            });
        }
```

Now when you build and run this code, every time you click the Envelope button a new item with the current date/time will be added to the list.
Go ahead and run the app. If you haven't followed all the changes you can get them at:
Stenotes_v5.zip

When you run the app, click the Envelope button numerous times and each time it will add a new list item.

You can see that I added so many that they no longer all fit on one screen.

The nice thing is that you can now swipe up or down and the list will scroll. You can see the scroll indicator bar on the right side in the previous snapshot.

Envelope Icon
Let's change the Envelope icon now, since it isn't a good indicator of what the button does for us.
The envelope icon is a resource provided by Android development environment and there are other icons too, so let's attempt to choose a better onw.

Envelope Icon Reference
First of all, to find where the Envelope image is referenced go to the main resource file for our MainActivity (activity_main.xml) and open it up.

Design Mode: activity_main.xml
This time make sure you are in design mode and then click the Envelope button one time in the graphic view.
Once you do that, right-click the Envelope button and a context menu will appear.

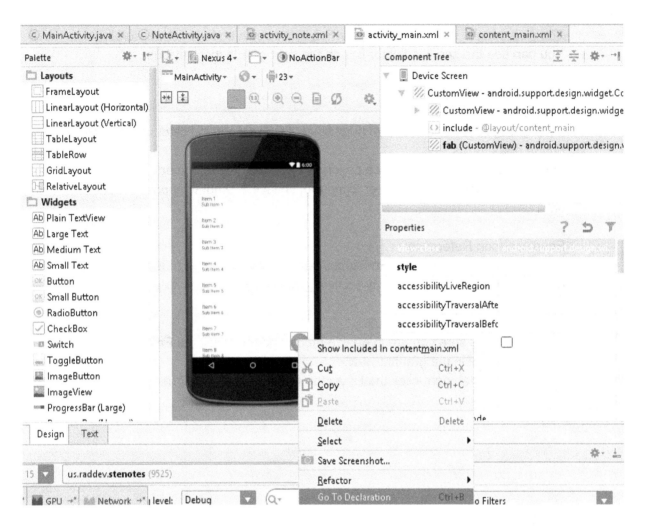

Choose the Go To Declaration menu item and Android Studio will take you to
the place in the XML file where the item is defined.

```xml
<android.support.design.widget.FloatingActionButton
    android:id="@+id/fab"
    android:layout_width="wrap_content"
    android:layout_height="wrap_content"
    android:layout_gravity="bottom|end"
    android:layout_margin="16dp"
    android:src="@android:drawable/ic_dialog_email" />
```

This is the layout definition of the FloatingActionButton which is named fab. The last line in the definition shows where the icon is loaded from.

```
android:src="@android:drawable/ic_dialog_email"
```

It is an odd reference, however, because my first thought was that the item would be found under the drawable folder under res in the project explorer.

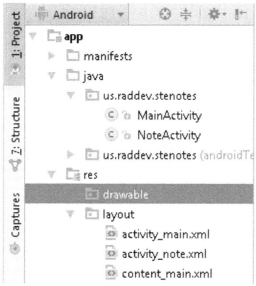

However, there is nothing in that folder yet.
I went out and looked at that folder from Windows File Explorer and there is nothing in there so I was confused.

Google It
I Googled the resource name and found a link to the Android Developers site which describes R.drawable and I found the item listed at:
http://developer.android.com/reference/android/R.drawable.html

Android APIs	API level: 23 ÷

android
android.accessibilityservice
android.accounts
android.animation
android.annotation
android.app
android.app.admin
android.app.assist
android.app.backup
android.app.job
android.app.usage

. . .

Classes

Manifest
Manifest.permission
Manifest.permission_group
R
R anim

Use Tree Navigation |← ←|

int	divider_horizontal_dim_dark
int	divider_horizontal_textfield
int	edit_text
int	editbox_background
int	editbox_background_normal
int	editbox_dropdown_dark_frame
int	editbox_dropdown_light_frame
int	gallery_thumb
int	ic_btn_speak_now
int	ic_delete
int	ic_dialog_alert
int	ic_dialog_dialer
int	ic_dialog_email
int	ic_dialog_info
int	ic_dialog_map
int	ic_input_add

Icon Name Prefix
Apparently the prefix of IC_ is an attempt to let us know it is an icon.
So, I'm guessing that the other IC_ items are icons also.

I browsed through them and found one named ic_menu_add.

Let's change the value to that one and see if we get a better icon.

```
android:src="@android:drawable/ic_menu_add"
```

```
<android.support.design.widget.FloatingActionButton
    android:id="@+id/fab"
    android:layout_width="wrap_content"
    android:layout_height="wrap_content"
    android:layout_gravity="bottom|end"
    android:layout_margin="16dp"
    android:src="@android:drawable/ic_menu_add" />
```

Go ahead and rebuild and run and let's see what it looks like.
You can get the code at:
Stenotes_v6.zip

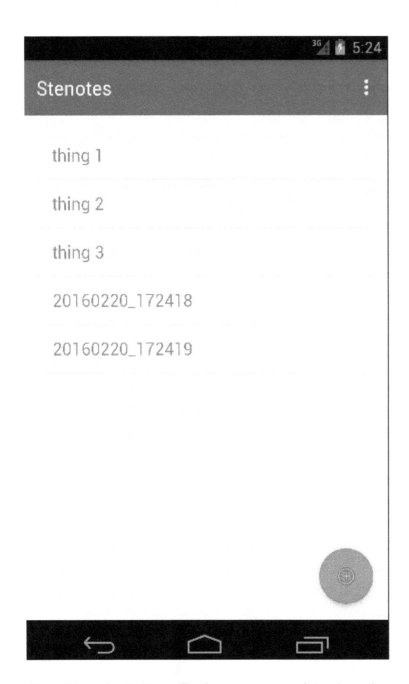

Now, it's a plus button. That's more appropriate since the + sign better indicates that it adds something. And, we've also learned a bit about some built-in resources that are available to us.

List of Notes

Now, we need to make our list show our list of notes.

However, we haven't stored a list of notes. We haven't even saved one note yet.

We need to allow the user to create new notes and we need to make sure we display the list of notes in our ListView.

Using the File System

For now we are going to save each of our notes into its own file on the Android device.

But, we also need a way to show the list of files that are available to the user. To do that, we are going to create a separate file which will contain the list of files which are available to the user. Along with the list of files we will store a title for each of the notes to help the user remember what is in the note.

That means we'll need to:
1. Create a file for each note
2. Create one file which contains the list of files and titles.

If we didn't store this information in a separate file then we'd have to search the file system for our note files each time and open them and get the titles out each time the user starts the app. Instead of doing that, we'll just store the information in one file which will list each note. That means we need to add the title and file name to the file which contains the list each time the user adds a new note.

That part is easy enough using the Java provided file functionality. However, we also need to allow the user to delete any note and that may prove to be a bit more difficult, since we'd have to find the item in our list file and then delete the file from the File system also.

Is There A Better Way?

So, yes, there are better ways to do what we are going to do with the list of files and storing them in a regular file. We could use a sqlite database, but for now we'll use the file system, simply as a way to help you get familiar with the file system. There are times when you want to store one or two values and all you need is a file so this way you'll learn how to do that.

Change NoteActivity Layout

We can see that we also want a title for each note so we need to provide the user with a place to add the title and we also need to allow the user to Save the new (or changed) note or Cancel the changes she has made.

Let's add a TextEdit and two buttons to our NoteActivity layout.

Open the activity_note.xml and make the following changes.

```xml
<?xml version="1.0" encoding="utf-8"?>
<LinearLayout
xmlns:android="http://schemas.android.com/apk/res/android"
    android:paddingBottom="@dimen/activity_vertical_margin"
    android:paddingLeft="@dimen/activity_horizontal_margin"
    android:paddingRight="@dimen/activity_horizontal_margin"
    android:paddingTop="@dimen/activity_vertical_margin"
    xmlns:tools="http://schemas.android.com/tools"
    tools:context="us.raddev.stenotes.NoteActivity"
    android:orientation="vertical"
    android:layout_width="match_parent"
    android:layout_height="match_parent"
    android:id="@+id/linearLayout">

<EditText
    android:layout_width="match_parent"
    android:layout_height="wrap_content"
    android:hint="Note title"
    android:id="@+id/titleText" />

<EditText
    android:layout_width="match_parent"
    android:layout_height="0dp"
    android:layout_weight="1"
    android:id="@+id/noteText"
    android:hint="Note text..."
    android:gravity="top"
    android:layout_below="@+id/titleText" />

    <LinearLayout
        android:orientation="horizontal"
```

```
        android:layout_width="match_parent"
        android:layout_height="wrap_content"
        android:gravity="right">
    <Button
        android:layout_width="wrap_content"
        android:layout_height="wrap_content"
        android:text="Cancel"
        android:id="@+id/cancelButton"
        />

    <Button
        android:layout_width="wrap_content"
        android:layout_height="wrap_content"
        android:text="Save"
        android:id="@+id/saveButton" />
    </LinearLayout>
</LinearLayout>
```

First of all we've changed our RelativeLayout into a LinearLayout.
LinearLayouts are nice because a provide an easy way to set up a group of
controls so they come one after another, either vertically or horizontally.

Our outermost LinearLayout is set to place the controls vertically with the
attribute :
```
android:orientation="vertical"
```
There are basically three vertical groups on the NoteActivity.

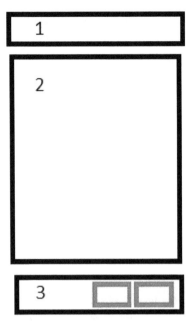

The last vertical group is further broken up into two horizontal groups by adding a nested LinearLayout which has it's orientation set to horizontal. This one contains two buttons (one for Cancel and one for Save).

If you make the changes to activity_note.xml and then switch to design view you'll see what the final layout looks like:

Also, notice that on the right side you can see the Component Tree which shows you that the outermost element is a LinearLayout which contains the two EditText controls and the nested LinearLayout. Further, you can see that the two buttons are contained in the inner LinearLayout and this LinearLayout is setup up for horizontal orientation.

Element Weight
The real magic of this layout come from one line which we've placed in the EditText control noteText.

```
android:layout_weight="1"
```

This tells the LinearLayout that this item has a maximum height (1 is max) and should have the maximum height possible while still allowing each of the other layout groups to appear on the this screen.

You can see that we actually set the height of this control to 0:

`android:layout_height="0dp"`

That tells the layout to draw the item's height based upon its weight. The weight is relative to the other controls which are contained within the same outer element. In our case the outer element is the LinearLayout.

You can see a lot more about LinearLayout and the example I drew from at the Google Android Developer site at:

http://developer.android.com/guide/topics/ui/layout/linear.html

What Is dp?
It stands for Density-independent Pixels. It is a way to measure the dots that make up a device's screen. Knowing their size is important to keeping things drawn in the right size on the screen.
There are different units which can be used for these sizes such as (px [pixels], pt [point] 1/72 of inch, mm [millimeter], etc).

Why Did We Use Weight?
We used weight instead of providing a specific width (number of dp, px, pt, etc).
Doing it this way tells the layout to render in such a way that the note EditText field should take up as much space as possible while leaving room for the top title EditText and the row of buttons at the bottom. It would be very difficult to mathematically calculate how many dp high this should be for every device so we let the system do that.

Landscape Mode
Now, when the device is rotated into Landscape mode, the layout will automatically calculate the height of the items, provide the maximum height possible for the note EditText while still displaying the title and the row of buttons at the bottom. You can test your Landscape layout versus your portrait layout very easily in Android Studio.

You simply open up the activity_note.xml and go to Design mode.

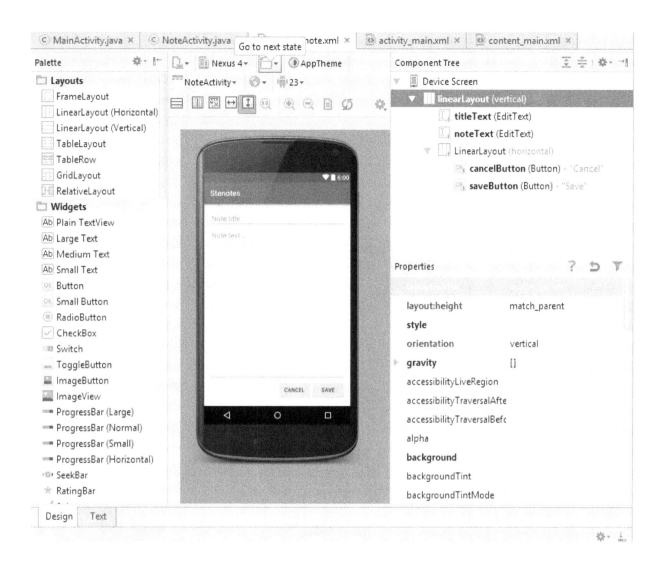

At the top of the design view there will be a button to the left of the AppTheme button which you can click. You can see the tooltip is displaying some information about the button : go to next state.

When you click that button it will flip it to landscape mode so you can see how your layout will render when your user rotates his device. Try it.

178

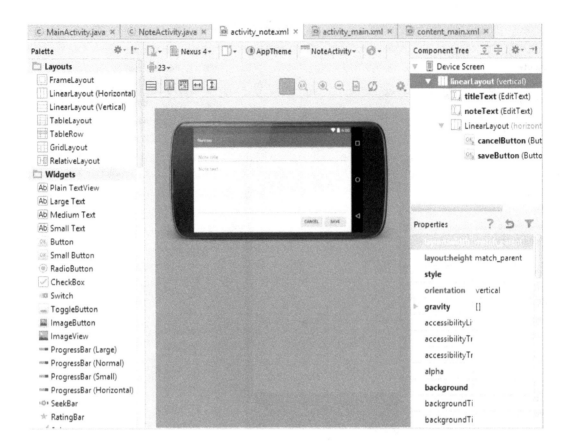

Because we weighted the note field, it takes up the appropriate amount of space and doesn't knock our other items out of view.

We'll go over more about how to manipulate layouts to keep them sized right as we develop our other apps in this book.

Now, let's switch back to our code and work on saving our note data to a file. The first thing to do is the easiest thing: add click handlers to our two buttons on our NoteActivity.

Add Click Handlers
Open up the NoteActivity.java file and move to the line just inside the NoteActivity class. We are going to add two member variables here which will allow us to reference the button objects we've created in the layout.

Add the following code:
```
private Button cancelButton;
private Button saveButton;
```

It will look like the following:

```
 C  MainActivity.java ×    C  NoteActivity.java ×    activity_note.xml ×    activity_main.xml ×    content_main.xm

    package us.raddev.stenotes;

  import ...

  public class NoteActivity extends AppCompatActivity {

      private Button cancelButton;
      private Button saveButton;

      public NoteActivity () { Log.d("NoteActivity", "Inside NoteActivity constructor..." ); }

      @Override
      protected void onCreate(Bundle savedInstanceState) {
          Log.d("NoteActivity", "In NoteActivity.onCreate()...");
          super.onCreate(savedInstanceState);
          setContentView(R.layout.activity_note);
          setTitle("Note - new");
```

Now, move to the last line of the onCreate() method. You can see that line in the previous screenshot. It's the line where we had previously set the title of our NoteActivity.

First we need to make sure our buttons reference our onscreen elements.
Add the following code:
```
cancelButton = (Button)findViewById(R.id.cancelButton);
saveButton = (Button)findViewById(R.id.saveButton);
```

It'll look like the following:

```java
package us.raddev.stenotes;

import ...

public class NoteActivity extends AppCompatActivity {

    private Button cancelButton;
    private Button saveButton;

    public NoteActivity () { Log.d("NoteActivity", "Inside NoteAct

    @Override
    protected void onCreate(Bundle savedInstanceState) {
        Log.d("NoteActivity", "In NoteActivity.onCreate()...");
        super.onCreate(savedInstanceState);
        setContentView(R.layout.activity_note);
        setTitle("Note - new");
        cancelButton = (Button)findViewById(R.id.cancelButton);
        saveButton = (Button)findViewById(R.id.saveButton);
```

Now our buttons are referencing layout objects. Let's set up each of them so they listen for the onClick() event.

You can copy/paste the setOnclickListener from the MainActivity fab object if you want.

That's because the setOnClickListener is the same code for both:

It'll look like:

```java
    .setOnClickListener(new View.OnClickListener() {
    @Override
    public void onClick(View view) {
        // our code goes here

    }
});
```

After we set them up for both buttons the code will look like:

```java
    @Override
    protected void onCreate(Bundle savedInstanceState) {
        Log.d("NoteActivity", "In NoteActivity.onCreate()...");
        super.onCreate(savedInstanceState);
        setContentView(R.layout.activity_note);
        setTitle("Note - new");
        cancelButton = (Button)findViewById(R.id.cancelButton);
        saveButton = (Button)findViewById(R.id.saveButton);

        cancelButton.setOnClickListener(new View.OnClickListener() {
            @Override
            public void onClick(View view) {
                // our code goes here
            }
        });

        saveButton.setOnClickListener(new View.OnClickListener() {
            @Override
            public void onClick(View view) {
                // our code goes here
            }
        });

    }
```

Of course, clicking the buttons still doesn't do anything because we haven't added any code to either onClick() function yet.

The Cancel button should check a value to determine if the note has been altered.
If the text has not been altered there is no reason to save it again, so we will simply close the NoteActivity to take the user back out to the MainActivity.

That's the easiest part of the code to write so let's do that work now.

Focus on the Cancel Button

For now, we are just focusing on the Cancel button. We want to present the user with a quick dialog box and allow her to decide if she really does want to lose her changes (instead of saving them).

The entire code for the cancel button's onclick will look like the following:

```
cancelButton.setOnClickListener(new View.OnClickListener() {
    @Override
    public void onClick(View view) {
        //view.getContext().getApplicationContext()
            new AlertDialog.Builder(view.getContext())
            .setTitle("Lose changes?")
            .setMessage("Are you sure you want to lose your changes to
this note?")
            .setPositiveButton(R.string.yes_button, new
DialogInterface.OnClickListener() {
                public void onClick(DialogInterface dialog, int which)
{
                    na.finish();
                }
            })
            .setNegativeButton(R.string.no_button, new
DialogInterface.OnClickListener() {
                public void onClick(DialogInterface dialog, int which)
{
                    // do nothing
                }
            })
                .setIcon(android.R.drawable.ic_dialog_alert)
                .show();
    }
});
```

```java
            cancelButton.setOnClickListener(new View.OnClickListener() {
                @Override
                public void onClick(View view) {
                    //view.getContext().getApplicationContext()
                        new AlertDialog.Builder(view.getContext())
                        .setTitle("Lose changes?")
                        .setMessage("Are you sure you want to lose your changes to this note?")
                        .setPositiveButton(R.string.yes_button, new DialogInterface.OnClickListener() {
                            public void onClick(DialogInterface dialog, int which) {
                                na.finish();
                            }
                        })
                        .setNegativeButton(R.string.no_button, new DialogInterface.OnClickListener() {
                            public void onClick(DialogInterface dialog, int which) {
                                // do nothing
                            }
                        })
                            .setIcon(android.R.drawable.ic_dialog_alert)
                            .show();
                }
            });
```

You can see that when the cancelButton is clicked we create a new
AlertDialog box.
We set the title, the message the user sees and then we set up the positive
button and the negative button. Normally these would have the text OK and
Cancel. However, I believe it makes it a little more readable and easier to
understand by using Yes and No instead.

Defining String Resources For Our Project.
Since I wanted the buttons to display the text "Yes" and "No" instead of "OK"
and "Cancel" I had to define my own two string resources for the project.
I did that by navigating in Solution Explorer down into the values folder and
opening up the strings.xml file.

184

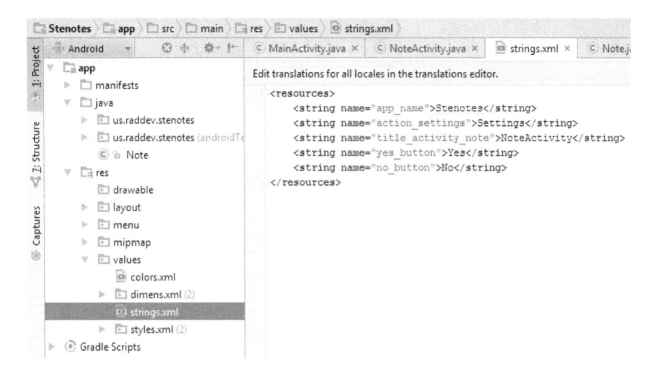

Edit translations for all locales in the translations editor.

```xml
<resources>
    <string name="app_name">Stenotes</string>
    <string name="action_settings">Settings</string>
    <string name="title_activity_note">NoteActivity</string>
    <string name="yes_button">Yes</string>
    <string name="no_button">No</string>
</resources>
```

You can see that I created two new strings named yes_button and no_button and set their string values appropriately.

Why Use String Resources

Once I create those, they are available to me from any of the Java classes throughout the app. This makes them easily available and insures that they are defined in one place and I won't misspell them along the way. Plus, if I want to change the "Yes" to "Affirmative" later then I only have to change it in one place.

This may not seem that important now, but if you have error messages and more detailed items it is an important programming practice to follow. This also makes it much easier if you decide to create a multilingual version of your app. You can load the appropriate string resource file for the user's location / language.

How Do You Reference These In Code?

As you can see, back in the code, you reference these by typing a reference to the name.

For example, R.string.yes_button. That R stands for Resource. Then, you ask for a string (resource) and provide the name. Android Studio will help you along the way as you type the

R. by displaying values you might want.

```
.setPositiveButton(R.string.
    public void onClick          no_button
        na.finish();             yes_button
    }                            action_settings
})                               app_name
.setNegativeButton(R.st          appbar_scrolling_v:
    public void onClick          title_activity_not(
        // do nothing            class
    }                            inst          expr
})                               instanceof    expr
        .setIcon(androi
```

Here, I've typed R.string. and Studio prompts me for the value I might want.

Notice that we've set up both the Yes button and the No button to have OnClickListeners also, so that when the user clicks them the button will do something.

```
.setPositiveButton(R.string.yes_button, new
DialogInterface.OnClickListener() {
   public void onClick(DialogInterface dialog, int which) {
       na.finish();
   }
})
.setNegativeButton(R.string.no_button, new
DialogInterface.OnClickListener() {
   public void onClick(DialogInterface dialog, int which) {
       // do nothing
   }
})
```

However, we haven't actually implemented any functionality in the NegativeButton.

That's because if the user says he doesn't want to lose his changes, we simply close the dialog box so we can see the NoteActivity again.
However, if the user clicks the Yes (he does want to lose changes) then we call a strange method:

```
na.finish();
```

What Canceling Does

This is simply the finish() method of our NoteActivity object which is currently displayed behind the dialog box. If the user is Canceling her work then she wants to go back to the MainActivity form since she's done. She is also indicating that she doesn't want to save any changes so we need to close the dialog and close the NoteActivity.

To close any activity, you call the built-in Activity method called finish().

In our case we are using an object named na to make that call.

That's because of the way we've constructed the cancelButton's onClickListener() method. We will see other ways of constructing that method later.

But for now, we had to have a reference to our NoteActivity object which is currently displayed on the screen.

To capture that reference I simply added a final variable to the top of the NoteActivity class which stores the this variable. Again, remember that the "this" variable contains a reference to the context to the current object you are working with.

If you look at the top of the file I've created and initialized this temporary na object in our NoteActivity class. I've initialized it to the this variable and made it final.

```java
    import android.view.View;
    import android.widget.Button;

    public class NoteActivity extends AppCompatActivity {

        private Button cancelButton;
        private Button saveButton;
        private final NoteActivity na = this;

        public NoteActivity () { Log.d("NoteActivity", "Inside NoteActivity

        @Override
        protected void onCreate(Bundle savedInstanceState) {
            Log.d("NoteActivity", "In NoteActivity.onCreate()...");
            super.onCreate(savedInstanceState);
            setContentView(R.layout.activity_note);
            setTitle("Note - new");
            cancelButton = (Button)findViewById(R.id.cancelButton);
            saveButton = (Button)findViewById(R.id.saveButton);

            cancelButton.setOnClickListener(new View.OnClickListener() {
                @Override
                public void onClick(View view) {
                    //view.getContext().getApplicationContext()
                    new AlertDialog.Builder(view.getContext())
```

What Does final Do?

The keyword final causes the object to contain a constant value which cannot be changed after it is initialized. This allows me to send this value into our OnClickListener for the cancelButton. The OnClickListener is constructed here on the fly (we can construct it differently and will see that later) so it requires that values sent into it are already initialized and will not change. The final keyword allows me to guarantee that I've fulfilled those requirements. And it provides me with a reference to our NoteActivity which we can use to call finish() to close our NoteActivity.

After all of this hard work, let's run the app so you can see what it can do at this point.

You can get the code at:
Stenotes_v7.zip

Run the app and you'll see our MainActivity.

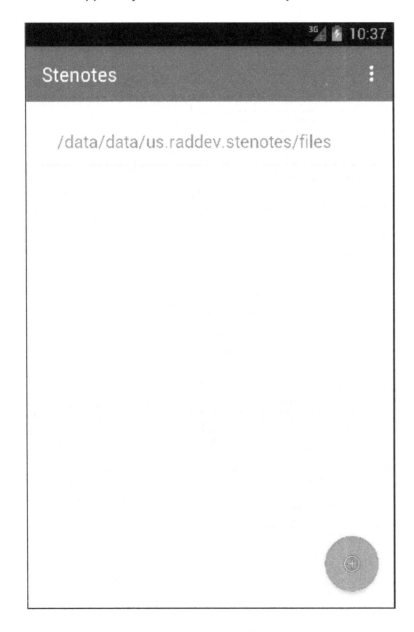

(**Note**: Our one list item reveals some other work I'm doing which is showing the space where we will eventually save our Note files.)

Next, click the (+) plus button and the NoteActivity will be displayed.

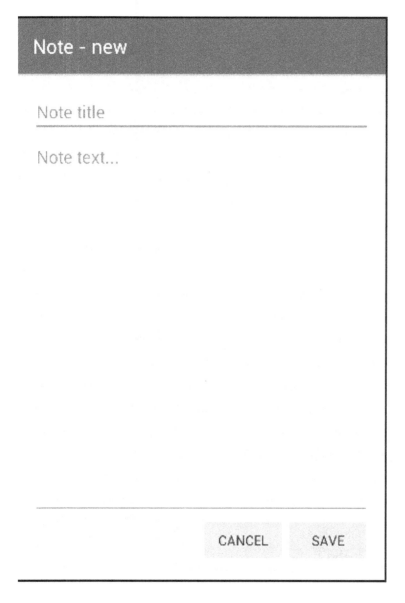

Click the CANCEL button and the dialog box we created will appear.

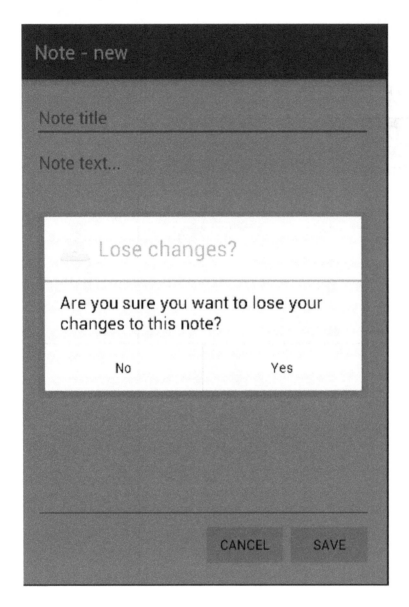

First, click the [No] button. The dialog box will disappear and you will be back on your NoteActivity. In this case the user would be able to continue editing her note without loss of data.

Now, click the [CANCEL] button again to display the dialog box. However, this time, click the [Yes] button.

When you do that, you will see two things:
1. the dialog box will close.
2. the NoteActivity will close and you'll be back at MainActivity

Next Steps

Now, we need to implement the Save button so users can save the notes they create.

However, as we look at the Note in our problem domain (more about this in the next chapter) we see that it is actually a thing which has some properties and some abilities. That means we should design a class for the note item because that will allow us to organize our code. Organizing our code allows us to develop it and do maintenance on it much easier.

We'll see more about how it can help in the next chapter, where we will finish our Stenotes application.

Chapter 6
Finishing Stenotes

Now we need to start thinking about our note object so we can separate it from our View (layout) code. Keeping our data separated into logical units (object) helps us keep our code organized.

OOP and Code Organization
Code organization is the main point of OOP (Object Oriented Programming). Organization of our code allows us to fix bugs faster (we know where to look) and add enhancements more easily. Enhancements are easier with organized code because you don't affect code which is already written when you add new features. That helps you to build your code in iterations adding functionality in layers.

However, to write code using OOP principles you have to do a bit of design. Where do you start? You start by finding the domain objects.

Domain Objects: What Are They?
The problem we are trying to solve is the domain of our problem. The objects we use to solve that problem are the domain objects. In our case we are attempting to create a easy to use note program which allows users to create new notes and provides a list of notes that the user has created.
We can often find domain objects by analyzing the words we have used to describe our project as we talk about it. The nouns we use often become the objects in our domain. In this case we keep using the word note.

What Is A Note?

We've described our note has having some text and a title. We also know that our note will be stored in a file so those three things end up defining our note object.

We might use a bit of UML (Universal Modeling Language) to draw our Note object something like the following:

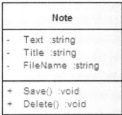

UML is a good quick way to communicate the properties and methods your domain object has in a quick small diagram. You can see that this is the Note object and it has Text, Title and a FileName where it is saved.

It also has two methods so it can Save its data and Delete itself from the system when necessary.

This is just a guess at how this will work, but it's a good start.

Pure Java Class : Can Be Used Anywhere

Also notice that we are going to create this object so it is a pure Java class. There is no Android-specific or View-specific code in this class. That means it could be re-used in another project very easily. These pure classes are also known as POJOs (Plain Old Java Objects) in the Java world.

Let's see how we add this basic class to our project.

Go to solution explorer and right-click the java folder and a menu will appear. Slide down over the New menu item and then over to the Java Class menu item and click it.

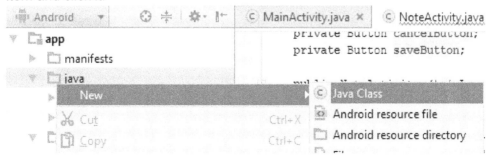

A dialog box will appear which is trying to guide you to create the Class in the correct folder.

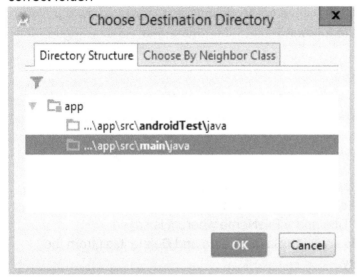

Make sure you have chose ..\app\src\main\java as shown in the previous picture and click the [OK] button.

A dialog will appear and you can type the name of our class in : Note

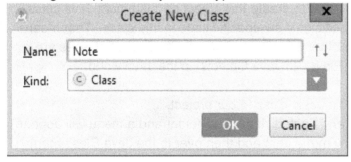

Click the [OK] button and Android Studio will create the empty class for you and open it in the editor.

First, we'll add our private properties:

```
private String text;
private String title;
private String fileName;
```

After you type those in, go ahead and right-click on the first one so we can let
Android Studio help us add a Getter and Setter for them.
When you right-click the item a menu will appear.

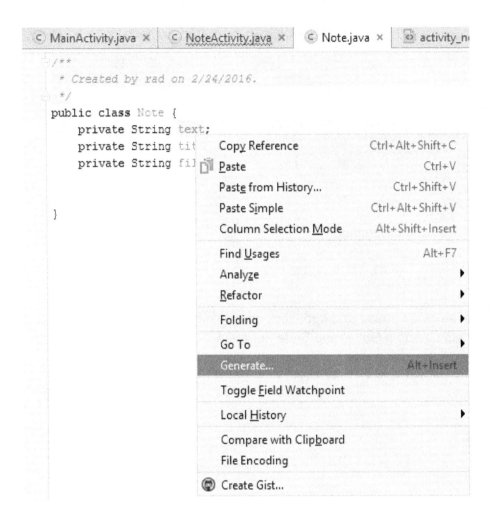

```
  /**
   * Created by rad on 2/24/2016.
   */
  public class Note {
      private String text;
      private String tit
      private String fil

  }
```

Copy Reference	Ctrl+Alt+Shift+C
Paste	Ctrl+V
Paste from History...	Ctrl+Shift+V
Paste Simple	Ctrl+Alt+Shift+V
Column Selection Mode	Alt+Shift+Insert
Find Usages	Alt+F7
Analyze	▶
Refactor	▶
Folding	▶
Go To	▶
Generate...	Alt+Insert
Toggle Field Watchpoint	
Local History	▶
Compare with Clipboard	
File Encoding	
Create Gist...	

Choose the Generate.... menu item and another menu will appear.

197

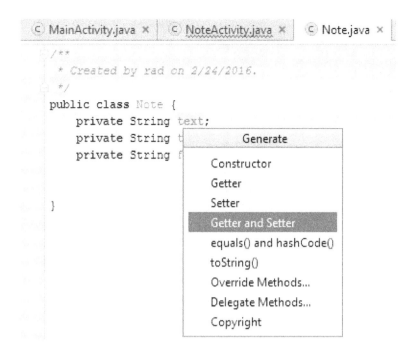

Choose the Getter and Setter menu item.

This will display another dialog box with all of your private variables.

Go ahead and hold the ALT key and click each of the items and they will highlight.

Then, click the [OK] button.

Your source code will be updated.

MainActivity.java × | NoteActivity.java × | Note.java ×

```java
/**
 * Created by rad on 2/24/2016.
 */
public class Note {
    public String getText() {
        return text;
    }

    public void setText(String text) {
        this.text = text;
    }

    public String getTitle() {
        return title;
    }

    public void setTitle(String title) {
        this.title = title;
    }

    public String getFileName() {
        return fileName;
    }

    public void setFileName(String fileName) {
        this.fileName = fileName;
    }

    private String text;
    private String title;
    private String fileName;


}
```

So far, we've simply added our three private properties and then made them available using Getter and Setter methods. If you would like more information on creating Java classes please see the following at my web site:

Now, let's generate a Constructor for the class. Again, you simply right-click in the code and choose the Generate… menu item. Then you choose Constructor from the Generate menu.

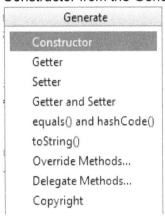

Generate
Constructor
Getter
Setter
Getter and Setter
equals() and hashCode()
toString()
Override Methods...
Delegate Methods...
Copyright

When you do that you'll see another dialog which asks you which fields you'd like to initialize when you construct the object:

Go ahead and choose all three (hold the ALT key to multi-select) and click the [OK] button.

Android Studio will add the following code for you:

```
public Note(String text, String fileName, String title) {
    this.text = text;
    this.fileName = fileName;
    this.title = title;
}
```

```
 * Created by rad on 2/24/2016.
 */
public class Note {
    public Note(String text, String fileName, String title) {
        this.text = text;
        this.fileName = fileName;
        this.title = title;
    }
}
```

Now, we can construct one of these objects by passing in values for text, filename and title and it will automatically set the object's values to the values you send in.

A Class Is a Template for An Object
We've created a template we can use over and over in our code to create Note objects.

But, we haven't actually created any code which uses the Class (template) to create a new Note object.

Note Object Generated from Note Class
Logically, it makes sense in our application to create a Note object when the NoteActivity is displayed on the screen.
That means the NoteActivity will contain a Note object.

Let's add a Note object to our NoteActivity so that when the user clicks the (+) FloatingActionBar button a new Note will be created also.

We will make the Note object a member variable of the NoteActivity class. When you go and begin to add the new private member variable of your type Note you will see that Android Studio will attempt to help you find the class.

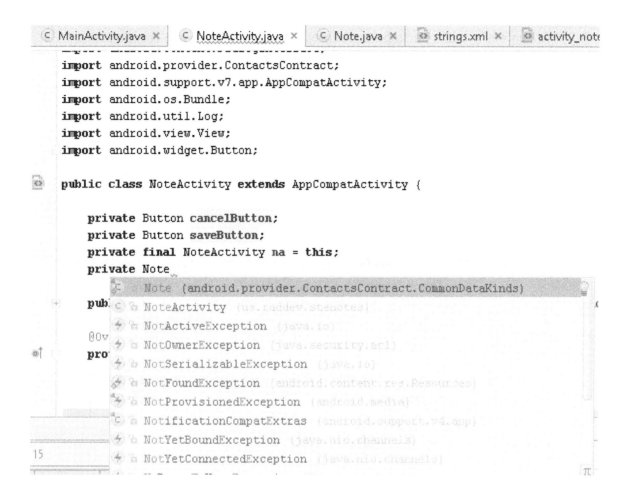

Package Problem

The problem is that none of those objects that Android Studio guesses is actually the one we want. We want our Note class which we just created in our project. Android Studio cannot find it though because we didn't place it in a good namespace (package) and Studio gets confused.

We need to add our Note to a package so Studio can differentiate our Note from other items with the word Note in them.

Adding A Package

We can easily add a package to our project. Go to solution explorer and right-click the Java folder and a menu will appear. Go down to the New... menu and then select the Package menu item which appears.

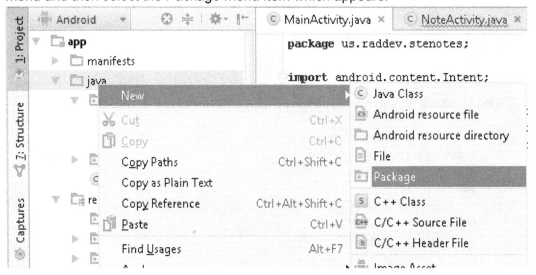

It will prompt you to select a folder you want the package to be created in. We will choose our main Java folder.

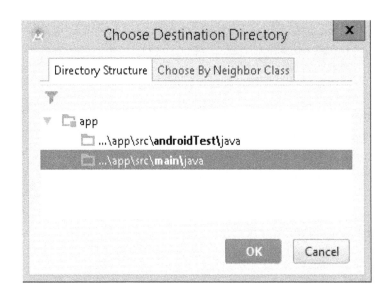

Click the [OK] button and it will ask you to provide a Package name.

I am going to name mine: us.raddev.domain (to hold my domain objects)

When you click the [OK] button the package will be created and you'll see it appear in the solution explorer.

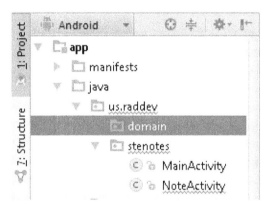

I've uncollapsed the us.raddev.stenotes package so you can still see that our two Activity classes (both are .java files) are in that package. There are no classes in our new us.raddev.domain package yet though.
Let's add our Note.java file to our new pacakge.

You can simply click on the Note.java file in solution explorer and drag it to the domain package and drop it.

You'll see some red box highlights appear around the target packages as you roll over them.

When you finally drop it, you will be prompted to make sure you really want to take this action.

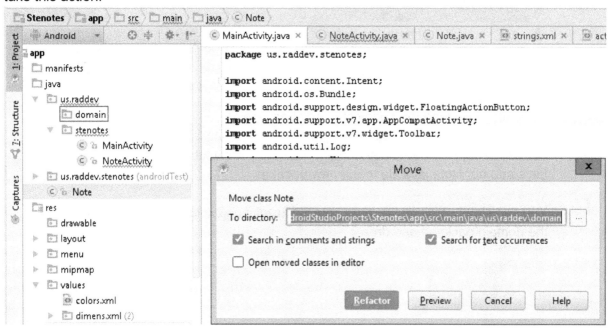

Since Android Studio knows that now the reference to the Note class will be different for anything that is already using it, it asks you if you want to search for places where it is currently used so it can refactor them. It's attempting to help you so any references that may already be using the Note class won't get all fouled up.

Leave the settings as they are and allow Studio to help you and click the [Refactor] button.

When you do that Android Studio provides a preview of what it thinks it needs to do, in the bottom panel window. It's a bit confusing at first, because the file isn't moved and the Studio view flashes and refreshes and looks like the following:

The bottom panel window is attempting to give you a preview of what it will do. You are supposed to click the [Do Refactor] or [Cancel] button.

Go ahead and click the [Do Refactor] button now.

You will see that the file is moved in solution explorer and if you scroll to the top of Note.java you will see that Studio has added a new package statement.

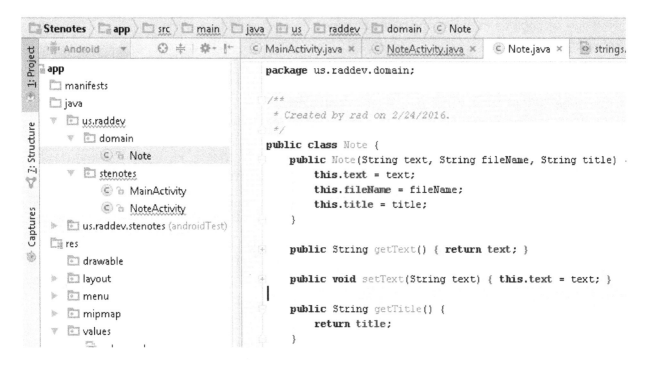

Now the Note.java class is packaged properly and will be reusable in other projects if we should like to use it and it'll show up in NoteActivity when we add our member variable.

Open up NoteActivity and let's try adding the Note member variable again. You can now see that it is one of the choices that Studio offers now.

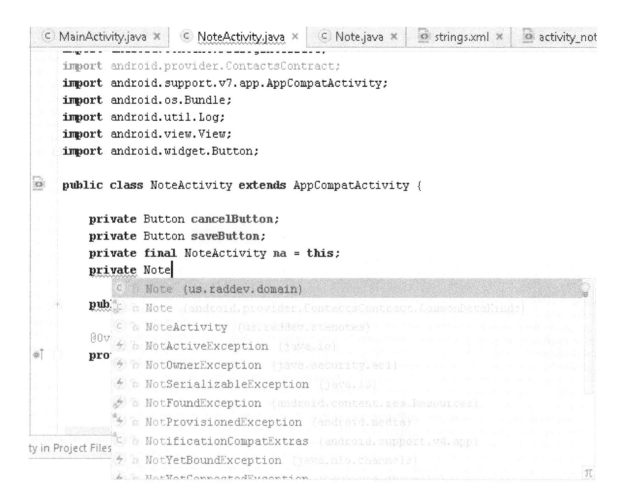

```java
import android.provider.ContactsContract;
import android.support.v7.app.AppCompatActivity;
import android.os.Bundle;
import android.util.Log;
import android.view.View;
import android.widget.Button;

public class NoteActivity extends AppCompatActivity {

    private Button cancelButton;
    private Button saveButton;
    private final NoteActivity na = this;
    private Note|
```

	Note (us.raddev.domain)
pub	Note (android.provider.ContactsContract.CommonDataKinds)
@Ov	NoteActivity (us.raddev.stenotes)
pro	NotActiveException (java.io)
	NotOwnerException (java.security.acl)
	NotSerializableException (java.io)
	NotFoundException (android.content.res.Resources)
	NotProvisionedException (android.media)
	NotificationCompatExtras (android.support.v4.app)
	NotYetBoundException (java.nio.channels)
	NotYetConnectedException

ty in Project Files

If you choose (double-click) our Note class from the list and allow Studio to add the item, then you will see that Studio also adds the import statement at the top of the file for you.

```java
import android.os.Bundle;
import android.util.Log;
import android.view.View;
import android.widget.Button;

import us.raddev.domain.Note;

public class NoteActivity extends AppCompatActivity {

    private Button cancelButton;
    private Button saveButton;
    private final NoteActivity na = this;
    private Note
```

We still need to add the name of our variable. Remember, the token following the word private is indicating the type that we are creating. In this case we are creating a type of us.raddev.domain.Note. However, we need to provide a variable name which we will use to reference this instance of our object.

Naming Conventions In Code
Go ahead and complete the line as follows:
```java
private Note _note;
```

Notice that I had you name the variable with a leading underscore _. That is because a good naming convention is to name member variables with leading underscores to indicate to code readers lately that this is a private member variable of the class we are viewing.

This concludes the declaration of our member variable but we still haven't instantiated a Note object or used one.

Let's do that now.

Instantiating the Note Class : Creating a Note Object

We could add the instantiation of the Note object in the NoteActivity constructor, but since we are already doing some work in the onCreate() method, we'll go ahead and do it there.

I'm adding the instantiation of the object to the current code right after line where we call setTitle().

So far, It looks like the following:

```
  C MainActivity.java ×    C NoteActivity.java ×    C Note.java ×    strings

        private Note _note;

        public NoteActivity () { Log.d("NoteActivity", "Inside I

        @Override
        protected void onCreate(Bundle savedInstanceState) {
            Log.d("NoteActivity", "In NoteActivity.onCreate()...
            super.onCreate(savedInstanceState);
            setContentView(R.layout.activity_note);
            setTitle("Note - new");
            _note = new Note();
```

Note Refactoring

Android Studio warns me (red squiggly underline) that something is wrong with my Note constructor call.

I remember that the constructor we created before, wants all three parameters (title, text and filename). However, now that I'm using the Note class I can see that when I first construct one, I don't have a couple of those parameters (title or text) since the user hasn't had the chance to fill them out yet.

I could pass in the location where I want the note file to be saved too, but now that I think about it I'd rather have the Note class do that for me. So, I'm going to alter the Note constructor so it takes zero parameters and generates a new filename for the file where it will store the text and title.

Let's alter the Note class now.

212

Remove All Parameters and Code

The first thing I've done is remove all the parameters and code from the constructor.

```
C MainActivity.java ×    C NoteActivity.java ×    C Note.java ×

    package us.raddev.domain;

    /**
     * Created by rad on 2/24/2016.
     */
    public class Note {

        public Note() {

        }
```

You can see we now have a constructor which takes no parameters and does nothing in the body of the method.

I want to add the code that generates a file name for our Note text.
I'm going to add a private method which will do that work and I'm going to call that method from the constructor. The method will be private because it will be called only from within this class (from the constructor). For now I'm going to "stub" out the code and then I can write the real code to do the work after.

Here's the stubbed out code.

```java
package us.raddev.domain;

/**
 * Created by rad on 2/24/2016.
 */
public class Note {

    public Note() {
        generateFileName();
    }

    private void generateFileName(){
        this.fileName = "generate file name here";
    }
}
```

The good thing about this stubbed out code is that it will build and run. Of course, it doesn't generate a valid file name or determine the correct storage location to store the file (full path) but it gets me started thinking about how I want to create this thing.

As I said, I need to know how and where to store the file on an Android device.

Android Storage
There are rules for storing files on Android devices in order to keep things organized and even more importantly to keep users secure from malicious apps which might try to read another app's data.

Context.getFilesDir()
We will learn more about advanced storage later, but for now we can use the simplest methods to store our data, because the data will only be used by our app.

That also means we do not have to add any additional permissions to our AndroidManifest.xml (more about the manifest and permissions later). The method we can use to get the storage location for our app is the Context.getFilesDir().

##
################

#################### SIDEBAR: AndroidManifest.xml
#############################

##
################

I came back and decided to add this sidebar about the AndroidManifest.xml
here because I discovered that some versions of Android do seem to require
us to include an item in the manifest to let the user know that we will be
reading and writing to the sandboxed storage which only our
app can write to.

I've added the value in the manifest in the code downloads so the app will
work on all of your devices, but I wanted to let you know a bit more about the
manifest does when I first mention it here in this chapter.

If you'll go to solution explorer and examine the folders you'll see the
manifests folder at the same level as the java folder. This manifest file
describes settings for your entire application.

Note: When I opened my project it took a moment while Gradle built and
Studio attempted to draw solution explorer before the manifests folder
appeared.

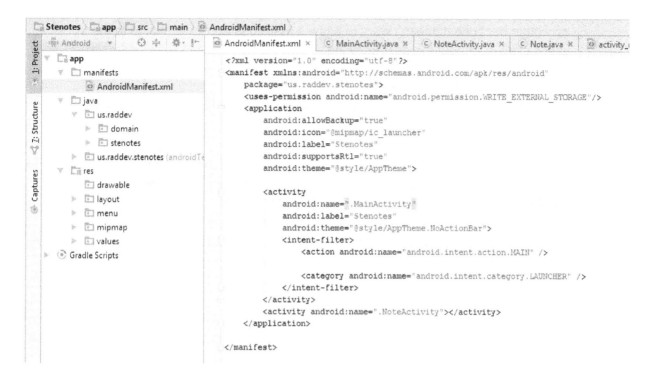

You can see that the manifest is another XML file. If you look about half way down the file you'll see an XML node named <activity> That describes main activity which launches when our app starts. We'll talk more about that in later chapters, but for know just know that is how the app knows which Activity to use to start when the app starts.

We are interested in the line near the top which is before the <application> node.

```
<uses-permission
android:name="android.permission.WRITE_EXTERNAL_STORAGE"/>
```

That is the item we had to add which gives the app permission to write to storage.

When these permissions (perms) are added it forces the app to warn the user that the app has the permission. This is to protect users from installing apps which have abilities they don't know about.

If you do not add this permission to the manifest then on newer versions of the OS (operating system) the app will crash. That's because it will throw an exception because it doesn't want to allow a malicious app to do things to the user's system without the user knowing.

Now, back to our work with writing a file to storage.
##
################

When we use the Context method getFilesDir() it returns the sandboxed (protected) app storage location that can only be read from and written to by our app.
Since we will use this protected storage space the Android system guarantees the data is protected and we do not have to add additional permissions.

Limitation of Context Object
The Context object is available to us from within our app and even our Activity classes within our app, however, it is not available to us from our Note class.

That means we are unable to call the Context.getFilesDir() from within our Note object directly. Since we cannot call that method from within our object, we will call the getFilesDir() and send the result into our Note activity's constructor. So, once again we will alter our Note constructor to take a String. We will also have to add a new member variable to our Note class to store the String.

How We'll Change the Code
Here are the three things we'll do now:
1. call getFilesDir() from NoteActivity to get the result (String representing the storage location for our app)
2. pass the value into the Note constructor
3. add a new member variable to our Note class so we can keep the value in our object.
4. set the member variable in our constructor.

Let's make those changes now.

I began typing the method call getFilesDir() and AndroidStudio attempted to help me.

```
C MainActivity.java ×   C NoteActivity.java ×   C Note.java ×   strings.xml ×   activity_note.xml ×

        private Button cancelButton;
        private Button saveButton;
        private final NoteActivity na = this;
        private Note _note;

        public NoteActivity () { Log.d("NoteActivity", "Inside NoteActivity constructor..." ); }

        @Override
        protected void onCreate(Bundle savedInstanceState) {
            Log.d("NoteActivity", "In NoteActivity.onCreate()...");
            super.onCreate(savedInstanceState);
            setContentView(R.layout.activity_note);
            setTitle("Note - new" );
            _note = new Note(getFilesDir);
            cancelButton  m    getFilesDir()                                          File
            saveButton =  m    getExternalFilesDir (String type)                      File
                          m    getExternalFilesDirs (String type)                     File[]
            cancelButton  m    getNoBackupFilesDir ()                                 File
                @Override
```

Notice in the picture that at the far right it says: File.
That is the type that is returned by getFilesDir().

Why getFilesDir() Is Available
Also notice that even though the getFilesDir() method is a member of the
Context object we do not have to provide a Context because the
AppCompatActivity (which NoteActivity is dervied from) is derived from a
Context and has all the abilities of the Context class available to it.

You can see the inheritance hierarchy of the AppCompatActivity in the
Google documenation.

AppCompatActivity

extends FragmentActivity

implements AppCompatCallback TaskStackBuilder.SupportParentable ActionBarDrawerToggle.DelegateProvider

java.lang.Object
  Ь android.content.Context
    Ь android.content.ContextWrapper
      Ь android.view.ContextThemeWrapper
        Ь android.app.Activity
          Ь android.support.v4.app.FragmentActivity
            Ь android.support.v7.app.AppCompatActivity

  ᵛ   Known Direct Subclasses

For more information see:
http://developer.android.com/reference/android/support/v7/app/AppCompatActivity.html

When I'm done typing my line is going to look like the following:

```
        _note = new Note(getFilesDir());
```

Notice that the getFilesDir() has a red squiggly underline and there is a lightbulb to the left. Android Studio is attempting to warn that our Note constructor doesn't take a parameter of this type.
That's okay, because the other hint Studio gave us reminded me that getFilesDir() returns and File object and I don't want to send in the File object to the constructor either. I only want the full path to the Files Directory as a String. Fortunately, there is a method I can call on the returned File object which will return the entire path called the absolute path.

If I go back into the editor and type a dot (. same as period) after the closing parenthesis Android Studio will attempt to show you available methods again. This time it shows me the one I want.

```
_note = new Note(getFilesDir().);
cancelButton = (Button)fin        CanWrite ()                              boolean
saveButton = (Button)findV   m    compareTo (File another)                     int
                             m    createNewFile ()                         boolean
cancelButton.setOnClickLis   m    delete ()                                boolean
    @Override                m    deleteOnExit ()                             void
    public void onClick(Vi   m    equals (Object obj)                      boolean
        //view.getContext(   m    exists ()                                boolean
           new AlertDialo     m    getAbsoluteFile ()                          File
                              m    getAbsolutePath ()                        String
                              m    getCanonicalFile ()                         File
                              m    getCanonicalPath ()                       String
                              m    getFreeSpace ()                             long  π
```

You can see that I'm choosing the getAbsolutePath() method and that (far right) it returns a String (representing that path).

That is exactly what I want to send in to my constructor so that later I can store my Note file at that location.

Here's the final code for the Note constructor which is in our NoteActivity.

```
_note = new Note(getFilesDir().getAbsolutePath());
```

You can see that we are creating a new Note by constructing it with a String which we get back after calling the getFilesDir() method which returns (in-place) a File object, which then calls the getAbsolutePath() method to return the String. Then that String is sent into our Note Constructor.

Now we just need to make sure we alter our Note constructor to handle this.

Switch over to your Note.java file in the editor and make the following changes.

```
public Note(String filePath) {
    this._fileRootPath = filePath;
    generateFileName();
}
private String _fileRootPath;
```

```
package us.raddev.domain;



/**
 * Created by rad on 2/24/2016.
 */
public class Note {

    public Note(String filePath) {
        this._fileRootPath = filePath;
        generateFileName();
    }
    private String _fileRootPath;

    private void generateFileName(){
        this.fileName = "generate file name here";
    }

    public String getText() { return text; }
```

You can see our constructor now takes a String.
I've then added a new member variable named _fileRootPath.
After that, we take the value sent into the constructor and store it in our member variable so we can use it later when the user saves her note text.

Ready to Capture Note Text
Now, we are ready to capture our Note text and title when the user hits the Save button.
To do so we need to implement our saveButton.onClick() to
   1. store the values from the View's title and text elements into our Note object.
   2. Have our Note object save itself to a file in our app storage.

Open up the NoteActivity.java and move down to the onClickListener() shown
in bold in the next image.

C MainActivity.java ×   C NoteActivity.java ×   C Note.java ×   ⊚ strings.xml ×   ⊚ activity_note.xml ×

```
                              }
                  })
                  .setNegativeButton(R.string.no_button, new DialogInterface.OnClickI
                          public void onClick(DialogInterface dialog, int which) {
                              // do nothing
                          }
                  })
                          .setIcon(android.R.drawable.ic_dialog_alert)
                          .show();
              }
          });

          saveButton.setOnClickListener(new View.OnClickListener() {
              @Override
              public void onClick(View view) {
                  // our code goes here
              }
          });
```

First of all we add the code to store the values from the View into our Note
object. It's very easy.
We do need to add a couple of private members which will allow us to get the
reference to the onscreen EditText elements. Add the following at the top of
NoteActivity:

```
private EditText _titleText;
private EditText _noteText;
```

Next, we'll initialize them so we can use these objects to get the values which
the user has typed into them on the Activity.

```
_titleText = (EditText) findViewById(R.id.titleText);
_noteText = (EditText) findViewById(R.id.noteText);
```

All of this newly added code now looks like:

```java
public class NoteActivity extends AppCompatActivity {

    private Button cancelButton;
    private Button saveButton;
    private EditText _titleText;
    private EditText _noteText;

    private final NoteActivity na = this;
    private Note _note;

    public NoteActivity () { Log.d("NoteActivity", "Inside NoteActivity constructor..." ); }

    @Override
    protected void onCreate(Bundle savedInstanceState) {
        Log.d("NoteActivity", "In NoteActivity.onCreate()...");
        super.onCreate(savedInstanceState);
        setContentView(R.layout.activity_note);
        setTitle("Note - new");
        _note = new Note(getFilesDir().getAbsolutePath());
        _titleText = (EditText)findViewById(R.id.titleText);
        _noteText = (EditText)findViewById(R.id.noteText);
        cancelButton = (Button)findViewById(R.id.cancelButton);
        saveButton = (Button)findViewById(R.id.saveButton);
```

Now we have references to our Activity EditText fields which is where the user will type his information.

Now, move back to saveButton.onClickListener() and add the following code.

```java
_note.setText(_noteText.getText().toString());
_note.setTitle(_titleText.getText().toString());
```

The code will now look like:

223

```
                    public void onClick(DialogInterface dialog, int which) {
                        na.finish();
                    }
                })
                .setNegativeButton(R.string.no_button, new DialogInterface.OnClickListener() {
                    public void onClick(DialogInterface dialog, int which) {
                        // do nothing
                    }
                })
                        .setIcon(android.R.drawable.ic_dialog_alert)
                        .show();
            }
        });

        saveButton.setOnClickListener(new View.OnClickListener() {
            @Override
            public void onClick(View view) {
                _note.setText(_noteText.getText().toString());
                _note.setTitle(_titleText.getText().toString());
            }
        });


    }
```

Data Still Not Saved To File

At this point, we still haven't saved the data to the file though.

Saving the data to the file is work that should be done for you by the Note class.

But to do so, we need to write that code. Let's open up the Note class again and add a new method that we'll call Save().

Add the following code:

```
public boolean Save()
{
    Log.d("Note.java","Saving...");
    try {
        OutputStreamWriter outputStreamWriter =
                new OutputStreamWriter(
                        new FileOutputStream(
                                new File(_fileRootPath +
"/"+fileName)));
```

```
        Log.d("Note.java", _fileRootPath + "/"+fileName);
        outputStreamWriter.write(title + "\n" + text);
        Log.d("Note.java", "after write...");
        outputStreamWriter.close();
        return true;
    }
    catch (IOException e) {
        Log.e("Note.java", "File write failed: " + e.toString());
        return false;
    }
}
```

```
    public boolean Save()
    {
        Log.d("Note.java","Saving...");
        try {
            OutputStreamWriter outputStreamWriter =
                    new OutputStreamWriter(
                            new FileOutputStream(
                                    new File(_fileRootPath + "/"+fileName)));
            Log.d("Note.java", _fileRootPath + "/"+fileName);
            outputStreamWriter.write(title + "\n" + text);
            Log.d("Note.java", "after write...");
            outputStreamWriter.close();
            return true;
        }
        catch (IOException e) {
            Log.e("Note.java", "File write failed: " + e.toString());
            return false;
        }
    }
```

First of all, notice that I added some logging so we can watch what the function does and make sure it works. But since I added this logging with a tag of "Note.java" you need to add the new tag to your filter. Remember how to do this? You Edit the filter configuration.

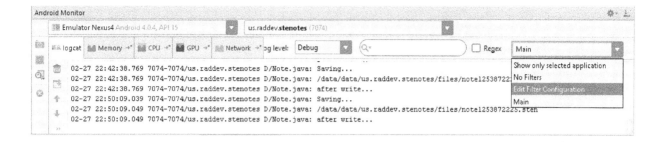

When you choose that you'll see the dialog where you can add the |Note.java to the filter.

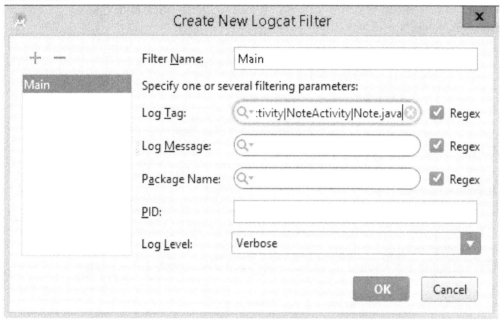

Click the [OK] button and logcat will display only the messages we want to see from our app.

The next thing you see in the code is where we create the OutputStreamWriter object and initialize it s we can write to our note file. To create the OutputStreamWriter we have to create a new FileOutputStream and we initialize the FileOutputStream with our _fileRootPath which will include our fileName.

```
OutputStreamWriter outputStreamWriter =
            new OutputStreamWriter(
```

```
                         new FileOutputStream(
                              new File(_fileRootPath +
"/"+fileName)));
```

After we create the OutputStreamWriter, all we need to do is call its write() method with the data we want to write. In our case, we write the Note title on the first line and the Note text after that.

Notice that I use the a "\n" in the call to the write() method. That writes a newline character so that after we write the title on the first line the rest of the text from the note will be on the lines following the first line. That will allow us to insure that our title is the first line for when we read these back in to display on the MainActivity list.

```
outputStreamWriter.write(title + "\n" + text);
Log.d("Note.java", "after write...");
outputStreamWriter.close();
```

After we write the file we have to make sure we call the close() method to make sure the file is closed properly.

Giving the File A Unique Name
But, let's take a step back because we haven't added the code which will give the file a unique name. We don't want to force the user to name every note file so we will generate the name for her.
We can do that using a standard Java File method called createTempFile().

This work of generating a unique file name is done when we construct our Note object. In our constructor we call the generateFileName() method.

You can see where the code is called from the constructor and what the actual method does in the following code listing:

```java
*/
public class Note {

    public Note(String filePath) {
        this._fileRootPath = filePath;
        generateFileName();
        Log.d("Note.java", _fileRootPath);
        Log.d("Note.java", fileName);


    }
    private String _fileRootPath;

    private void generateFileName(){
        try {
            Log.d("Note.java","Generating file name");
            this.fileName =
                    File.createTempFile("note",
                    ".sten",
                    null).getName();
            Log.d("Note.java", fileName);
        }
        catch (Exception ex)
        {
            Log.d("Note.java", ex.getMessage());
        }
    }
}
```

The core code which generates the file name for us is:

```java
this.fileName =
        File.createTempFile("note",
        ".sten",
        null).getName();
```

You can see that the result of calling the createTempFile is stored in our member variable named fileName.

When we call the File.createTempFile() method we have to supply three arguments but the documentation says the last one can be null if not used. That is the path to the file and we don't need it so we do pass in null.

The first argument is a prefix for the file so that every file will be prefixed with the word "note" so we can determine easily that these are our Note files.

The second argument is a suffix. In this case I am adding a file extension of ".sten" to indicate that the file is for our Stenotes app.

FileName Examples: Pattern
When the method is called it will generate files which have the following pattern:
note<randomUniqueNumber>.sten
For example:
note1253872225.sten
note2523363453.sten
note6842348373.sten

Since this work is done when the object is constructed, the filename value can be used at any time after that. That's why when the user hits the Save button and the Note.Save() method is called the filename is already generated and ready to save the text in.

List All Files
Well, we could run the code at this point and generate a new Note file and save it. However, we wouldn't be able to see the list of files that are available. So let's add the code that will also list the files for us and then we'll run the code.

MainActivity For File List
When the application starts it needs to get the list of files so we want the MainActivity to call getFilesDir() and find all the files which are named <anything>.sten. Then, when it finds each one, we want it to add them to the list. Finally, once they display on the list, we want each Note to load again in the NoteActivity whenever the user touches one in the list.

loadFileList()

The first thing we want to do is add a function named loadFileList() to the MainActivity. This is where we will attempt to load each of the *.sten files found into the listview.

For now, we'll just put the filename in the list, but we'll update this to display the title because that will provide the user with a better idea of what the note contains.

MainActivity.java × | NoteActivity.java × | Note.java × | AndroidManifest.xml ×

```java
private void loadNoteFileList()
{

    try {
        String rootPath = getFilesDir().getAbsolutePath();
        adapter.add(rootPath);
        File f = new File(rootPath);
        File file[] = f.listFiles();
        for (int i=0; i < file.length; i++)
        {
            adapter.add(file[i].getName());
            Log.d("MainActivity", "FileName:" + file[i].getName());
        }

        adapter.notifyDataSetChanged();
    }
    catch (Exception ex)
    {
        Log.d("main", ex.getMessage());
    }
}
```

The first thing we do is get the rootPath to our apps file storage. This is that same call to the getFilesDir() that we did in the Note class.

Next, you can see that we add the rootPath value to the adapter just so we can see it for reference in the list. Later we will remove this code. It's just for testing.

Get Files In Directory

Next we new up a File object using our rootPath. The File object provides an easy way to get the files in a directory by calling its listfiles() method which returns an array of File objects. The array will contain one File for each file found in the target directory.

Next we run a for loop based upon the number of objects in the file[] array. If there were no files this for loop will not run at all.
However, if there is one or more file in the target directory then we get the name of the file using the file object and an index value named i :
file[i].getName()
We pass that value to the adapter.add() method to insert the file name into our listview.
Finally, after we iterate through all the files we call the adapter.notifyDataSetChanged() method so the listview will update on the screen.

I ran the app and added two notes and here is what it looks like so far:

You can run the app now too, by getting the code at:
stenotes_v8.zip
Keep in mind that you can create new notes, but you cannot edit them or reload them yet, since we haven't added the onclick functionality for handling the situation when a note is clicked from the listview.

Let's do that work now.

Go back to the MainActivity.java file in the Studio editor and add the following code after our fab.onClickListener:

```java
listView.setOnItemClickListener(new AdapterView.OnItemClickListener()
{
    public void onItemClick(AdapterView<?> parent, View view,
                            int position, long id) {
        Log.d("MainActivity", "item clicked");
    }
});
```

```
            loadNoteFileList();

            Toolbar toolbar = (Toolbar) findViewById(R.id.toolbar);
            setSupportActionBar(toolbar);

            FloatingActionButton fab = (FloatingActionButton) findViewById(R.id.fab);
            fab.setOnClickListener(new View.OnClickListener() {
                @Override
                public void onClick(View view) {
                    Log.d("MainActivity", "in onClick...");
                    Intent i = new Intent(MainActivity.this, NoteActivity.class);
                    Log.d("MainActivity", "after new Intent()...");
                    startActivity(i);
                    Log.d("MainActivity", "after startActivity");
//                    SimpleDateFormat sdf = new SimpleDateFormat("yyyyMMdd_HHmmss");
//                    String outItem = sdf.format(Calendar.getInstance().getTime());
//                    adapter.add(outItem);
//                    adapter.notifyDataSetChanged();
                }
            });

            listView.setOnItemClickListener(new AdapterView.OnItemClickListener() {
                public void onItemClick(AdapterView<?> parent, View view,
                                        int position, long id) {
                    Log.d("MainActivity", "item clicked");
                }
            });
    } // onCreate() closing bracket
```

As you can see, the listView's onClickListener is set up quite a bit differently than the way we have to set up a button click listener.

That's because we don't want to know when the ListView itself is clicked, but we want to know when the item within the list is clicked and that is a bit different.

At this point, when you run the program and click an item all you get is an "item clicked" message in your Logcat. We want to reload the Note and display it on our NoteActivity so there is more work to do. We will revisit this item onClickListener further onward in this chapter. But for now, let's see what we need to do to the Note class.

Altering the Note Class Again

Now that we know we want to load a Note which already exists we actually need a different constructor for our Note object. Right now, we have the one Note constructor which takes a String representing a path where we want to save our new files.

However, in this case we want to pass in a filename and have the Note object load our existing data.

Method Overloading

There is a feature of Java classes called Method overloading which allows you to call the same method (in this case our constructor) with different parameter types or a different number of parameters so that the code will do different things.
Method overloading will suit us fine, however, you cannot have two methods with the same signature.

What's the Signature of a Method?

The signature of a method is based upon its name and it's number and type of parameters.
For example our current Note constructor has a signature of:
```
public Note(String filePath)
```

The method is named Note and it takes one string.
We cannot have another method with that signature or the class will not compile.
The following will not work:
```
public Note(String fileName)
```

Even though we are changing the name of the parameter, Java can only differentiate if the types or number of arguments is different

We could create another constructor which takes two strings:
```
public Note(String filePath, String fileName)
```

Or, we could create a new constructor which takes a String and an integer
```
public Note(String filePath, int fileCount)
```

Since we now want to differentiate between the constructors when we are loading a file or creating a new file, we need to pass in a different type or a different number of parameters to overload our constructor.

Send In a File Type
I suggest we send in a File (Java.io.File) for our new constructor since we will not need generateFileName() to be called in our new constructor.

Let's add the following new constructor to our Note class code:
```
public Note(File existingNote){
    loadNote(existingNote);
}
```

This simply constructs our Note object using a passed in Java.io.File (existingNote) which we will construct from our NoteActivity onCreate() method. We'll look at that code in a moment.
After that we call a private Note class method we are going to add right now, called loadNote().
This is the code which will load the note back in from the original file.
Here's a view of the entire loadNote() method.

```java
        private void loadNote(File existingNote){
            try {
                BufferedReader r =
                        new BufferedReader(
                                new InputStreamReader(
                                        new FileInputStream(existingNote)));
                StringBuilder inString = new StringBuilder();
                String line;
                int lineCounter = 0;
                while ((line = r.readLine()) != null) {
                    if (lineCounter == 0)
                    {
                        Log.d("Note.java", "line : " + line);
                        title = line;
                    }
                    else {
                        inString.append(line);
                    }
                    lineCounter++;
                }
                if (inString.toString() != "")
                {
                    text = inString.toString();
                }
            }
            catch (FileNotFoundException fnf)
            {
                Log.e("Note.java", fnf.getMessage());
            }
            catch (IOException iox)
            {
                Log.e("Note.java", iox.getMessage());
            }
        }
```

I've made loadNote() private because it is never called from outside the Note
class. This is an internal method called when the object is constructed.

Exception Handling
The first thing you'll notice is that the entire method is wrapped in a
Try...Catch... block.
That's because creating the FileInputStream can throw a FileNotFound
exception and Java forces you to write safe code that handles that situation.

237

It's also because readline() method of the BufferedReader can throw an IOException (can't read from file, etc) so you have to code for that also.

Read From File
The first thing we have to do is read from the File that has been passed in. That's the original Note that we want to see onscreen again.

To do that work we have to construct a BufferedReader object which I simply name r.
However, to construct the BufferedReader I have to construct a new InputStreamReader and to construct the InputStreamReader I have to attach the input stream to some physical thing such as a http stream or file. Of course, in our case we are attaching it to our note file. This is where we used our passed in reference of the File which has a full path to the actual filename in the Android storage.

StringBuilder
Once we build the BufferedReader up we are ready to read data from the file, but for our purposes we also build up a StringBuilder which allows us to create large strings very quickly.

I create a String variable named line to hold each line which will be read in. I also add a lineCounter simply because I want the first line to be loaded into the title variable of our Note object.

Reading From the File
You can see that the work of reading from the file is all done on the while loop line.

```
while ((line = r.readLine()) != null)
```

This line calls the readLine() method of the BufferedReader (r). Each time it reads a line it checks to see if the return from readLine() was null. If it is then it means the end of the file has been reached and there is no more data to read.

First Line of File Is Title

Since the first line of the file is the Note Title and we only want to load the title one time I implement a line counter and set the title only when the lineCounter == 0.

Rest of Lines Are Note Text
The rest of the file is our Note text so the else case handles that by appending to the StringBuilder each time we read a line:

```
inString.append(line);
```

Finally, right before the loadNote() method returns, it sets the Note text field to the value that has been built up in the StringBuilder so that the Note text is completely loaded from the file and ready to be displayed on screen.
The code makes one check just to insure that the StringBuilder isn't just an empty string. Then it sets the text value of the Note.

```
if (inString.toString() != "")
{
    text = inString.toString();
}
```

That's all there is to it in the Note class, but now we need to do some work to make sure the loaded Note displays in the NoteActivity properly.

Switch back over to the NoteActivity class file and take a look at the onCreate() method.

```
C MainActivity.java ×    C NoteActivity.java ×    C Note.java ×    AndroidManifest.xml ×    activity_note.xml ×

        private EditText _noteText;

        private final NoteActivity na = this;
        private Note _note;

        public NoteActivity () { Log.d("NoteActivity", "Inside NoteActivity constructor..." ); }

        @Override
        protected void onCreate(Bundle savedInstanceState) {
            Log.d("NoteActivity", "In NoteActivity.onCreate()...");
            super.onCreate(savedInstanceState);
            setContentView(R.layout.activity_note);
            setTitle("Note - new");
            _note = new Note(getFilesDir().getAbsolutePath());
```

Right now you can see (on last line of previous image) that every time onCreate is called (any time the NoteActivity is launched) then we load up a new Note and initialize it with a new file name. However, now we only want to do that work if the (+) add note button is clicked on MainActivity.

We want to do something different if a previously created note is clicked from the MainActivity Note ListView. But, how do we do that?

That's right, we need to go back to our MainActivity and finish up our onSetItemClickedListener.

That method is now going to contain the following code:

```java
listView.setOnItemClickListener(new AdapterView.OnItemClickListener()
{
    public void onItemClick(AdapterView<?> parent, View view,
                            int position, long id) {
        Log.d("MainActivity", "item clicked");
        Object o = listView.getItemAtPosition(position);
        String fileName=(String)o;
        Log.d("MainActivity", "fileName : " + fileName);
        Bundle bundle = new Bundle();
        bundle.putString("noteFileName", fileName);
        Intent i = new Intent(MainActivity.this, NoteActivity.class);
        i.putExtras(bundle);
        startActivity(i);
    }
});
```

```
        loadNoteFileList();

        Toolbar toolbar = (Toolbar) findViewById(R.id.toolbar);
        setSupportActionBar(toolbar);

        FloatingActionButton fab = (FloatingActionButton) findViewById(R.id.fab);
        fab.setOnClickListener(new View.OnClickListener() {
            @Override
            public void onClick(View view) {
                Log.d("MainActivity", "in onClick...");
                Intent i = new Intent(MainActivity.this, NoteActivity.class);
                Log.d("MainActivity", "after new Intent()...");
                startActivity(i);
                Log.d("MainActivity", "after startActivity");
            }
        });

        listView.setOnItemClickListener(new AdapterView.OnItemClickListener() {
            public void onItemClick(AdapterView<?> parent, View view,
                                    int position, long id) {
                Log.d("MainActivity", "item clicked");
                Object o = listView.getItemAtPosition(position);
                String fileName=(String)o;
                Log.d("MainActivity", "fileName : " + fileName);
                Bundle bundle = new Bundle();
                bundle.putString("noteFileName", fileName);
                Intent i = new Intent(MainActivity.this, NoteActivity.class);
                i.putExtras(bundle);
                startActivity(i);
            }
        });
    } // onCreate() closing bracket
```

You can see the first thing we do inside the onItemClick() method is get the item at the position in the list that was clicked and store it in a generic Object o.

Next, we convert the value to a String and store it in a variable named fileName. We know that each item in the list is a String representing the filename where the Note is stored so this works.

Android Bundles

Next, we create a new Bundle object.

This is one of the standard ways to pass values from one Activity to another. In our case we want to pass the value of the file name from the MainActivity to the NoteActivity.

After we new up the Bundle we call a method it provides called putString() which allows us to store a String in the Bundle which we can later retrieve on the other Activity.

```
bundle.putString("noteFileName", fileName);
```

putString : Name-Value Pair

When we call putString, the first parameter is the name we will use to later retrieve the value. The second parameter is the value that we want to send. In our case we are sending in the file name so we can retrieve it in the NoteActivity.

Next, we create our new NoteActivity Intent just as we do when the user clicks the (+) button.

```
Intent i = new Intent(MainActivity.this, NoteActivity.class);
```

After that, we add our new Bundle to the Intent object by calling the putExtras() method.

```
i.putExtras(bundle);
```

Then, we start the activity just as we did when there was no Bundle.

```
startActivity(i);
```

Each time a user clicks an item in the list it will send the fileName across to the NoteActivity. However, that means we need to do something with the value. For that, we need to switch back to our NoteActivity and change our onCreate().

We need to delete the line in NoteActivity onCreate() we mentioned before:

```
_note = new Note(getFilesDir().getAbsolutePath());
```

We'll replace it with the following lines:

```
Bundle bundle = getIntent().getExtras();
if (bundle != null) {
    String fileName = bundle.getString("noteFileName");
```

```
        _note = new Note(new File(getFilesDir() + "/" +fileName));
        Log.d("NoteActivity", bundle.toString());
    }
    else {
        _note = new Note(getFilesDir().getAbsolutePath());
    }
```

The top portion of NoteActivity onCreate() will now look like:

| C MainActivity.java × | C NoteActivity.java × | C Note.java × | AndroidManifest.xml × | activity_note.xml × |

```
    private EditText _noteText;

    private final NoteActivity na = this;
    private Note _note;

    public NoteActivity () { Log.d("NoteActivity", "Inside NoteActivity constructor..." ); }

    @Override
    protected void onCreate(Bundle savedInstanceState) {
        Log.d("NoteActivity", "In NoteActivity.onCreate()...");
        super.onCreate(savedInstanceState);
        setContentView(R.layout.activity_note);
        setTitle("Note - new");

        Bundle bundle = getIntent().getExtras();
        if (bundle != null) {
            String fileName = bundle.getString("noteFileName");
            _note = new Note(new File(getFilesDir() + "/" +fileName));
            Log.d("NoteActivity", bundle.toString());
        }
        else {
            _note = new Note(getFilesDir().getAbsolutePath());
        }

        _titleText = (EditText)findViewById(R.id.titleText);
        _noteText = (EditText)findViewById(R.id.noteText);
        cancelButton = (Button)findViewById(R.id.cancelButton);
        saveButton = (Button)findViewById(R.id.saveButton);
```

The first thing we do in the newly added code is load up the Bundle by grabbing it off the Intent which is started.
```
Bundle bundle = getIntent().getExtras();
```
If there was no Bundle added, as in the case that the user clicked the add new note (+) button then the Bundle will be null and the else path will be

executed and a new Note object will be loaded and a new filename will be generated. In that case the Title and the Text EditText boxes will be empty on the screen.

However, if the bundle object exists then we pull the string off the bundle using its name (noteFileName) and the getString() method of the Bundle object.

```
String fileName = bundle.getString("noteFileName");
_note = new Note(new File(getFilesDir() + "/" +fileName));
```

After we get the String from the Bundle we can then call the new Note constructor which takes a File object by newing up a File object which will point to our existing file in storage.

When we do that the Note fields Title and Text will be loaded up with the appropriate data.
The only thing left to do is display the values on the screen by loading the values into the titleText and noteText EditText objects.

Back to Activity LifeCycle
This is where our knowledge of the Activity LifeCycle will help us. We know that when the Activity starts up we want to load the values that are in the Note object into the on screen elements so we add some simple code to our onStart() method of the NoteActivity.

```
        }

        @Override
        public void onStart()
        {
            super.onStart();
            Log.d("NoteActivity", "onStart()...");
            if (_note != null) {
                _titleText.setText(_note.getTitle());
                _noteText.setText(_note.getText());
            }
        }
    }
```

You can see that now we check to insure the _note object isn't null. If it is null then it has no values and we don't need to do any work.
Then, if the _note object is valid we go ahead and call the setText() methods on each of the EditText boxes with the values which are in the Note object. That displays the values which are in the Note file.

This creates complete functionality with the ability to create, read and update Notes from a note list.
You can run the code by getting the code:
Stenotes_v10.zip

More For Another Time
You have a working app which will allow you to create and edit notes.
However, there is much more work to be done on this for it to be ready for production release.

Additional Features
Some of the features would be just nice to have but others are probably strong requirements to make it more useful and easy to use.
Here's the list of things that I can think of that need to be added for sure:
  1. Alter the ListView so it displays the title text of the Note

245

2. If the user is viewing a note but doesn't change it and hits the Cancel don't bother her with the dialog asking if she wants to save changes, because there haven't been any.
3. Fix the problem with the NoteActivity not properly displaying CrLf (Carriage Return & LineFeed ie Newlline) from the file.
4. Change the NoteActivity Title text (top of Activity) so that it doesn't say New, if it's old note you are editing / viewing again.
5. Handle the situation if the user has created a new note and typed in a new title and new text but then hits the device's back button. In that case, the note is lost, because the Save button was never hit.
6. What if the app goes into Pause mode or Stop while user is editing a note? He will probably lose his data. Make decisions about what to do in that case.
7. Allow users to longClick (hold) a note in the listview and then choose to delete it if they want to.

BONUS ITEM -- Using ADB
ADB (Android Debug Bridge) : Running Linux System Commands
Finally, I want to show you how to see the files you have created in the Android storage location.
However, to do that you need to use the command line tool ADB which is installed at the location where you installed your Android SDK.

Most likely they are installed at : %localappdata%/Android/sdk

You can enter that exact string in the navigation edit box at the top of File Explorer and hit <ENTER> and it should take you to this location.

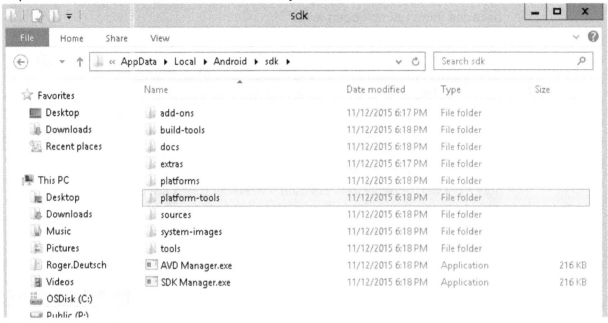

After that, hold your Shift key and right-click the \platform-tools directory and a menu will appear.

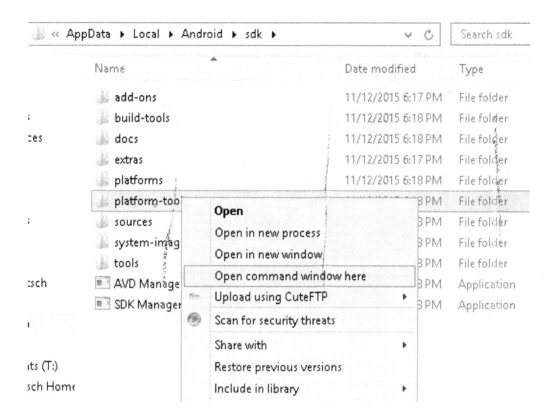

Choose the [Open command window] here menu item and a console window will open and you will be in the platform-tools directory.

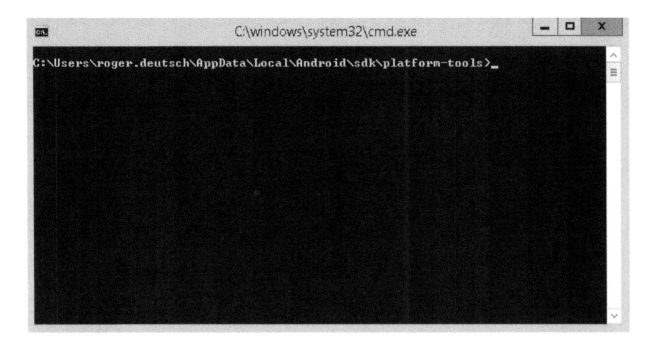

```
C:\windows\system32\cmd.exe
C:\Users\roger.deutsch\AppData\Local\Android\sdk\platform-tools>_
```

Now type the following and press <ENTER>:

adb shell ls -al /data/data/us.raddev.stenotes/files/ <ENTER>

Note that the path I'm attempting to list for is the same path shown in our application listview (highlighted in blue at the top of the following screen shot).

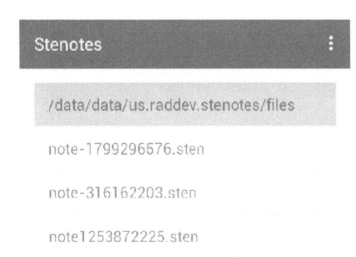

Once you run the ADB command, you will see something like the following:

```
C:\Users\roger.deutsch\AppData\Local\Android\sdk\platform-tools>adb shell ls -al
/data/data/us.raddev.stenotes/files/
-rw-------    app_45    app_45         89 2016-02-28 17:06 note-1799296576.sten
-rw-------    app_45    app_45         45 2016-02-27 23:45 note-316162203.sten
-rw-------    app_45    app_45         73 2016-02-27 22:50 note1253872225.sten

C:\Users\roger.deutsch\AppData\Local\Android\sdk\platform-tools>_
```

We have done a Linux ls (list files) with parameters telling it to show all files in long form in the target directory. These are the files which contain the notes we have created in our program.

Summary
This has been a huge chapter and you've followed along you've grown serious Android Dev chops.
You know a bit about:
Android Storage
Writing and Reading files from Android Storage
Bundles and how you can pass data across Activities.
The Activity lifecycle.

Most importantly, you know how a real Android app is built. Even if you stopped going forward in this book at this point you have enough knowledge to build many of your own apps. But don't stop there's way more to learn and advance your skills.

What's Next?
Android Intents are powerful and there are built-in Intents which you can implement your code on top of to get text from SMS messages, use pictures from the camera and even do things when the phone rings. We'll look into some of the more interesting Intents and learn how to build our own Intent to grab text from any screen we are reading so we can store quotes and text in a database for research purposes. That way, if you're reading a book you

can save quotes from the book in your own list / database and call up those quotes later when you want to reference them.

Chapter 7

Building QuoteCap:Android Intents & Sqlite Database

We are going to build an app in this chapter which will allow a user to capture text as she is reading and save it to a sqlite database on her device. To do this, we will have to add an Intent which can be launched when the user selects text she is reading from any other app (web browser, Kindle app, etc).

I'm going to call the app QuoteCap (Quote Capture). The app will allow the user to:

1. set up categories so he can organize his quotes
2. add a note which will be saved along with the quotes in case there is additional information he wants to remember
3. allow user to add a heading to each quote
4. All quotes and notes will be saved in a sqlite database on the device, however, since we want to allow the user to use this information further, we are going to provide a way to print by posting the data to a web API,
5. The app will also provide a way to get the data out of the device for use in other documents like MS-Word or LibreOffice.

You've Learned A Lot : Accelerate
Since you've learned so much already and you are familiar with Android Studio this book can accelerate as we go because you already know how to

do the basics. You'll see that I speed things up quite a bit, but if you forget how to do something, just do a review of the previous chapters and it'll clear it up.

Creating QuoteCap
Go to AndroidStudio and create a new project named QuoteCap. When you create the project and you are choosing the Activity template, go ahead and choose [Empty Activity]. We don't need the menu and the buttons since our Activity will be fairly simplistic with only one main Activity for configuring the app.

You can download this project if you don't want to create it:
quoteCap_v01.zip

Run First Time
After create the new app project (or download it) I always like to run it on my target emulator, just to insure that everything is set up and working as I expect.

Here's a snapshot of the simple program running.
You can see that it adds that Hello, world! string which we'll need to remove.

Configuring QuoteCap
We need allow the user to

1. display, add, delete a list of categories which will be provided to her when she uses QuoteCap to save a quote.
2. A way to page through the quotes the user has saved.

That's it for the most part, because most of our functionality will be presented on a dialog box which the user will interact with.

App Walk-through

Let's take a walk through of the completed app so you can see what I mean. This app will be a service to other apps since it is more about collecting that quotes.

##

Setup Our App As An Intent

The first thing we want to do is set up our app as an Intent so that when text is copied our app will show up as one of the choices where the text can be sent.

To do that, we need to alter our AndroidManifest.xml.

Go to Solution Explorer and open up the AndroidManifest.xml in the Studio editor.

Intent Filter

You can see there is already one section of the AndroidManifest.xml which contains an <intent-filter>. Notice that the intent-filter is nested inside the Activity which has a name of :

.MainActivity. Obviously, this refers to the MainActivity in our app. The nested Intent Filter adds a launcher to the application which tells the system that there is an Activity which will be started when the app is started. That's how MainActivity gets displayed when we start our application.

We want to add another intent-filter which will look like the following:
<intent-filter>
        <action android:name="android.intent.action.SEND" />
        <category android:name="android.intent.category.DEFAULT" />
        <data android:mimeType="**text/plain**" />
    </intent-filter>

This tells the system that our application allows text to be sent to it. Since, we've nested the intent-filter under our MainActivity, when the text is sent to our app then the MainActivity will be brought to the front. That will allow the user to do something with the text in our app.

Go ahead and add the new intent so our AndroidManifest.xml looks like the following now:

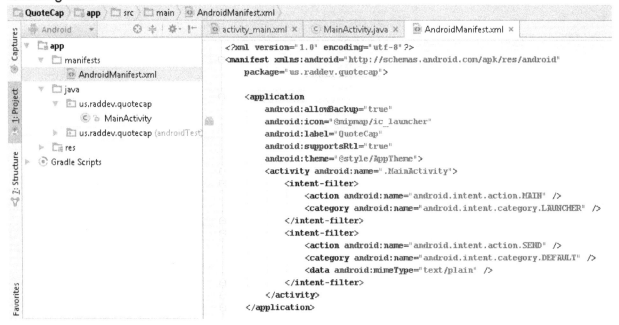

App Already Does Something

Even though we've done very little, the app already does something interesting. Since we've now told the AndroidManifest to register the app as accepting incoming text, the app will now appear when a user clicks the Share menu item. Let's run the app and see it in action.

You can get the code at:
QuoteCap_v02.zip

Once you build app, go ahead and run it so it'll get installed onto your device emulator. However, for the test that we are going to do now, the app does not need to be running.
As a matter of fact, once the app starts, go ahead and click the back arrow and the app will be suspended and probably stop.

After that, start up the Android Browser on your emulator.

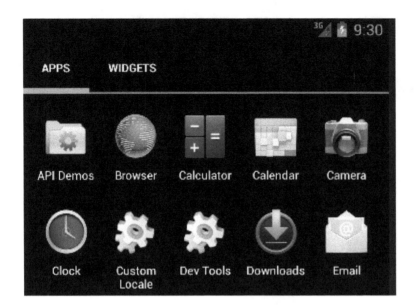

After the browser comes up, go to a web site that has some text.

I went to http://en.wikipedia.org (english version of wikipedia).

You can go to any site you like. I just know that wikipedia will load relatively fast and will have some text for me to select.

Bristol Temple Meads, the city's oldest and largest railway station

Bristol is a city in South West England. With an estimated population of 442,500 in 2015, it is the second most populous city in Southern England and the eighth in the UK. Iron Age hill forts and Roman villas were built near the confluence of the Rivers Frome and Avon, and around the beginning of the 11th century the settlement was known as Brycgstow (Old English for "the place at the bridge"). Bristol received a royal charter in 1155, and became a county in 1373. A major

Click on the text somewhere in the article and hold.

If you hit only text when you click, then the two selector tags will appear and you can move them to select more or less text.

Today's featured article

Bristol Temple Meads, the city's oldest and largest

Bristol is a city in South West England. With an estimated population of 442,500 in 2015, it is the second most populous

However, if you happen to hit one of the links, you'll first be presented with a menu:

Today's featured article

https://en.m.wikipedia.org/wiki/
Hill_fort

Open

Open in new tab

Save link

Copy link URL

Select text

Brycgstow (Old English for "the place at the
bridge"). Bristol received a royal charter in
1155, and became a county in 1373. A major
commercial port from the 12th century, it was
the starting place for early voyages of

If that happens, choose the last menu item [Select text] and then the two
selector tags will appear.
Just make sure you select some text. In either case, when you select text
then at the top of the browser app you'll see some buttons appear which
allow you to do something with your selection.

Today's featured article

Bristol Temple Meads, the city's oldest and largest railway station

Bristol is a city in South West England. With an estimated population of 442,500 in 2015, it is the second most populous city in Southern England and the eighth in the UK. Iron Age hill forts and Roman villas were built near the confluence of the Rivers Frome and Avon, and around the beginning of the 11th century the settlement was known as Brycgstow (Old English for "the place at the bridge"). Bristol received a royal charter in

The first choice is the checkmark icon which simply indicates that you are done.
The second choice is [Select all] which allows you to select all the text currently displayed.
The third choice is the paper over paper icon which indicates that you can copy the text.
The fourth and final choice is the additional menu button.

The fourth one is the one we want to select.
Click that one and additional menu choices will appear.

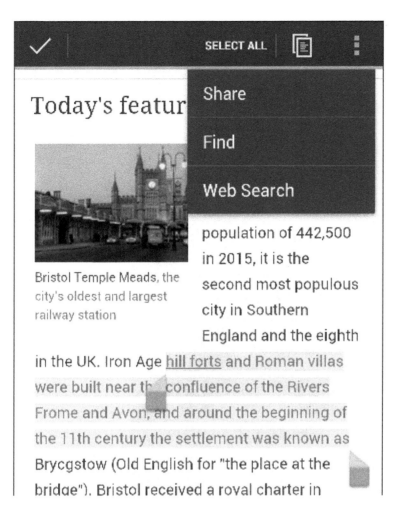

Today's featur

Share

Find

Web Search

Bristol Temple Meads, the city's oldest and largest railway station

population of 442,500 in 2015, it is the second most populous city in Southern England and the eighth in the UK. Iron Age hill forts and Roman villas were built near the confluence of the Rivers Frome and Avon, and around the beginning of the 11th century the settlement was known as Brycgstow (Old English for "the place at the bridge"). Bristol received a royal charter in

Share is the menu item we want. Click the Share menu item now and you will see a list of apps that are registered on the device which accept text.

Look at that! QuoteCap is available.

Go ahead and click it.

When you do, it isn't quite fantastic, yet.

As a matter of fact, the Browser crashed on my emulator when I clicked. But, that's not normal and it isn't related to our app.

Once I clicked the [OK] button the QuoteCap MainActivity came to the front, but of course we haven't written any code to handle the incoming text yet so nothing happens.

Let's add the code to get the incoming text now. We'll display it on the MainActivity just so we can see it does something for now.

Go to Android Studio and open up the activity_main.xml.

You can see that it is currently a RelativeLayout. Highlight the top tag and type LinearLayout and Studio will change the bottom one for you so we will now have a LinearLayout.

Next, move down to the TextView element and add an id to it named mainText so we can reference the control in code.

```xml
<?xml version="1.0" encoding="utf-8"?>
<LinearLayout xmlns:android="http://schemas.android.com/apk/res/android"
    xmlns:tools="http://schemas.android.com/tools"
    android:layout_width="match_parent"
    android:layout_height="match_parent"
    android:paddingBottom="16dp"
    android:paddingLeft="16dp"
    android:paddingRight="16dp"
    android:paddingTop="16dp"
    tools:context="us.raddev.quotecap.MainActivity">

    <TextView
        android:layout_width="wrap_content"
        android:layout_height="wrap_content"
        android:id="@+id/mainText" />
</LinearLayout>
```

Also, remove the line which sets the text to "Hello, world!" since we don't care about displaying that text any more.

Let's Capture the Text

Now let's write the code that captures the text. Open up the MainActivity.java file and go to the onCreate() method.

We're going to add the following code:

```java
public class MainActivity extends AppCompatActivity {

    TextView tv;

    @Override
    protected void onCreate(Bundle savedInstanceState) {
        super.onCreate(savedInstanceState);
        setContentView(R.layout.activity_main);
        tv = (TextView)findViewById(R.id.mainText);
        // Get intent, action and MIME type
        Intent intent = getIntent();
        String action = intent.getAction();
        String type = intent.getType();

        if (Intent.ACTION_SEND.equals(action) && type != null) {
            if ("text/plain".equals(type)) {
                handleReceivedText(intent); // Handle text being sent
            }
        }
    }
}
```

You can see that the first thing we do is get a member variable (tv) set up to hold our reference to our TextView since that is where we are going to display our incoming text.

Of course the first two lines of our onCreate() method were generated for us by the project template. Then the third line is where we actually instantiate our TextView from our layout item we just added.

Finally, we see some of the code that works with the incoming Intent. I snagged this code right out of the Google Android development documentation at :
http://developer.android.com/training/sharing/receive.html

The first line gets the incoming Intent.
```java
Intent intent = getIntent();
```

Once we get the Intent we need to grab the Intent Action and Type from it to make sure we handle it properly.

```
String action = intent.getAction();
String type = intent.getType();
```

After we do that, we can decide what to do based upon the action being a SEND action and the type being "text/plain". We need to know the type because obviously we can't display picture data in our TextView.

Once, we've determined the type, we can do whatever we want with the data, it's nice to split that work up by calling a method. In our case we call the handleReceivedText() method and send it the Intent.

That's the code which will do the work of retrieving the actual text and displaying it in our TextView.

```
        if (Intent.ACTION_SEND.equals(action) && type != null) {
            if ("text/plain".equals(type)) {
                handleReceivedText(intent); // Handle text being sent
            }
        }
    }

    private void handleReceivedText(Intent intent){
        String outText = intent.getStringExtra(Intent.EXTRA_TEXT);
        Log.d("MainActivity", outText);

        tv.setText(outText);
    }
```

You can see, it is very easy to get the text. We just call the intent's built-in method called getStringExtra and we pass it a predefined static String (Intent.EXTRA_TEXT). That item is defined by the Android libraries.

We store the value returned from getStringExtra() in our local variable outText and finally pass that to our TextView tv method setText() to display it on our MainActivity. That's all there is to it.
Let's run the app and share some text to it.

You can get the code at:
QuoteCap_v03.zip

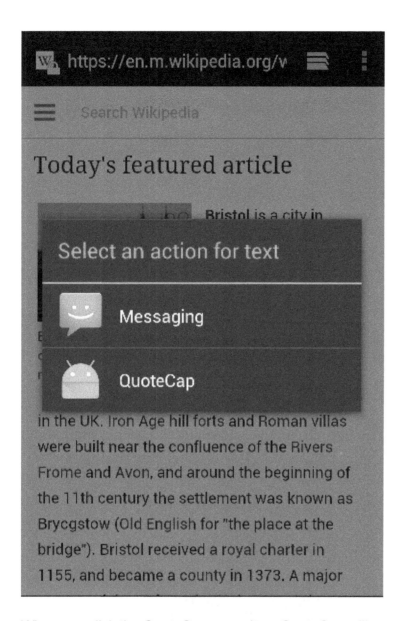

When you click the QuoteCap menu item QuoteCap will come to the front and the text you selected will be displayed on the MainActivity.

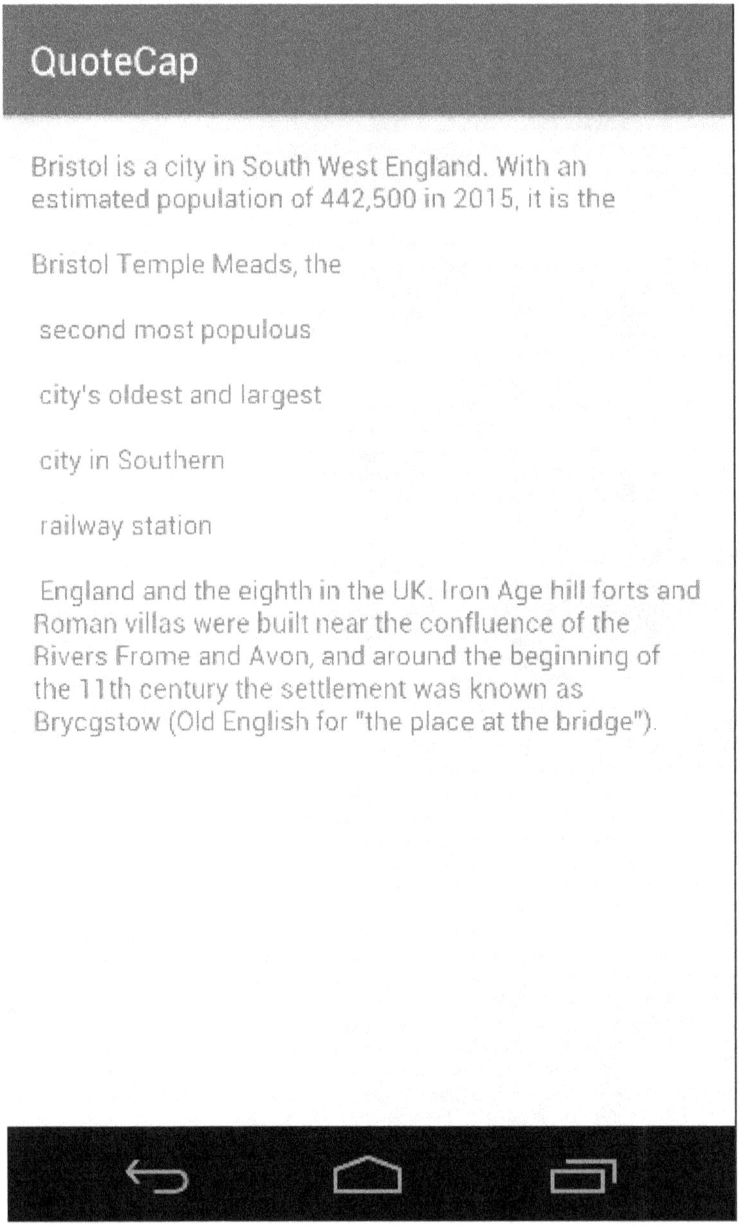

Bristol is a city in South West England. With an
estimated population of 442,500 in 2015, it is the

Bristol Temple Meads, the

second most populous

city's oldest and largest

city in Southern

railway station

England and the eighth in the UK. Iron Age hill forts and
Roman villas were built near the confluence of the
Rivers Frome and Avon, and around the beginning of
the 11th century the settlement was known as
Brycgstow (Old English for "the place at the bridge").

That's not too bad for the small amount of code we've written so far.

Odd Formatting : Line Breaks

You can see that there is also some kind of translation going on with CrLf (Carriage-Return Line-Feed) characters, because there are some odd breaks in the text that wasn't in the original.

As a programmer you will find that it is these little things that are cause for a lot of extra (and unexpected) code that you have to write.   It's another reason that there are "no simple apps".

Of course, this program doesn't do much for us because we aren't saving the data anywhere. This time, we have more information we want to save than we did with Stenotes.   What I mean is that we want to be able to save a few different kinds of information this time.
I'm thinking we want to save:
1. The captured text
2. a title for the text
3. source of the text (book name, html link, etc)
4. extra notes related to the text
5. category for the captured text (the list will be managed by the user)

If we capture all this information about each quote then later, it'll be much easier to remember where it came from. We will also create a way to page through these quotes in our app so we can review them more easily and these fields will help us remember the context of why the quote was important to us in the first place.

We will allow any of the fields to be empty (except the captured text field) so the user will be able to capture text very quickly without much intrusion from our app if they don't want to save all the other info.

Since all of this information creates a structure which we might refer to as a Quote which has properties like text, title, source, notes and category, you can easily see that this Quote thing is a good candidate for a Domain object. It is also a good candidate to be a table in a database. That's where we're heading with this app.   We are going to save our data in a local Sqlite (pronounced Sequel-Light or Sequel-ite) database.

What Is Sqlite?

Here's a quote from http://sqlite.org

SQLite is a software library that implements a self-contained, serverless, zero-configuration, transactional SQL database engine. SQLite is the most widely deployed database engine in the world. The source code for SQLite is in the public domain. More...

Here's what those terms mean to us.

Self-contained: That just means you don't have to install anything else to use it.

Serverless: Sqlite runs right on your device and saves all data locally. No need for a network or Internet connection.

Zero-configuration: Install it and use it. There's not a bunch of setup work to do.

Transactional: Each action on the database is limited to a small size and tracked to relieve worries about losing data if the app or device crashes.

Most Widely Used Database Engine In the World
Just in case you think that is an exaggeration, because maybe you've never heard of Sqlite, here are just a few places Sqlite is used. If you're running Windows, you have Sqlite databases on your machine. If you're using an iPhone or iTunes you have Sqlite databases.
Here's the amazing info from the Sqlite site:

Most Widely Deployed and Used Database Engine

SQLite is likely used more than all other database engines combined. Billions and billions of copies of SQLite exist in the wild. SQLite is found in:

- Every Android device
- Every iPhone and iOS device
- Every Mac
- Every Windows10 machine
- Every Firefox, Chrome, and Safari web browser
- Every instance of Skype
- Every instance of iTunes
- Every Dropbox client
- Every TurboTax and QuickBooks
- PHP and Python
- Most television sets and set-top cable boxes
- Most automotive multimedia systems
- Countless millions of other applications

Why Not Store QuoteCap Data In A File?
The SQL part of the Sqlite name stands for Structured Query Language. That is a standard way to query (question) a database about its data. Once we design our tables (structured storage used in relational databases) and store our data in the database, there is a structured way to query the database to obtain information which will answer our questions.

For example, if we implement the category field and choose a category for every quote stored then later we can filter our data down to a specific category very easily using SQL. However, imagine if all that data were just stored in a file and we had to parse through it every time we wanted to see just the quotes in specific category. It would be very difficult work and every query would be custom programming. SQL and Sqlite allows us to do that work much more easily.
However, of course there is the initial creation of the database and learning how to use Sqlite in our Android development.

The good news is that Android has made it very easy to use Sqlite. Let's get started on creating our database and writing code to save our data to it.

Designing Our Quote Table
Since we are saving our data in a structured way it's as if we are placing our data in storage boxes. That means we have to decide ahead of time what size box we need for each field (column). In our case, size relates to number of bytes (characters). I am going to choose some arbitrary numbers for these and change them later if I need more space in a particular field.

For now, our table will end up being something like the following:
ID : unique id for row, will be auto-generated (more later)
Title: 100 bytes
Text: 5000 bytes (this is the actual quote text we're copying from the other source) Average size of English word is 5 bytes, this means you get about 1000 words.
Source: 500 bytes trying to allow for title, link, author name, etc.

Notes: 5000 bytes - if you're a researcher like I am, you'll want some space to type what you were thinking about when you grabbed the quote

Category: 500 bytes - this should be relatively short so it can show up easily.

Created: Date - I like to know a history of what I was reading so we'll add this field too so that when we create an entry we grab the date. This way there is a bit of history to the research you are doing.

That will give you a rough idea of what we will be creating in code.

Using Sqlite Means Creating a Sqlite Class

The easiest and most direct way to create our database is to use the SqlLiteHelper class provided by the Android libraries.

To use that class we have to create our own class to extend SqlLiteHelper. Let's do that now.

Go to solution explorer and right-click the us.raddev.quotecap package item and a context menu will appear. Slide over the [New] menu item and click the [Java Class] menu item.

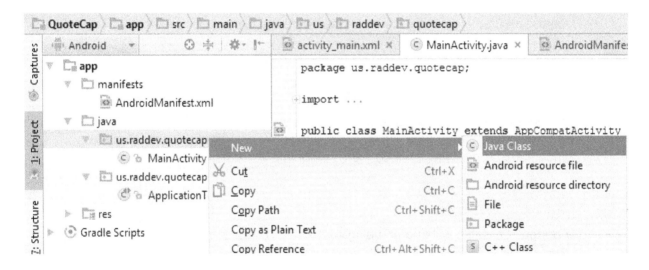

A dialog box will appear asking you what you want to name your class.

Let's call it QuoteDatabaseHelper.

After you type the name, click the [OK] button.

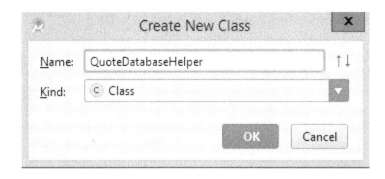

When you do, Android Studio will generate the QuoteDatabaseHelper.java
file and open it in the editor for you.

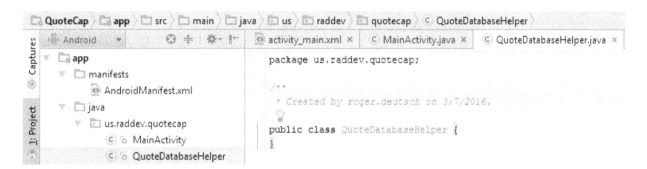

Notice that Android Studio placed our new class in our app package since we
had right-clicked that package when we created the class. It has also added
the correct package name at the top of our new file. This makes sense
because this class will be specific to code we are writing for this app and it
being in the same package namespace is good.

Getting Functionality That Is Already Written
When we extend a class we get the advantage of obtaining code that is
already written in a library and can make our development cycle much faster.
That's what we want to do with our QuoteDatabaseHelper class.

Begin typing the extends keyword after the class name and as you type the
name of the class we want to extend (SqliteOpenHelper) you will see that
Android offers it as a choice.

Choose the SqliteOpenHelper item or completely type it yourself.

When you do that Android Studio will probably kind of flash and redraw the editor window and you'll see a red lightbulb appear on the left side of the editor window. Studio has looked into the code you are extending and it knows there are methods that need to be implemented.

If you click the down arrow which appears next to the red lightbulb you will see that Studio offers to help.

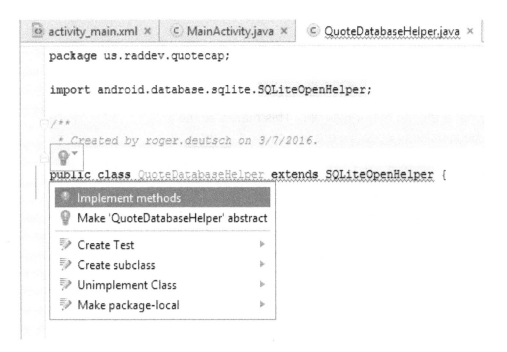

Click the [Implement methods] item.
When you do, a dialog box will appear requesting you pick the methods you want to implement and override.

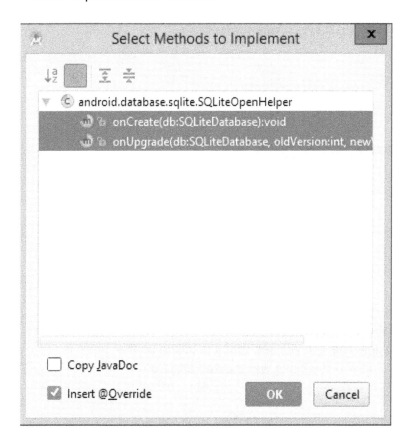

Go ahead and click the [OK] button because we do want to implement / override both of these methods.

Now your code will look like the following:

```
package us.raddev.quotecap;

import android.database.sqlite.SQLiteDatabase;
import android.database.sqlite.SQLiteOpenHelper;

/**
 * Created by roger.deutsch on 3/7/2016.
 */
public class QuoteDatabaseHelper extends SQLiteOpenHelper {
    @Override
    public void onCreate(SQLiteDatabase db) {

    }

    @Override
    public void onUpgrade(SQLiteDatabase db, int oldVersion, int newVersion) {

    }
}
```

However, you can see that Studio is complaining at me about something. If
you float over the red squiggly line you will see that it is telling us that there is
no default constructor available in the class we're extending from.

```
 */
public class QuoteDatabaseHelper extends SQLiteOpenHelper {
```

There is no default constructor available in 'android.database.sqlite.SQLiteOpenHelper'

This is Studio's best guess about something that seems to be going wrong.
It wants us to implement a constructor in our derived class.
Let's try to get Studio to help us to generate the constructor for us.
Right-click somewhere in the editor and a context menu should appear.
Choose the [Generate...] menu item.

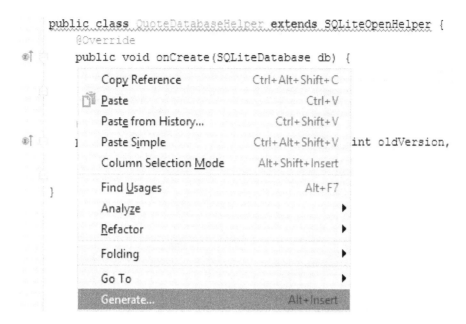

```
public class QuoteDatabaseHelper extends SQLiteOpenHelper {
    @Override
    public void onCreate(SQLiteDatabase db) {
```

Copy Reference	Ctrl+Alt+Shift+C	
Paste	Ctrl+V	
Paste from History...	Ctrl+Shift+V	
Paste Simple	Ctrl+Alt+Shift+V	int oldVersion,
Column Selection Mode	Alt+Shift+Insert	
Find Usages	Alt+F7	
Analyze	▶	
Refactor	▶	
Folding	▶	
Go To	▶	
Generate...	Alt+Insert	

As we have seen in the past another menu titled, Generate, will appear. We obviously want to choose the [Constructor] menu item.

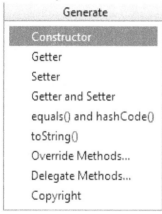

When you do another dialog box will appear because there are two choices of constructors that you need to choose from.

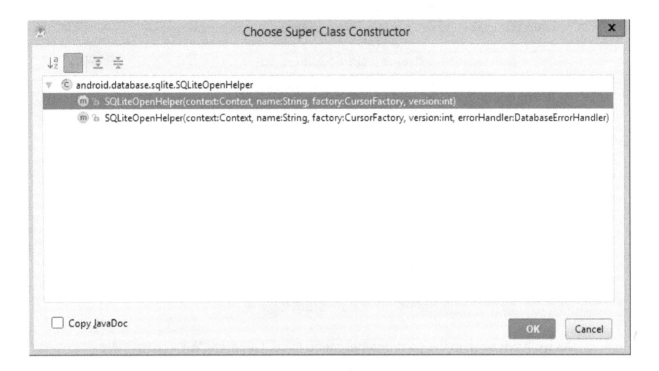

I had to stretch that window so you could see all the parameters that the 2nd constructor takes.
We want the 1st parameter because it will suit our needs. We will talk more about why we chose that one as we move further into the code. For now, choose that one and click the [OK] button.

Now Studio will be satisfied with your code and no more mean red squigglies.

```java
import android.content.Context;
import android.database.sqlite.SQLiteDatabase;
import android.database.sqlite.SQLiteOpenHelper;

/**
 * Created by roger.deutsch on 3/7/2016.
 */
public class QuoteDatabaseHelper extends SQLiteOpenHelper {
    public QuoteDatabaseHelper(Context context, String name, SQLiteDatabase.CursorFactory factory,
                              int version) {
        super(context, name, factory, version);
    }

    @Override
    public void onCreate(SQLiteDatabase db) {

    }

    @Override
    public void onUpgrade(SQLiteDatabase db, int oldVersion, int newVersion) {

    }
}
```

Now that we have our QuoteDatabaseHelper stubbed out we need to switch gears a bit and create our Quote object so we can begin to assign it the correct properties and methods to keep our development work separated properly.

Quote : Domain Object
Let's design our Quote object, it will basically look like as if we take the Quote database fields and turn them into properties.

Here's a quick class diagram to show what our Quote class should look like:

284

```
                   Quote
  -   ID  :int
  -   Title  :String
  -   Text  :String
  -   note  :String
  -   Source  :String
  -   CategoryId  :int

  +   Save()  :void
  +   Delete()  :void
```

Most of those fields probably look like what you expect. However, the CategoryId may have thrown you. You may have expected a Category which was a String so we could add a String which represents a category.
However, in the case of a Category the best way to implement a solution is a separate table which contains a list of all possible Categories.

The table would look something like the following. It's very simple and only requires two columns (one for ID and one for the category String)

ID (Int)	CATEGORY (String)
1	None
2	History-North America
3	History-Europe
4	Science-Biology
5	Science-Computer
6	Science-Astronomy
7	Math-Algebra
8	Math-Trigonometry
9	Literature-Western
10	Literature-SciFi

We will provide the user with some way of managing these categories so they can add and delete them.

One of values will then be used in the data rows when the user saves a new Quote.

That data will look like what is shown in the following table. Notice that I've cut out some fields that would actually be in the Quote table because I want it to fit on the page/screen nicely.
Also, please imagine that the Text field has much data in it as represented by "data…".

Quote Table Example

ID(Int)	Title	Text	CategoryId
1	Super cool	data…	1
2	extra	data…	1
3	more	data…	1
4	WWII	data…	2
5	Cells	data…	4
6	2(n)*6	data…	7

Now, imagine what I have to do if I decide that I want to change the text for the Category with the ID = 1. I only have to edit that in one place in the database. I would go to the Category table and change it from None to "Miscellanous" and then I'd be done.

But, what if my Quote table had looked like the following:

ID(Int)	Title	Text	Category (string)
1	Super cool	data…	None
2	extra	data…	None
3	more	data…	None
4	WWII	data…	History-North America
5	Cells	data…	Science-Biology
6	2(n)*6	data…	Math-Algebra

Now, I'd have to update all three rows (and anywhere else that the Category "None" is used.
It's also more of a pain because you have to search where the Category = "None" for the change.

This is a form of normalizing your database and though we've only touched on it slightly you will hear more about it if you continue development work. Normalizing your database is done so you don't have redundant data that you'd have to edit in several tables if you change one piece of data. It's another form of code organization.

Let's go add our Quote class and then we'll see how and where we will put our code that will create our Sqlite tables for us.

Adding the Quote Class
We want to add the Quote class to our app package so go and right-click the package in solution explorer just like you did when we added the QuoteDatabaseHelper class.

Name our new class Quote and click the [OK] button.

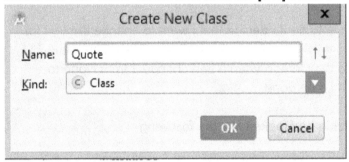

Studio will create the file for you and open it in the editor.
After that, we want to add all the properties and getter and setters.

Go ahead and add the following properites:
```
private int _id;
private String _title;
private String _text;
private String _note;
private String _source;
private Date _created;
private int _categoryId;
```

Next add the getters and setters for each of those.

Studio will do the work for you if you right-click the editor and choose Generate...

After that you can choose [Getter and Setter]

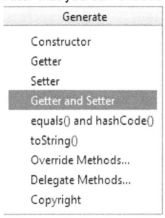

When you do, Studio will prompt you for which properties you want to generate them for.

Choose all of them and click the [OK] button.

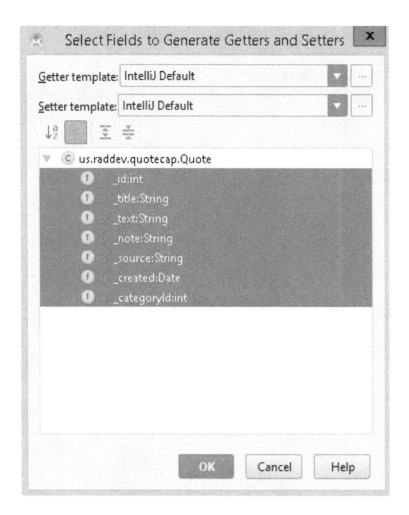

I'll do the work too and if you want you can get the code up to this point at:
QuoteCap_v04.zip

Some Talk About Our App Design

Previously we only displayed the incoming text on the MainActivity. Now, we want to instantiate a new Quote object and set the Text value when the text comes in.

That helps me know that I want a constructor which takes the incoming text and sets our Quote.Text property with that value.

Let's add that constructor now and then we'll also add UI elements to our MainActivity so the user can set the other elements of the Quote object manually -- by typing those values in.

After the user sets all the values she wants to on the form, she should be able to press a save button to save the data to the database so we'll add a Save button to MainActivity also. Once the user successfully saves her data we should close our Activity, since our
Since, it could be that the user decides not to Save the value, we'll also add a Cancel button which will close the form so the app he was sharing from is in the front again.

Focus On the Simpler Parts First
Now that we've separated out the Quote object from the rest of the app we can focus on the simpler parts of the UI first. Most of the elements of our Quote object are very easy to deal with, but the Category item is going to take a bit of work. That's because it is a dropdown list (in Windows UI) and called a Spinner on Android. There's no straight-forward way to use the Spinner because it's selectable values are loaded from somewhere else (String list or, as in our case the database). Since there's more to do with the Spinner, for now we will get everything else hooked up and then we'll take care of the Category select list.

Importance of SOC : Separation of Concerns
This is why it is so important to separate the various parts of your app as much as you can. If you do it properly then you can work on the parts you want and move forward in your project. You will be able to work on parts of development in isolation from the other parts and it will help you so you don't get blocked on some difficult piece.

Focus On One Thing At A Time
In the case of QuoteCap we are able to work on our database, Quote class and the User Interface (UI) all completely separately from each other. That allows us to concentrate on one thing at a time and makes development much easier.

The rest of the elements in our Quote object can all be displayed as EditText elements and the Created (Date) element can simply be a TextView element since we don't want to allow the user to be able to edit that item.

Of course, we also need the two buttons (Save & Cancel) which will allow the user to Save or Cancel her changes.

Next Steps For QuoteCap

This has been a long chapter so let's take a break and then re-group in the next chapter and start in with setting up the layout. After that we'll instantiate our Quote object and save its data to the database. Then we'll work on the Spinner for the Categories.

Chapter 8
QuoteCap: Altering the Layout

Layouts can be somewhat difficult to work with until you learn all the attributes you can use. We can't go over every attribute in this book or we'd never get our apps written. (I'm planning on writing a follow-up book which will touch upon advanced features and more focus on layouts next.)

ScrollView Root Node
For now, one of the easiest layouts to use which nicely fits our purposes is the LinearLayout.
However, if you make your root node is a LinearLayout and the user fills in a lot of text in one of your text boxes, the rest of your UI elements will disappear off the screen. The LinearLayout does not support scrolling by default.

Swipe Up For More
That's why i'm creating a root node that is a ScrollView which will wrap our LinearLayout. The user won't even notice the ScrollView is there unless she makes a long entry into one of the text boxes and the buttons at the bottom disappear. Then she can swipe up and see the rest of the screen.

First let's take a look at what the final UI looks like and then I'll show you the layout XML and talk about it a little.

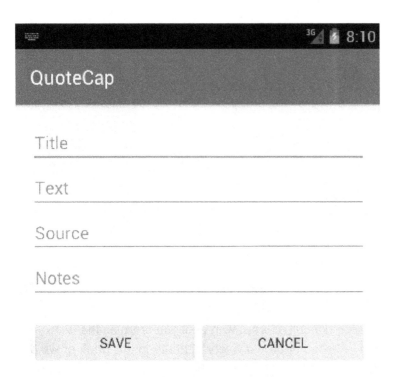

Initially there is plenty of space for everything to fit on this screen. However, if the user puts a large amount of text in one or more of those fields, the buttons will disappear off the bottom of the screen. Adding the root ScrollView layout XML which acts as a container to the rest of the layout solves this problem.

Here's an example of what I'm talking about.

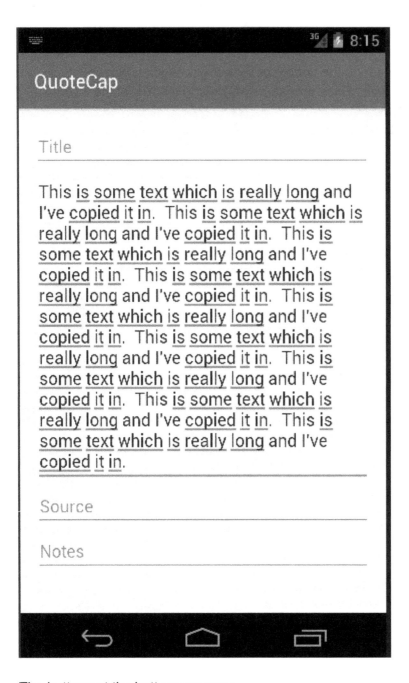

The buttons at the bottom are gone.

If you didn't have a root node of ScrollView, then the user wouldn't be able to scroll the buttons back into view.

You can get the code up to this point at:
QuoteCap_v05.zip

Here's what the layout XML looks like.

```xml
<?xml version="1.0" encoding="utf-8"?>
<ScrollView
     xmlns:android="http://schemas.android.com/apk/res/android"
     xmlns:tools="http://schemas.android.com/tools"
     android:layout_width="match_parent"
     android:layout_height="match_parent"
     android:paddingBottom="@dimen/activity_vertical_margin"
     android:paddingLeft="@dimen/activity_horizontal_margin"
     android:paddingRight="@dimen/activity_horizontal_margin"
     android:paddingTop="@dimen/activity_vertical_margin"
     tools:context="us.raddev.quotecap.MainActivity">
     <LinearLayout
          android:layout_width="match_parent"
          android:layout_height="match_parent"
          android:orientation="vertical">

          <EditText
               android:layout_width="match_parent"
               android:layout_height="wrap_content"
               android:hint="Title"
               android:id="@+id/titleText"/>
          <EditText...>
          <EditText...>
          <EditText...>
          <TextView
               android:layout_width="match_parent"
               android:layout_height="wrap_content"
               android:id="@+id/createdTextView"/>
          <LinearLayout
               android:layout_width="match_parent"
               android:layout_height="wrap_content"
               android:orientation="horizontal">
          <Button
               android:layout_width="0dp"
               android:layout_height="wrap_content"
               android:layout_weight=".5"
               android:text="Save"
               android:id="@+id/saveButton"/>
          <Button
               android:layout_width="0dp"
               android:layout_height="wrap_content"
               android:layout_weight=".5"
               android:text="Cancel"
               android:id="@+id/cancelButton"/>

          </LinearLayout>
     </LinearLayout>
</ScrollView>
```

First of all, please notice that it was difficult to get the entire layout structure into one manageable snapshot so I collapse the EditText items which were all similar. Just know that each of those EditText elements represent the following fields :

1. Text
2. Source
3. Notes

They are all defined the same way except for their hint and id values.

Hint Attribute

The hint attribute is a String value that allows you to set a message the user can see when the EditText control is empty. The text that appears is slightly lighter than text that has been entered and it serves to provide the user with an idea of what is supposed to go in the EditText field.

You can see those values in the original snapshot of the QuoteCap.

ScrollView Root Node

You can also see that the ScrollView is set as the root node of our layout XML.

Immediately after I've defined the ScrollView opening tag I've added a LinearLayout and the important attribute (to make the layout easy) is the orientation="vertical". Since I've made each of the child controls to have their width="match_parent" and height="wrap_content" it means that they will be the width of the MainActivity (minus margin padding).

Nested LinearLayout For Buttons

Then, near the bottom (where I add the two buttons) you will see that I add another LinearLayout to contain the two buttons and I set that one to orientation="horizontal". That's because I want the buttons to both be on the same vertical row. To do that I also set each of the buttons' layout-weight=".5" giving them half of the width of the containing horizontal container (LinearLayout).

It's a simple way to setup our layout and now that we have it, we can move back to working with our Quote object.

Let's move back to our MainActivity.java file and add a Quote object as a member variable.

You can see that we added the _quote variable at the top of the MainActivity class.
Then, we instantiate our new Quote object down in the handleReceivedText() method (highlighted in the following example).

```
activity_main.xml ×   strings.xml ×   © MainActivity.java ×   © Quote.java ×   © 

    import android.util.Log;
    import android.widget.ArrayAdapter;
    import android.widget.Spinner;

    public class MainActivity extends AppCompatActivity {

        private Quote _quote;

        @Override
        protected void onCreate(Bundle savedInstanceState) {
            super.onCreate(savedInstanceState);
            setContentView(R.layout.activity_main);

            // Get intent, action and MIME type
            Intent intent = getIntent();
            String action = intent.getAction();
            String type = intent.getType();

            if (Intent.ACTION_SEND.equals(action) && type != null) {
                if ("text/plain".equals(type)) {
                    handleReceivedText(intent); // Handle text being sent
                }
            }
        }

        private void handleReceivedText(Intent intent){

            String outText = intent.getStringExtra(Intent.EXTRA_TEXT);
            Log.d("MainActivity", outText);
            _quote = new Quote(outText);
        }
    }
```

We used our constructor which takes a String (the passed in text which we grabbed from the Intent).

Now, our object is in memory. However, with this code change we are no longer displaying the quote text on the screen. That's not very useful so let's add the code to do so.

Databinding : Objects & Views
Very often when we have an object in memory we allow a user to type values into screen elements to alter the values. However, keep in mind that the screen elements EditText, Spinners, etc. are not tied (or bound) to the properties in the object.
This poses a challenge that when the user changes the value on screen we need to do something to change the value in the object. This software challenge is generally referred to as databinding.

We are going to add the official way to bind our Quote object to our view (layout) by following the very well documented guide at:
http://developer.android.com/tools/data-binding/guide.html

Alter Gradle to Include Databinding Library
The first thing we have to do is include the helper databinding library in our project build.
To do that, we need to expand the Gradle Scripts tree node in solution explorer. When you do that you will actually see there are two build.gradle files under that node.
We want to alter the one that says (Module: app) after it.

When you double-click that node it'll open the Gradle build script up in the editor.

We need to tell the project that we want to build the Android binding code into our project and to do that we add a script directive which looks like:

```
dataBinding {
    enabled = true
  }
```

Go ahead and add it into the script at the to and it'll look like the following:

```
apply plugin: 'com.android.application'

android {
    compileSdkVersion 23
    buildToolsVersion "23.0.2"

    dataBinding {
        enabled = true
    }
    defaultConfig {
        applicationId "us.raddev.quotecap"
        minSdkVersion 15
        targetSdkVersion 23
        versionCode 1
        versionName "1.0"
    }
    buildTypes {
        release {
            minifyEnabled false
            proguardFiles getDefaultProguardFile('proguard-android.txt'), 'proguard-rules.pro'
        }
    }
}

dependencies {
    compile fileTree(dir: 'libs', include: ['*.jar'])
    testCompile 'junit:junit:4.12'
    compile 'com.android.support:appcompat-v7:23.1.1'
}
```

You can see the portion we added has its beginning ending curly braces
highlighted in light blue.

Go ahead and build your app just to make sure it builds okay.
You can get the app with the changes up to this point at:
QuoteCap_v06.zip

Mapping the Object to the Layout
Now we have to tell the Layout about our Quote object and map each layout
element to a Quote object property. It's not difficult.

302

The binding documentation explains that we have to add a new root element to our layout, which is simply a generic <layout> tag. Then immediately after we add the new root element we add a data node which will describe where to find our Quote class via package name.

Open up activity_main.xml (layout file) in your editor again and make the changes so it looks like the following:

```xml
<?xml version="1.0" encoding="utf-8"?>
<layout xmlns:android="http://schemas.android.com/apk/res/android">
    <data>
        <variable name="quote" type="us.raddev.quotecap.Quote"/>
    </data>
    <ScrollView
        xmlns:tools="http://schemas.android.com/tools"
        android:layout_width="match_parent"
        android:layout_height="match_parent"
        android:paddingBottom="@dimen/activity_vertical_margin"
        android:paddingLeft="@dimen/activity_horizontal_margin"
        android:paddingRight="@dimen/activity_horizontal_margin"
        android:paddingTop="@dimen/activity_vertical_margin"
        tools:context="us.raddev.quotecap.MainActivity">
        <LinearLayout
            android:layout_width="match_parent"
            android:layout_height="match_parent"
            android:orientation="vertical">

            <EditText
                android:layout_width="match_parent"
                android:layout_height="wrap_content"
                android:hint="Title"
                android:id="@+id/titleText"/>
        <EditText...>
        <EditText...>
        <EditText...>
```

Notice that I added the <layout> (notice the lowercase L) tag to wrap the entire existing layout.

I also ripped the original namespace definition from the ScrollView and pasted it up to the <layout> tag.

Data Element and Variable
You can also see that we added this new <data> element which contains a reference to our Quote object. Notice also that we do provide a name to refer to our object. However, make note that this is not the same value which is used in our MainActivity.java file. This is variable name will only be used in the layout.

Mapping Quote Properties to Layout Elements
Now, we do the very easy work of mapping each Quote property to a layout element.
To do so we use the variable name we just created in the layout file <data> element (quote) and a special syntax which consists of a few characters @{ }
That's the at symbol then open curly closed curly.
An example using our quote object would be :
@{quote._text} or @{quote._title}

It's that easy. Of course, we add these to each layout element where appropriate and we set the element's text property.
A full example will look like the following:
android:text="@{quote._title}"
or
android:text="@{quote._source}"

Double-quotes
Take note that these directives are surrounded by double-quotes. That's very important.

Created Date : Use toString()
Also notice that we have to use the toString() call on the quote._created property because we are setting the text property of the TextView element and it knows that it expects a String type.

Once they are all mapped up, the layout will look like the following:

```xml
<EditText
    android:layout_width="match_parent"
    android:layout_height="wrap_content"
    android:hint="Title"
    android:text="@{quote._title}"
    android:id="@+id/titleText"/>
<EditText
    android:layout_width="match_parent"
    android:layout_height="wrap_content"
    android:hint="Text"
    android:text="@{quote._text}"
    android:id="@+id/textText"/>
<EditText
    android:layout_width="match_parent"
    android:layout_height="wrap_content"
    android:hint="Source"
    android:text="@{quote._source}"
    android:id="@+id/sourceText"/>
<EditText
    android:layout_width="match_parent"
    android:layout_height="wrap_content"
    android:hint="Notes"
    android:text="@{quote._note}"
    android:id="@+id/noteText"/>
<TextView
    android:layout_width="match_parent"
    android:layout_height="wrap_content"
    android:text="@{quote._created.toString()}"
    android:id="@+id/createdTextView"/>

<LinearLayout
    android:layout_width="match_parent"
    android:layout_height="wrap_content"
    android:orientation="horizontal">
    <Button
        android:layout_width="0dp"
        android:layout_height="wrap_content"
        android:layout_weight=".5"
        android:text="Save"
        android:id="@+id/saveButton"/>
```

Go ahead and build again to insure the code compiles properly.

You can get the code up to this point at:

QuoteCap_v07.zip

Now, there's just one more simple thing to do and we can run it and try it out.

Add Binding Class and Bind

We have to add the code to our MainActivity.java which does the binding of our actual object to the Binding utitlity object. The Binding utility object is the one that does the work of binding the two things (object and UI elements) together.

Generated Class From Your Specific Code

Now, this is the interesting or odd or possibly magical part about how this works.

When you build the utility class the compiler inspects your code and classes and builds an additional class for you to use.

How Does It Name the Generated Class?

It names that class by flipping the name of your associated layout file around. In our case, our layout file is named activity_main.xml. The compiler inspects the XML and finds the root is a <layout> tag and that it contains a <data> tag and knows it needs to do something special since we've included the databinding reference in our Gradle build file.

The compiler looks at the name of your layout file (acitvity_main.xml) removes all underscores (_) and the file extension (.xml) uppercases each word in the file name (ActivityMain) and then adds the word Binding to generate the final name of ActivityMainBinding.

You can see (next image) the import for the class is added at the top of our MainActivity.java file.

However, you cannot see that generated class in the solution explorer.

You May Encounter Odd Problems

Since this code is generated you may see some odd problems as Android Studio attempts to build the code, but cannot build the code until it generates this class, which it needs to build our code.

I suggest you do a Rebuild about three times. It's seems to be the nature of Studio and generated classes. Studio was giving me all kinds of errors.

Incorrectly Documented at Google Site
Also, as of this writing (2015-03-11) the Google documentation at the link I provided earlier uses a layout file named main_activity.xml (which breaks the Studio convention) and causes the example class to be named differently than it is in our app.

Using the Static Class DataBindingUtil
When you call DataBindingUtil.setContentView() and pass in the resource to your layout (R.layout.activity_main) it will instantiate a object of type ActivityMainBinding.

After that you can call the generated method setQuote() on the binding object. It will look like the following: binding.setQuote(quoteObject). The setQuote() method is also generated as the compiler inspects your code and knows the type that you are binding. If your target object had been named Book then this method would be generated as setBook(). Quite amazing and helpful.

The binding instantiation we will do inside the onCreate() of our MainActivity class.
Then we'll call the setQuote() method of the binding object in our handleReceivedText() method where we instanatiate our Quote object.

binding.setQuote(_quote);

Notice that we create a member variable named _binding so we can initialize the object in the onCreate() method and then call setQuote() on the _binding object in the handleReceivedText() method.

It'll all look like the following:

```java
import android.os.Bundle;
import android.util.Log;

import us.raddev.quotecap.databinding.ActivityMainBinding;

public class MainActivity extends AppCompatActivity {

    private Quote _quote;
    private ActivityMainBinding _binding;

    @Override
    protected void onCreate(Bundle savedInstanceState) {
        super.onCreate(savedInstanceState);
        setContentView(R.layout.activity_main);

        _binding = DataBindingUtil.setContentView(this, R.layout.activity_main);
        // Get intent, action and MIME type
        Intent intent = getIntent();
        String action = intent.getAction();
        String type = intent.getType();

        if (Intent.ACTION_SEND.equals(action) && type != null) {
            if ("text/plain".equals(type)) {
                handleReceivedText(intent); // Handle text being sent
            }
        }
    }

    private void handleReceivedText(Intent intent){

        String outText = intent.getStringExtra(Intent.EXTRA_TEXT);
        Log.d("MainActivity", outText);
        _quote = new Quote(outText);
        _binding.setQuote(_quote);
    }
}
```

Everything is complete and we are ready to run.

You can get the code up to this point at:
QuoteCap_v08.zip

What Does the Binding Do For Us So Far?
Right now, the binding will automatically set the value in the EditText (text) that represents the Quote.Text value. That means when we fire this thing up and grab text from the browser now it will use the Intent to send the text into our app and our app will set instantiate the new _quote object with the text (setting the Quote.Text property). When the object's text property gets set, the binding will automatically set the value displayed on screen in the EditText field which represents the Quote.Text property. If the user types anything in any of the text boxes now, the _quote object will automatically have its associated property updated. That means we are ready to save the data from the object into our database without having to write a bunch of code that checks to see if the values in the screen elements have changed. Instead the binding keeps track of the values and keeps them in sync for us.

Try It Out
Run the app, copy some text, share it with QuoteCap and you'll see that the Text EditText element will be automatically filled with the value and ready to be saved.

reverse depicts an eagle with wings
outstretched. The Coinage Act of 1873, which
stopped the minting of silver dollars, was
reversed by a series of laws supporting
production of the Morgan dollar. The Bland–
Allison Act of 1878 required the Treasury to
purchase between two and four million dollars'

In this last snapshot of the QuoteCap screen you can see that the text we copied from the web browser is displayed in the Text layout field. All this work is done for us by the binding. If the user changes the text, the _quote object is automatically updated since the layout element is bound to the object.

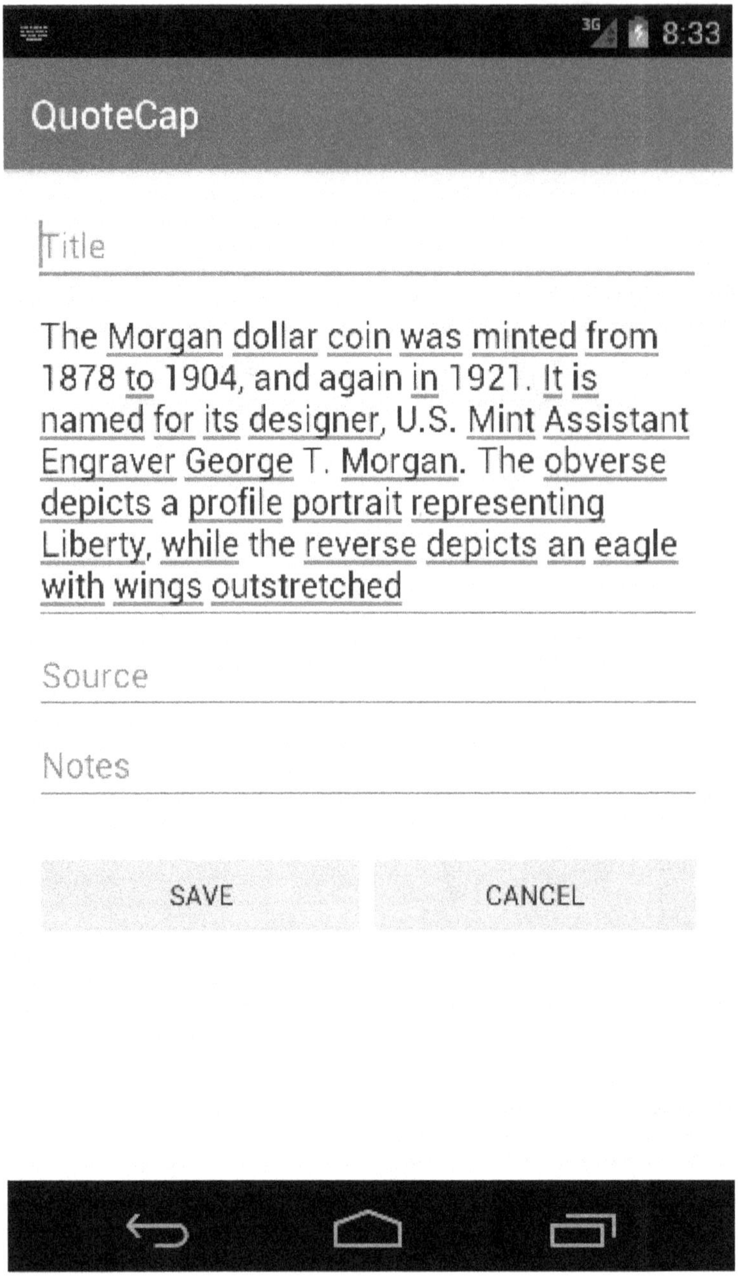
8:33
QuoteCap
Title
The Morgan dollar coin was minted from 1878 to 1904, and again in 1921. It is named for its designer, U.S. Mint Assistant Engraver George T. Morgan. The obverse depicts a profile portrait representing Liberty, while the reverse depicts an eagle with wings outstretched
Source
Notes
SAVE
CANCEL

Now, we can focus on the work to save our Quote object our Sqlite database.

Alter QuoteDatabaseHelper
The first thing we want to do is slightly alter our QuoteDatabaseHelper class to make a few things more clear.
Go ahead and open the QuoteDatabaseHelper.java in the Studio editor and let's make those changes.

A Note About Constant Values
First of all we are going to add some values that we want to make sure cannot be changed anywhere else in our program after we initialize them.
With a normal variable like:
float PI = 3.1415926F
Somewhere else in your code you or another programmer could change that accidentally :
PI = 3.333;
Nothing will warn you that the value (which should be constant and never changed) has been changed.
Java provides a way to make a variable name a constant so that your program will not compile if you change the value anywhere else in the code after you initialize it.
We are going to use a lot of constants in the database code because things like table names, column names and the file name of the database really shouldn't ever change while the code is running.

Developer Conventions For Organization
We use common formatting as a convention (a way) of organizing our code and making it more obvious when you look at the code what is going on. In the case of constant variables, we use all uppercase letters with each word of the variable name seperated by underscores _.
For example:
LIGHT_SPEED = 186000; // miles per second

Now, when you see variables within code that are formatted like that, you will know they are constants that have been defined for your use. That makes it easier to know what is going on in code.

Here are our first two constants that we want to add to our QuoteDatabaseHelper:

```
public static final int DB_VERSION = 1;
public static final String DB_NAME = "quote.db";
```

The keyword to create a constant in Java is final. We do not want the DB_VERSION to change while the app is running nor do we want the file name where the database is stored to change so it makes sense that they are constants.

Notice also that these two constants are also marked as public (we can get to them outside the class, but of course only for reading since they cannot have their value changed). However, we have also marked these two constants as static, which means they are global values to the package they are in. These are at times also referred to as Class Variables, because you can get to them via the class (not the instance of an object). That means we can get to these values by typing the following code:
String myString = QuoteDatabaseHelper.DB_NAME;
Normally, we would have to instantiate a class and then use the object to get to the value, but since these are static variables we get to them via the class.

Now, let's alter our QuoteDatabaseHelper constructor also.
It'll clean it up and make it a bit easier to instantiate our QuoteDatabaseHelper since we'll only have to send in a Context object.

```
public QuoteDatabaseHelper(Context context) {
    super(context, DB_NAME, null, DB_VERSION);
}
```

Using Our Constants
Previously, we were passing in all four items, but now, we just want to pass in the Context object (more later).

We still have to provide all four items to the super class but now, two of them are coming from the constants we just created.

Creating the Database
Now we want to look into creating our database schema (tables and table layout with columns).
To do that we are going to need to create another helper class. But instead of switching to the creation of that class and then coming back, let's first alter our onCreate() method which will use some constansts that we are going to create in our new class. It's only two lines of code and it will only make sense after we build the other class but for now add the code and then I'll explain how it is used. Go ahead and alter the QuoteDatabaseHelper onCreate() method so it looks like the following:

```
@Override
public void onCreate(SQLiteDatabase db) {
    db.execSQL(QuoteDatabaseContract.SQL_CREATE_QUOTE);
    db.execSQL(QuoteDatabaseContract.SQL_CREATE_CATEGORY);
}
```

When you add that code Android Studio is going to complain at you because the class and those two constants (SQL_CREATE_QUOTE and SQL_CREATE_CATEGORY) do not exist and Studio is trying to warn you that it cannot build properly. That's fine for now. Let's go create the class which will contain these items.

The Contract Class: Public Constant Class
The Google dev docs (http://developer.android.com/training/basics/data-storage/databases.html)
suggest that you use a convention of creating a public class which is marked final (constant) to define all the SQL you will use to create your tables. Again, you don't want your tables to be altered while the app is running so this is a good way to insure that the values aren't changed by accident.

Choose Correct Package

We are going to add our new class to our package us.raddev.quotecap (same as the Quote class and the QuoteDatabaseHelper) so go ahead and walk through the steps to add a new class and name it QuoteDatabaseContract. Make sure you mark the class as public and final.

Once you add the final modifier the class will look like the following:

```
package us.raddev.quotecap;

public final class QuoteDatabaseContract {


}
```

Now, we are going to add an empty constructor so no one accidentally instantiates the class.
And we are going to add the code which defines our Quote table and our Category table.

These two classes are inner classes to our Contract class and are both derived from the BaseColumns class. This class will add an extra field named _ID to our table definitions that we can use as a primary key on our tables.

Once we add the inner classes which define our tables the class will look like the following:

```java
package us.raddev.quotecap;

import android.provider.BaseColumns;

public final class QuoteDatabaseContract {
    public QuoteDatabaseContract() {
    }

    /* inner classes define tables */
    public static abstract class QuoteTableDef implements BaseColumns {
        public static final String TABLE_NAME = "quote";
        public static final String COLUMN_NAME_TITLE = "title";
        public static final String COLUMN_NAME_TEXT = "text";
        public static final String COLUMN_NAME_SOURCE = "source";
        public static final String COLUMN_NAME_NOTES = "notes";
        public static final String COLUMN_NAME_CATEGORY_ID = "categoryId";


    }


    public static abstract class CategoryTableDef implements BaseColumns {
        public static final String TABLE_NAME = "category";
        public static final String COLUMN_NAME_NAME = "name";
    }
}
```

Next, we need to add our constants which will define the action that occurs when the db.execSQL() methods will take when they are called with the constants from the QuoteDatabaseHelper.onCreate() method.

Ugly String Code
However, before I show you this extremely ugly code I need to explain why it is so ugly.
You see, Sqlite requires the table definition and creation to be done using strings. The strings which are used to define the table are very long and

repetitive because the strings are using commands that Sqlite will use to create the table.

First I will show you the code and then I will show you what that code expands to as a string so you'll better understand what is happening.

```java
public final class QuoteDatabaseContract {
    public QuoteDatabaseContract() {
    }

    private static final String TEXT_TYPE = " TEXT";
    private static final String INT_TYPE = " INTEGER";
    private static final String COMMA_SEP = ",";
    public static final String SQL_CREATE_QUOTE =
            "CREATE TABLE " + QuoteTableDef.TABLE_NAME + " (" +
                    QuoteTableDef._ID + " INTEGER PRIMARY KEY," +
                    QuoteTableDef.COLUMN_NAME_TITLE + TEXT_TYPE + COMMA_SEP +
                    QuoteTableDef.COLUMN_NAME_TEXT + TEXT_TYPE + COMMA_SEP +
                    QuoteTableDef.COLUMN_NAME_SOURCE + TEXT_TYPE + COMMA_SEP +
                    QuoteTableDef.COLUMN_NAME_NOTES + TEXT_TYPE + COMMA_SEP +
                    QuoteTableDef.COLUMN_NAME_CATEGORY_ID + INT_TYPE + COMMA_SEP +
            " )";

    public static final String SQL_CREATE_CATEGORY =
            "CREATE TABLE " + CategoryTableDef.TABLE_NAME + " (" +
                    CategoryTableDef._ID + " INTEGER PRIMARY KEY," +
                    CategoryTableDef.COLUMN_NAME_NAME + TEXT_TYPE + COMMA_SEP +
                    " )";



    /* inner classes define tables */
    public static abstract class QuoteTableDef implements BaseColumns {
        public static final String TABLE_NAME = "quote";
        public static final String COLUMN_NAME_TITLE = "title";
        public static final String COLUMN_NAME_TEXT = "text";
        public static final String COLUMN_NAME_SOURCE = "source";
        public static final String COLUMN_NAME_NOTES = "notes";
        public static final String COLUMN_NAME_CATEGORY_ID = "categoryId";

    }

    public static abstract class CategoryTableDef implements BaseColumns {
        public static final String TABLE_NAME = "category";
        public static final String COLUMN_NAME_NAME = "name";
    }
}
```

320

You can see we've added five new static final strings to our QuoteDatabaseContract class.

Three of those are private so they are only used inside the QuoteDatabaseContract. The last two are public and we use them outside the class in our QuoteDatabaseHelper in the onCreate() method.

First Three Private Strings
The first three private strings are simply chunks of strings we will use repetitively while building the two larger strings.

You can see that we reference these strings in when creating the other two strings (SQL_CREATE_QUOTE and SQL_CREATE_CATEGORY). Keep in mind that the two public strings are used in our onCreate() method on the database where we execute some sql using db.execSQL().

Take a close look at each of the two public strings and notice that they each start out with the same text which is: "CREATE TABLE "

Create Database, Create Tables
These are strings which become the Sqlite commands to create the tables when the database is initially created on the device.

Creating Tables Means Defining Columns
To create the table, we provide a name and then we provide the name and type of each column name that we want created in the table.

To create one string which contains the entire CREATE TABLE definition when there are numerous columns ends up being quite a long string. That's why we've broken it up into substrings that we concatenate (append) together.

The final string that is created for the creation of the Quote table looks like the following:

CREATE TABLE quote (_id INTEGER PRIMARY KEY,title TEXT,text TEXT,source TEXT,notes TEXT,categoryId INTEGER,)

The string for the Category table is quite a bit shorter simply because it only has two columns:

CREATE TABLE category (_id INTEGER PRIMARY KEY,name TEXT,)

You can see that basically each column has its name and then its data type (TEXT, INTEGER, etc).,

What Does the Contract Class Give Us
Keep in mind, the Contract class doesn't give us a whole lot. You don't have to add the class and you could put your Database creation and table creation string generating code somewhere else.
This is the convention that Google suggests and it keeps your code more organized.
Basically it provides a encapsulated (protected) area where your creation strings can be defined and since we implement the BaseColumns Interface we get the additional ID value for free in our tables. I'm mentioning this because often development things like this lead to confusion because they seem like the professional devs have some hidden reason for these types of structures, but often it is just an attempt at organization. Organization isn't as obviously important when you are starting out coding, but when you are on a large team it becomes extremely important so your developers aren't wasting all their time searching for the things they need to build their apps.

Our database is now defined with two tables (Quote & Category) but we still haven't added the code which will actually create the quote.db file and the tables within it yet.
Let's do that now and then let you run the app.

Create Database First Time
Move back to the MainActivity.java class and add a new member variable like the following:
```
private QuoteDatabaseHelper _quoteDBHelper;
```

That gives us a member which we can use to store a reference to our QuoteDatabaseHelper which we will end up using to read and write to the database with.

Go to the bottom of the MainActivity onCreate() method and add the following line of code to instantiate an instance of the QuoteDatabaseHelper:

```
_quoteDBHelper = new QuoteDatabaseHelper(getApplicationContext());
```

Your MainActivity onCreate() will now look like the following. You'll also see the two Log.d() calls where I output the string values of those create table constant strings.

```
 QuoteDatabaseContract.java ×    QuoteDatabaseHelper.java ×    strings.xml ×    MainActivity.java ×

    public class MainActivity extends AppCompatActivity {

        private Quote _quote;
        private ActivityMainBinding _binding;
        private QuoteDatabaseHelper _quoteDBHelper;

        @Override
        protected void onCreate(Bundle savedInstanceState) {
            super.onCreate(savedInstanceState);
            setContentView(R.layout.activity_main);

            _binding = DataBindingUtil.setContentView(this, R.layout.activity_main);
            // Get intent, action and MIME type
            Intent intent = getIntent();
            String action = intent.getAction();
            String type = intent.getType();

            if (Intent.ACTION_SEND.equals(action) && type != null) {
                if ("text/plain".equals(type)) {
                    handleReceivedText(intent); // Handle text being sent
                }
            }
            Log.d("MainActivity", QuoteDatabaseContract.SQL_CREATE_QUOTE);
            Log.d("MainActivity", QuoteDatabaseContract.SQL_CREATE_CATEGORY);
            _quoteDBHelper = new QuoteDatabaseHelper(getApplicationContext());
        }
    }
```

ApplicationContext

We send in the Application Context so that the database is bound to the ApplicationContext which is a Singleton class (only one of them exists in app).

Let's run the app to insure it works.
You can get the code up to this point at:
QuoteCap_v09.zip

However, once you run the app, it still will not create the database. Just calling the QuoteDatabaseHelper constructor doesn't actually generate the database file (quote.db).

To create the database we need to call the method
_quoteDBHelper.getWriteableDatabase().
However, we want to do that work in the Quote class in our Save() method.
Let's add that code just to make it create our database file.
Open up the Quote.java file and add the following

```java
public void save(QuoteDatabaseHelper qoh){
    Log.d("MainActivity", "in Quote.Save()...");
    SQLiteDatabase db = qoh.getWritableDatabase();

}
```

We went ahead and added a parameter of QuoteDatabaseHelper so we can pass it in from our Activity so we can use the object we've already created. I write to the logcat just so I can insure the code is running as expected. It's a good idea just so you can verify that the code is running as expected and it'll save you a lot of wasted time tracking down problems in your code that are related to a method simply not being called.

Now we need to add the onClick handler to our button in the MainActivity. Switch over to the MainActivity.java in the editor and we'll add that code. This is just like the work we did in the Stenotes app to get a button working.

First, we add a _saveButton member variable to our MainActivity.

```
private Button _saveButton;
```

Next, we initialize the Button by loading a reference to the screen element using findViewById().
```
_saveButton = (Button)findViewById(R.id.saveButton);
```

Finally, we set up our onClickListener.
```
_saveButton.setOnClickListener(new View.OnClickListener() {
    @Override
    public void onClick(View view) {


    }
});
```

All together it looks like the following:

```java
        private ActivityMainBinding _binding;
        private QuoteDatabaseHelper _quoteDBHelper;
        private Button _saveButton;

        @Override
        protected void onCreate(Bundle savedInstanceState) {
            super.onCreate(savedInstanceState);
            setContentView(R.layout.activity_main);

            _binding = DataBindingUtil.setContentView(this, R.layout.activity_main);
            _saveButton = (Button)findViewById(R.id.saveButton);
            // Get intent, action and MIME type
            Intent intent = getIntent();
            String action = intent.getAction();
            String type = intent.getType();

            if (Intent.ACTION_SEND.equals(action) && type != null) {
                if ("text/plain".equals(type)) {
                    handleReceivedText(intent); // Handle text being sent
                }
            }
            Log.d("MainActivity", QuoteDatabaseContract.SQL_CREATE_QUOTE);
            Log.d("MainActivity", QuoteDatabaseContract.SQL_CREATE_CATEGORY);
            _quoteDBHelper = new QuoteDatabaseHelper(getApplicationContext());

            _saveButton.setOnClickListener(new View.OnClickListener() {
                @Override
                public void onClick(View view) {

                }
            });
        }
```

Now we add the code to the onClickListener that we want to run when the user clicks the [Save] button.

```java
_saveButton.setOnClickListener(new View.OnClickListener() {
    @Override
    public void onClick(View view) {
        if (_quote == null)
        {
            _quote = new Quote();
            _binding.setQuote(_quote);
        }
        _quote.save(_quoteDBHelper);
    }
```

326

```
});
```

Notice that we check to see if our member _quote is null. If the user started up the application without copying text to share, then the _quote has not yet been initialized and the binding has not been set either, so we have to do that here. After that we simply call the save() method of our Quote object.

We Need an Empty Constructor

This code is almost complete, however, Studio will warn you that you do not have an implementation for a Quote constructor that takes 0 parameters. In the case when the user starts the app directly she hasn't copied in any text so we don't have any text to use to initialize the Quote.Text parameter. Let's go add the empty constructor to the Quote class and then run the app.

I generated the empty constructor and it looks like:

```
© Quote.java ×    © QuoteDatabaseHelper.java ×    © MainActivity.java ×

Q▾                              ↑  ↓  ⊤ₙ ⊤ₙ ⊠ₙ ▣ ▣ □ Match Case □ R

    import java.util.Date;

    /**
     * Created by roger.deutsch on 3/7/2016.
     */
    public class Quote {
        public int get_id() { return _id; }

        public Quote() {
        }

        public Quote(String _text) { this._text = _text; }

        public void set_id(int _id) { this._id = _id; }

        public String get_title() { return _title; }

        public void set_title(String _title) { this._title = _title; }
```

You can get the code at:
QuoteCap_v10.zip

Run the code and then click the [Save] button. When you do, the app will determine if the database has been created on the device (more in a moment). The database hasn't been created so it will attempt to create it on your device at a sandboxed* location in your storage under your program's app installation directory.

*Sandboxed location means protected area that the Android OS only allows the registered app to read from. No other app can steal the data by reading from this location.

Errors and Crashes When Attempting to Run
I want to show you what happened the first time I ran the code and hit the Save button.
Note: If you've obtained the code from QuoteCap_v10.zip you will not encounter this problem because I fixed it before zipping up the project for you. However, if you've followed along and made the changes your app will crash.

QuoteCap crashed and I saw the following in my Logcat:

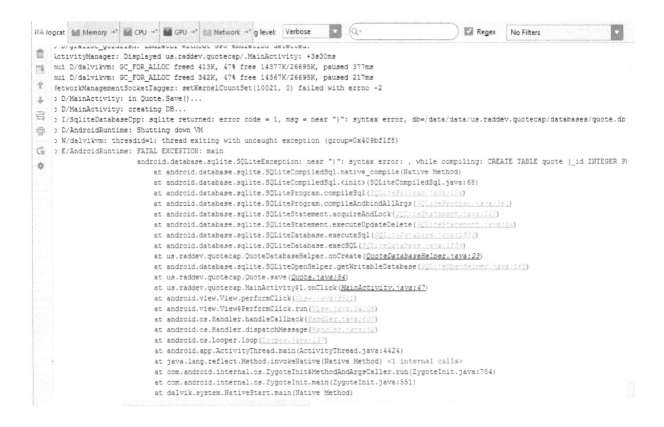

Most books won't show you code crashing and yet that is what you'll spend a lot of time as a developer looking at.

I see that it was a FATAL EXCEPTION. I then notice that it tells me I had a:

```
SqliteException near ")": syntax error , while compiling
: CREATE TABLE quote...
```

Then it shows the entire constant String that we've pieced together for our quote table creation SQL.

There is obviously an error in the String.
When I scroll far to the right in logcat I see the the problem, but I know it is a problem because of over 23 years of development experience and staring at

errors and trying to figure them out. If I were a new developer I may not know what it means.

Here's what it looked like at the far right:

```
while compiling: CREATE TABLE quote (_id INTEGER PRIMARY KEY,title TEXT,text TEXT,source TEXT,notes TEXT,categoryId INTEGER, )
```

Do you see the problem? It's quite subtle. There is a trailing comma -- a comma after the last field. I'm sure that is what is choking it.

Let's go back to our QuoteDatabaseContract class and look at the place where we create this String.

```
 C  Quote.java  ×      app  ×     C  QuoteDatabaseContract.java  ×     C  QuoteDatabaseHelper.java  ×    C  M
```

```java
    private static final String TEXT_TYPE = " TEXT";
    private static final String INT_TYPE = " INTEGER";
    private static final String COMMA_SEP = ",";
    public static final String SQL_CREATE_QUOTE =
            "CREATE TABLE " + QuoteTableDef.TABLE_NAME + " (" +
                    QuoteTableDef._ID + " INTEGER PRIMARY KEY," +
                    QuoteTableDef.COLUMN_NAME_TITLE + TEXT_TYPE + COMMA_SEP +
                    QuoteTableDef.COLUMN_NAME_TEXT + TEXT_TYPE + COMMA_SEP +
                    QuoteTableDef.COLUMN_NAME_SOURCE + TEXT_TYPE + COMMA_SEP +
                    QuoteTableDef.COLUMN_NAME_NOTES + TEXT_TYPE + COMMA_SEP +
                    QuoteTableDef.COLUMN_NAME_CATEGORY_ID + INT_TYPE + COMMA_SEP +
            " )";

    public static final String SQL_CREATE_CATEGORY =
            "CREATE TABLE " + CategoryTableDef.TABLE_NAME + " (" +
                    CategoryTableDef._ID + " INTEGER PRIMARY KEY," +
                    CategoryTableDef.COLUMN_NAME_NAME + TEXT_TYPE + COMMA_SEP +
                    " )";
```

See those COMMA_SEP items? They each represent a comma character (char). We need to remove the last COMMA_SEP from each of our table creation strings. I'll remove them now and the code will look like:

```
                  }
        private static final String TEXT_TYPE = " TEXT";
        private static final String INT_TYPE = " INTEGER";
        private static final String COMMA_SEP = ",";
        public static final String SQL_CREATE_QUOTE =
                "CREATE TABLE " + QuoteTableDef.TABLE_NAME + " (" +
                        QuoteTableDef._ID + " INTEGER PRIMARY KEY," +
                        QuoteTableDef.COLUMN_NAME_TITLE + TEXT_TYPE + COMMA_SEP +
                        QuoteTableDef.COLUMN_NAME_TEXT + TEXT_TYPE + COMMA_SEP +
                        QuoteTableDef.COLUMN_NAME_SOURCE + TEXT_TYPE + COMMA_SEP +
                        QuoteTableDef.COLUMN_NAME_NOTES + TEXT_TYPE + COMMA_SEP +
                        QuoteTableDef.COLUMN_NAME_CATEGORY_ID + INT_TYPE +
                " )";

        public static final String SQL_CREATE_CATEGORY =
                "CREATE TABLE " + CategoryTableDef.TABLE_NAME + " (" +
                        CategoryTableDef._ID + " INTEGER PRIMARY KEY," +
                        CategoryTableDef.COLUMN_NAME_NAME + TEXT_TYPE +
                " )";
```

Now the code should run without any problems.

When you start the app and click the [Save] button you have no indication
that the database has been created. Since your app doesn't crash you may
assume it has been created, but we are developers and developers have to
know exactly what happens when code runs. Let's take a look at how we can
see the database file (quote.db) which was created for us.

Where Is the Database Created?
As I mentioned before the system will create the database for you in a
protected sandbox, just like it did when you created your files for the Stenotes
app.

We can use the ADB (Android Debug Bridge) to take a look at the file system
of any connected device including the device emulator which is running.

Again, remember, you'll have to open a command prompt and change directory to your %localappdata%\Android\sdk\platform-tools\ directory on Windows systems (notice those are backslashes between the folder names in the path).

Run ADB
When you finally get to that directory you can run the adb.exe tool which can help you connect to a device or emulator which is running and connected to the computer.

You can use ADB to run a Linux ls (list) command on the device. This allows you to see the files which are on the device.
Once you get to the target (platformtools) directory type the following command and hit <ENTER>

```
adb shell ls -al data/data/us.raddev.quotecap/ <ENTER>
```

Notice that these are forward slashes (Linux uses forward slashes as separators).
When you run that command you will see something like the following if you've already run QuoteCap and pressed the [Save] button:

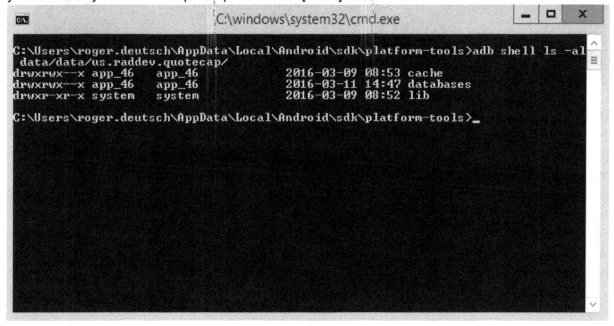

If you look to the far left, you'll see some letters (drwxrwx). The first letter lets you know the item is a Directory. You can see there is a databases directory. Let's add that to our path that we send to the ls command and try again.

```
adb shell ls -al data/data/us.raddev.quotecap/databases
<ENTER>
```

After running that command you see that there are two files in the directory. One is the expected quote.db and the other is a Sqlite system file named quote.db-journal. According to the Sqlite documentation the extra -journal file holds information related to database transactions (inserts, deletes, etc) in order to allow them to be rolled back. You can read more about that at http://sqlite.org.

Let's go back to the application now and continue our work saving our data in the database.

Let's go ahead and add the code to save our Quote object to the database now.

However, we aren't going to be able to know it's saved yet, because nothing particularly special happens on the screen. However, I'll show you how to use the ADB again to query the database from the command line.

Saving A Record to the Database

Open up the Quote.java file in the editor again and move down to the save() method. We'll add some code which will write the _quote object to the database.

##
################

###################### SIDEBAR : Things That Should Work
##########################

##
################

At this point I actually went on a diversion because I discovered that two-way binding on Android is not free.

What Is Two-Way Binding?

Two-way binding means two things:

1. when you change the value in the object, the UI element is automatically updated.
2. When you change the value in the UI (a user types a value into an EditText box) then the value in the object is updated.

The Challenge of Two-Way Binding

A serious challenge with two-way binding is that you can get into a situation where the value gets updated on the screen which updates the object so the binding thinks it needs to update the value on the screen which thinks it needs to update the object. You get the point. It can easily fall into a circular (recursive) loop.

I have also worked extensively with AngularJS and its two-way binding works as smooth as butter so I am spoiled and annoyed that we have to do more work to handle this thing that should be handled well in the subsystem (Android libraries) we are building on.

Workaround Took Hours of Research
I finally found a workaround and I am able to add the code for two way binding and I will explain it to you. However, there is still a bug related to it and it is quite a bit of code I still want to explain it to you and I definitely want it to work properly in QuoteCap. Also, there are other ways we could've solved this. Maybe you'll look at the code and think of a better way.

First of all, the bug that you'll see is that when you set the value in the object and the onscreen element is supposed to update, then the EditText box will leave the cursor at the beginning of the EditText box, even though it should relocate itself to the end of the text that is entered into the EditText. There are ways around this and there are numerous StackOverflow.com answers but many of them only work sometimes.

How We'll Proceed From Here
Here's how I'm going to proceed.
1. First I'm going to give you the code with just the Quote.Text field implemented with two-way binding.
2. I'll let you run the app and save some records to the database.
3. I'll show you the command line ADB to query the database

Then I'll implement two-way binding for the rest of the fields and give you the updated code but I won't show you all of that code since it is exactly the same as the rest.
##
#################
##
#################

QuoteCap With Text Field Two-Way Binding
First of all, let me give you the working code which implements two-way binding for just the Text field. You can get the code at:
QuoteCap_v11.zip

Let's do a quick review of how the code is set up now. We'll go over the changes to MainActivity and the Quote class and then see a couple changes in the layout file.

```
MainActivity.java ×    activity_main.xml ×    Quote.java ×

public class MainActivity extends AppCompatActivity {

    private Quote _quote;
    private ActivityMainBinding _binding;
    private QuoteDatabaseHelper _quoteDBHelper;
    private Button _saveButton;
    private Button _cancelButton;

    @Override
    protected void onCreate(Bundle savedInstanceState) {
        super.onCreate(savedInstanceState);
        setContentView(R.layout.activity_main);

        _binding = DataBindingUtil.setContentView(this, R.layout.activity_main);
        _saveButton = (Button) findViewById(R.id.saveButton);
        _cancelButton = (Button) findViewById(R.id.cancelButton);

        // Get intent, action and MIME type
        Intent intent = getIntent();
        String action = intent.getAction();
        String type = intent.getType();

        if (Intent.ACTION_SEND.equals(action) && type != null) {
            if ("text/plain".equals(type)) {
                handleReceivedText(intent); // Handle text being sent
            }
        } else{
            _quote = new Quote();
            _binding.setQuote(_quote);
        }
        Log.d("MainActivity", QuoteDatabaseContract.SQL_CREATE_QUOTE);
        Log.d("MainActivity", QuoteDatabaseContract.SQL_CREATE_CATEGORY);
        _quoteDBHelper = new QuoteDatabaseHelper(getApplicationContext());
```

336

In MainActivity, the first thing of importance is that when MainActivity is started (onCreate()) we check if there is an Intent of the text type. If there is we can initialize our Quote object using the Intent text.

However, if there is no Intent, the user has started the app directly and there is no text to use to initialize the _quote object. In that case we new up an empty object and set up the binding.

After that we log the information about the Tables we are going to create and then we initialize our _quoteDBHelper so that when we finally call getWriteableDatabase() we will be able to obtain a reference to the database. Of course, if the database hasn't been created yet then it will be at that time.

Continuing down through the MainActivity.java file you can see that we've implemented some code for both the [Save] button click and the [Cancel] button click.

```
        _quoteDBHelper = new QuoteDatabaseHelper(getApplicationContext());


        _saveButton.setOnClickListener(new View.OnClickListener() {
            @Override
            public void onClick(View view) {
                Log.d("MainActivity", "Saving _quote...");
                if (_quote == null)
                {
                    _quote = new Quote();
                    _binding.setQuote(_quote);
                }
                _quote.save(_quoteDBHelper);
            }
        });
        _cancelButton.setOnClickListener(new View.OnClickListener() {
            @Override
            public void onClick(View view) {
                Log.d("MainActivity", "CANCEL BUTTON");
                if (_quote == null) {
                    _quote = new Quote();
                }
                _binding.unbind();
                _quote.set_text("This changes the object value");
                _binding.setQuote(_quote);


            }
        });
    }
```

Of course the [Cancel] button isn't really doing the work that it will do in the
end. Instead we are using it to show how that when you change the bound
object that it will change the EditText element automatically.

Over in the Quote class I've made two getter/setter accessors for the _text
property bindable by adding the @Bindable decorator. This attribute added
to those properties is part of hooking up the binding from the layout to our

Quote class. Again, this tells the compiler to add in some additional functionality into our class.

Quote.java × MainActivity.java × activity_main.xml ×

```
public String get_title() {
    return _title;
}

public void set_title(String _title) {
    this._title = _title;
}

@Bindable
public String get_text() {
    return _text;
}

@Bindable
public void set_text(String _text) {
    this._text = _text;
}
```

Along with those changes I've also added a TextWatcher object named textChanged which is called when the screen element (EditText) is updated. This is how we keep the object in sync with the value that the user types on the screen.

```
        private int _categoryId;

    public void save(QuoteDatabaseHelper qoh) {
        Log.d("MainActivity", "in Quote.Save()...");
        SQLiteDatabase db = qoh.getWritableDatabase();

        ContentValues values = new ContentValues();
        values.put(QuoteDatabaseContract.QuoteTableDef.COLUMN_NAME_TEXT, _text);

        long newRowId = db.insert(
                QuoteDatabaseContract.QuoteTableDef.TABLE_NAME,
                null,
                values);

        Log.d("MainActivity", "newRowId : " + String.valueOf(newRowId));
    }

    public final TextWatcher textChanged = new TextWatcher() {
        @Override
        public void afterTextChanged(Editable s) {
            if(!s.toString().equalsIgnoreCase(_text))
                set_text(s.toString());
        }

        @Override
        public void beforeTextChanged(CharSequence s, int start, int count, int after) {}

        @Override
        public void onTextChanged(CharSequence s, int start, int before, int count) {}
    };
```

For this to work it has to be wired up on the layout so we've changed the
EditText element for the Quote._text item so that it has a new attribute.

```
                  auuiuiu.mill-  rrere
            android:text="@{quote._title}"
            android:id="@+id/titleText"/>
        <EditText
            android:layout_width="match_parent"
            android:layout_height="wrap_content"
            android:hint="Text"
            android:text="@{quote._text}"
            bind:addTextChangedListener="@{quote.textChanged}"
            android:id="@+id/textText"/>
        <EditText
            android:layout_width="match_parent"
            android:layout_height="wrap_content"
            android:hint="Source"
            android:text="@{quote._source}"
            android:id="@+id/sourceText"/>
```

We've added the following line to our EditText which represents the text field of the Quote object onscreen:

```
bind:addTextChangedListener="@{quote.textChanged}"
```

This lets the system know that we want the method quote.textChanged to be called any time this screen element changes. That's how we are notified of the change that the user makes so we can make sure the Quote object _text property is updated.

Running and Testing QuoteCap
If you run the app now you can again, grab a quote from the browser and share/copy it over to QuoteCap. Once you do that, you can click the [Save] button and the data will be saved in the database. However, you won't be able to tell the data was saved because we don't yet have a way to view the data. I will show you how you can query the database using an ADB shell command.

Go ahead and run the app, type some text in and click the save button.

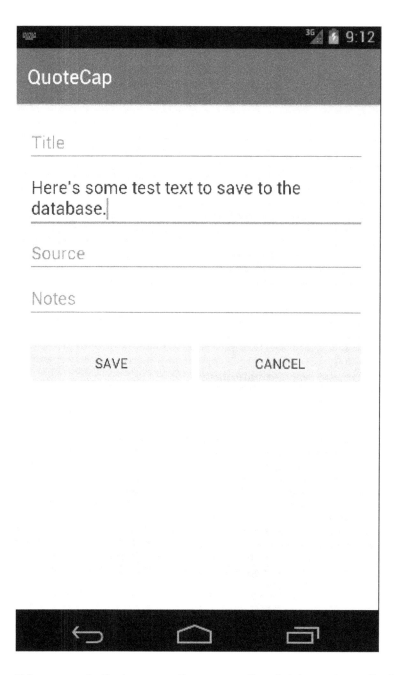

When you do that we can then query the database to verify that the data was saved.

Back at our command prompt for ADB we want to run the following command:

```
adb shell sqlite3
data/data/us.raddev.quotecap/databases/quote.db 'select *
from quote' <ENTER>
```

It'll look like the following:

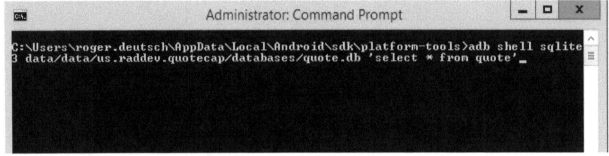

You can see that we are running a command named sqlite3. That is name of the sqlite executable which is installed on the device. It is the actual sqlite program which does all the work of creating and updating your database.

When you hit the <ENTER> button you will see your data:

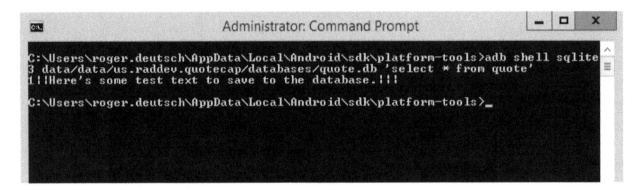

You can see the "Here's some test text to save to the database" is what I typed in QuoteCap.
Each field is separated by a pipe symbol | .

If you haven't pressed the [Save] button or it fails to create the database for some reason you may see an error like the one in the next screen shot that states: "unable to open database file".

That's because the file doesn't exist for some reason.

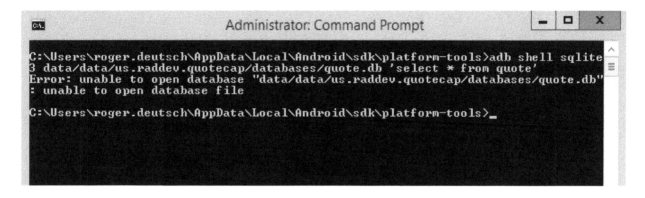

Now, we have a working copy of our app which creates the database and binds the one field but there is a lot more work to do. Right now, if you don't change the text and you keep pressing the [Save] button then it will simply insert a new row into the database every time you hit the button.
That's not what we really want. Instead we would want to update the last inserted record. That will take more work however.

Of course none of the other fields are saved in the database either so we need to fix that.
I'm going to set up the rest of the databinding so all fields will be updated both ways and they will be saved to the database. You can get that code at: QuoteCap_v12.zip

We've covered plenty for this chapter. However, we need to complete this app and we will in the next chapter. I want to add a few things like allowing the user to view the quotes that have been saved and save any updates the user has made to fields. There are a few things to work out like how to insure you update a record which has already been saved in the database instead of saving a new record. It's all related to using the rowId that comes back from the sql insert.   We also need to see how to deal with the Create Date / Time value in Sqlite.

Chapter 9

QuoteCap : Finishing the App – Finding Bugs In APIs

A lot has happened in the small space between the last chapter and this one. In my world, where I am writing this book I stumbled upon a problem with the QuoteCap application related to the way we are sharing text from other apps.

Summary of the Problem
The quick explanation of the problem is that the first time you share text from an app, the text will come over as expected via the Intent. However, each time after that you will find that even though you select new text in the external app the same original text is copied to QuoteCap.

I've documented the problem at StackOverflow.com at:
http://stackoverflow.com/questions/36039304/android-sharing-data-and-receiving-text-from-3rd-party-app-why-doesnt-my-app

A few people have chimed in, but no one else has really talked about this issue.
Unfortunately, the best answer out there which is supposed to work (override onNewIntent()) does not work at all.

Behaves Differently On Different API Levels

Also, you will see that this feature works entirely differently on different API Levels (Android versions). It seems that running Android 5.0 (API Level 21) and above solves the problem and it works as expected. However, we are running API Level 15 (Android 4.0.4) in our dev environment and targeting that version since it targets the greatest number of users. I myself have a Galaxy Core Prime phone running Android 4.4 and it behaves the improperly on that version also.

Building On Top of APIs
I spent a couple of days working through the issue and it was very interesting at times, but it also put me behind on my schedule. This is the challenge of building on top of any API (Application Programming Interface). As developers we are dependent upon certain functionality to work as documented and when it doesn't we have to find ways to work around the problems. However, that means we end up spending more time to get to the same place we should've already arrived at.

The Benefit of Reading Launch Your Android App
This is one of the benefits of reading this book. As a developer who is beginning to learn Android programming you could become stuck on issues like this and just think you are doing something wrong. I'm also going to show you the workaround which will help you understand how to create workarounds in your own code. It'll help you to think more creatively when you come up against a roadblock.

Get the Code
First of all, you can get the code with all the latest changes at:
QuoteCap_v14.zip

Here's what the app looks like with a sample entry added:

QuoteCap

PREV   NEXT

Title for entry
_____

This is where the main text for each entry
goes.
_____

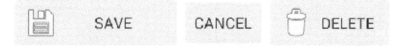
Source info goes here.
_____

Any notes you want to make about the
entry can go here.
_____

SAVE   CANCEL   DELETE

As you can see, most of the functionality need for the complete app has been added.
The user can save, edit and delete entries and can cancel an entry - which will throw away any added data and return her to the last entry in the list.

Of course, when a user decides to delete an entry she is warned with a dialog box which requires confirmation before the entry is deleted.

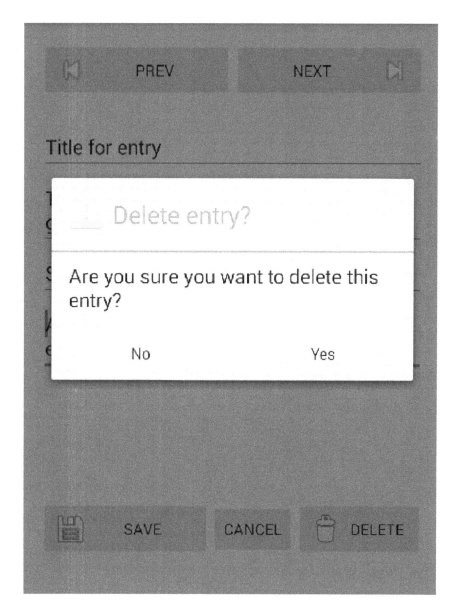

The code to do that was taken directly from our Stenotes app.

Images on Buttons
I've also implemented the simple and available icons from the Android dev libraries to display icons on the buttons where appropriate. This is as simple

as adding a new android attribute to our buttons such as in the case of our Save button like the following:

```
android:drawableLeft="@android:drawable/ic_menu_save"
```

This is a nice feature which draws the icon to the left of the Button's text.

Layout and Scroll Ability

You will also see that I've implemented the layout in such a way that the fields are scrollable but the buttons stay in place at the top and bottom. This way the content we are attempting to work with can be scrolled while our buttons stay in view at all times even if the content takes up more room because of long entries.

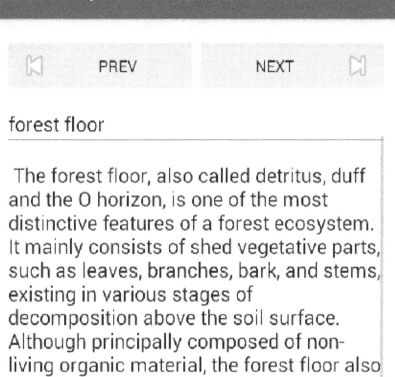

QuoteCap

⏮ PREV   NEXT ⏭

forest floor

 The forest floor, also called detritus, duff and the O horizon, is one of the most distinctive features of a forest ecosystem. It mainly consists of shed vegetative parts, such as leaves, branches, bark, and stems, existing in various stages of decomposition above the soil surface. Although principally composed of non-living organic material, the forest floor also teems with a wide variety of fauna and flora

wikipedia daily article

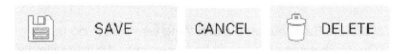

💾 SAVE   CANCEL   🗑 DELETE

You can see that I took that snapshot in mid-scroll (scroll indicator on far right) and yet, even while scrolling all of our buttons stay in view.

This is a simple matter of how we arrange our containers in the layout so that the LinearLayouts containing the buttons at the top and bottom of the layout are actually outside the ScrollView and each of those LinearLayouts are set with gravity and weight settings that make them float to the top and bottom of the view.

Let's dig down through the details of all the code now so you can see how this app works.

Let's go through our MainActivity class and walk through the functionality found in each of the Button clicks.

```java
_saveButton.setOnClickListener(new View.OnClickListener() {
    @Override
    public void onClick(View view) {
        Log.d("MainActivity", "Saving _quote...");
        if (_quote == null)
        {
            _quote = new Quote();
            _binding.setQuote(_quote);
        }
        // if the method returns true a record was inserted
        // and that means we want to update our lastRecordId
        // otherwise we don't because we already have that value
        if ( _quote.save(_quoteDBHelper)) {
            lastRecordId = _quote.get_id();
        }
    }
});
```

When the user clicks the Save button the first thing we need to do is determine if the Quote object is null (hasn't been set yet). If it is we simply new one up and bind it to the View so the values will be set properly.

If the Quote object is already instantiated then we attempt to save it to the database.

To do so we call the Quote object's save() method while passing in the QuoteDatabaseHelper which we will use in the save() method to get a writeable copy of the database.

Nested Inside if Statement
You can see that we've nested the call to the save() method inside an if statement. That's because I've made the save() method return a boolean which will indicate whether or not it has issued an update command or an insert command to the database.

Insert Versus Update
An insert command means that the record is a new database row which we are adding to the database. However, an update means that the record has previously been added but now we are changing some of the values in row to reflect changes the user has made.

Determining Insert or Update
In the case of a new Quote record being added to the database the _id value will be 0 because we haven't received a value from the database yet. Remember, the _id is a unique value generated by the Sqlite database itself. It generates a new value for us for this column because of the way we defined it in our QuoteDatabaseContract class which looked like the following:

```
QuoteTableDef._ID + " BIGINT PRIMARY KEY,"
```

That column is defined as a BIGINT (64-bit integer which is a primary key). That tells the database to handle generating the value itself.
It also guarantees that our ID value will be greater than zero. That makes it easy to determine if our Quote has ever been saved before, because the Quote._id value is initialized to zero (Java default for member variables). Only after loading a Quote from the database is the Quote._id ever initialized to a value greater than zero.

Let's take a closer look at the Quote.save() method now.

```java
public boolean save(QuoteDatabaseHelper qoh) {
    Log.d("MainActivity", "in Quote.Save()...");
    SQLiteDatabase db = qoh.getWritableDatabase();
    boolean isInsert = false;
    ContentValues values = new ContentValues();
    values.put(QuoteDatabaseContract.QuoteTableDef.COLUMN_NAME_TEXT, _text);
    values.put(QuoteDatabaseContract.QuoteTableDef.COLUMN_NAME_TITLE, _title);
    values.put(QuoteDatabaseContract.QuoteTableDef.COLUMN_NAME_SOURCE, _source);
    values.put(QuoteDatabaseContract.QuoteTableDef.COLUMN_NAME_NOTES, _note);
    if ( _id > 0) {
        //String[] selectionArgs = { _title,_text,_note,_source };
        db.update(
                QuoteDatabaseContract.QuoteTableDef.TABLE_NAME,
                values,
                "_id = " + String.valueOf(this._id),
                null);
    }
    else {
        long newRowId = db.insert(
                QuoteDatabaseContract.QuoteTableDef.TABLE_NAME,
                null,
                values);
        this._id = newRowId;
        isInsert = true;
    }

    Log.d("MainActivity", "newRowId : " + String.valueOf(this._id));
    return isInsert;
}
```

Immediately you can see that the method takes one parameter (QuoteDatabaseHelper) and returns a boolean.

You can see that I have some logging statements in here so I can follow the code a bit more easily while it is running. However, the first line of code that is more interesting is where we use the QuoteDatabaseHelper.

getWriteableDatabase

You can see that we use the QuoteDatabaseHelper because it provides a built-in method named getWriteableDatabase(). That method will return a SqliteDatabase to us which we can use to do our insert and update work.

```
SQLiteDatabase db = qoh.getWritableDatabase();
```

If we were only wanting to read records from the database we would've called the getReadableDatabase(). We'll see more about this later when we examine the [Previous] and [Next] button code.

SQLiteDatabase Methods
The entire reason we get a SQLiteDatabase instance is because it provides helper methods we can use to work with our database.

The first thing we do is initialize our isInsert boolean value (which we will return to the caller) so that it is false. In other words, if this is an update then the isInsert will stay false otherwise we'll set it to true.

The next thing you see is that we set up a new variable of type ContentValues.

```
ContentValues values = new ContentValues();
values.put(QuoteDatabaseContract.QuoteTableDef.COLUMN_NAME_TEXT,
_text);
values.put(QuoteDatabaseContract.QuoteTableDef.COLUMN_NAME_TITLE,
_title);
values.put(QuoteDatabaseContract.QuoteTableDef.COLUMN_NAME_SOURCE,
_source);
values.put(QuoteDatabaseContract.QuoteTableDef.COLUMN_NAME_NOTES,
_note);
```

This is another helper class provided by the Android libraries so you can set up the values which will be stored in the database row.

You can see that after we instantiate a new ContentValues container we then call the put() method multiple times. The put() method takes two parameters:
1. A String representing the name of the value (in our case, it's our column name)

2. The actual value of the item (in this case it is the matching property in our Quote class)

This creates a simple name-value pair collection which then can be used in our call to the SqliteDatabase insert() or update() method.

Now that we've set up the values which the new Quote row will be updated with or the previously created Quote row will be set to we can simply call the appropriate method (insert or update) to do our work.
However, to determine if it should be an insert or update, we simply check the value of our Quote._id field. If it is greater than 0 then we know the quote object has previously been saved to the database and we call update(), otherwise we call insert().

Updating the Quote
Once we determine the update should occur we run the following code:

```
db.update(
        QuoteDatabaseContract.QuoteTableDef.TABLE_NAME,
        values,
        "_id = " + String.valueOf(this._id),
        null);
```

As I said earlier, the main reason we instantiated the SQLiteDatabase object is so we can use its methods and you can see that we use it now to call update().

The update() method takes three parameters, however, we don't need to use the last one so we can send in a null* value.

*If you are a newer developer you can read more about what null means at my website where I'll be adding numerous articles on introductory development topics.

The first parameter to the update() method is simply a String which contains the name of the table you want to update. Since we created constants for all of these values earlier, now we can use them again:

```
QuoteDatabaseContract.QuoteTableDef.TABLE_NAME
```

That's the QuoteTableDef table name which is a String containing the value "quote".

The second parameter is the values object we just instantiated and initialized with values from our quote object.
Finally, the third parameter is a String representing a SQL Where clause.
I have created a String by adding two strings together. We want the row to be updated to have a Where clause which follows a pattern like the following:
"_id = <number>"

I use the Quote._id value to create the String and since the _id value is a long (integer) value I have to convert the value to the String and I use the static method String.valueOf() to do that for me.

This creates a dynamic String which creates a good Where clause so that only the record we want to update gets its values changed. If we did not add a Where clause and we ran the update, then all the records in the database would be updated with the same values.

After everything is set up the update() method will set all the column values properly. It's actually all quite easy.

The code which runs when we insert a new quote record is only slightly different.

```
long newRowId = db.insert(
      QuoteDatabaseContract.QuoteTableDef.TABLE_NAME,
      null,
      values);
this._id = newRowId;
isInsert = true;
```

You can see that the call to insert() has a slight different order of parameters. Again, the first parameter is our constant String representing the name of our table.
In the case of our insert() the second parameter represents the nullColumnHack value.

That is an odd thing which can help you add a completely empty row to a Sqlite table.
In our case, we never want to add a completely empty row so I set the value to null since we don't want to use the parameter.

The last parameter is the same values object we previously instantiated and initialized. This is the nice thing about this code is that it uses the exact same values object so we just pass it into whichever method (update or insert) we end up calling.

Also, notice that the insert() method also returns the IDENTITY value (generated _ID) that Sqlite has just created to insert our new row. We need to save that value so we can store it in our current quote object. You can see we save it in the newRowId variable and then store it in our object by setting the this._id = newRowid. This insures that if the user clicks the [Save] button twice, then the second time, the update() method will be called instead, since the quote object's _id value will then be greater than zero.

Finally, since this is an insert and we have added a new record we set the isInsert boolean to true so we can return it to our calling method.

Back in the MainActivity onClick of the [Save] button you will see that we use the boolean to determine whether or not we need to update our lastRecordId value.

```
if ( _quote.save(_quoteDBHelper)) {
    lastRecordId = _quote.get_id();
}
```

You can see if the _quote.save() method returns true then we set the lastRecordId value.
We do that as a simple way to know the lastRecordId as a reference point for paging through records in the quote database. A bit more about that later.

That's it for the [Save] button.
Let's take a look at the [Cancel] button now.

Cancel Button : Designing What It Does

First of all I had to decide what I wanted the Cancel button to do. What does it mean to Cancel in this context? I decided there should be a way to erase a current entry that has been made. Sometimes you might capture text and then decide you do not want it. Here's a couple of screen shots of what I was thinking.

First, let's go over how the app works.
Suppose you are looking at the daily featured article at wikipedia on your phone. You can select text and click the Android Share menu button.

 Search Wikipedia

Today's featured article

Amir Hamzah (1911–1946) was an Indonesian poet and national hero. Born into an aristocratic Malay family in the Sultanate of Langkat, Sumatra, he began writing poetry while still a teenager.

Though his works are undated, the earliest are from around 1930, when he first travelled to Java for schooling. He continued writing while studying in Surakarta and Batavia. He helped

When you do, Android will display the various apps which have registered the Text Intent.

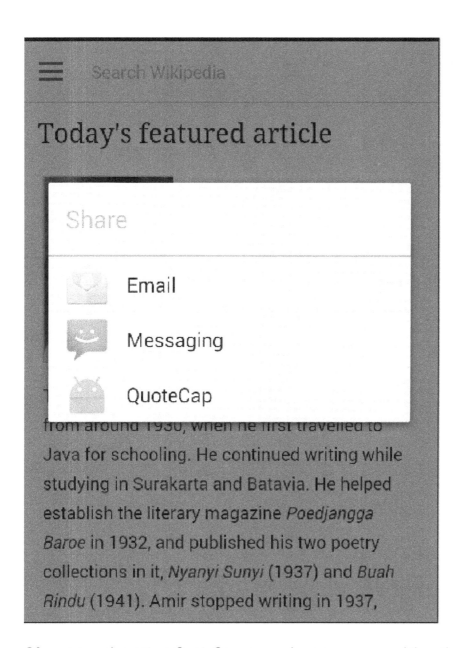

Of course, we've set up QuoteCap so we choose our app and then the selected text automatically added to our text field.

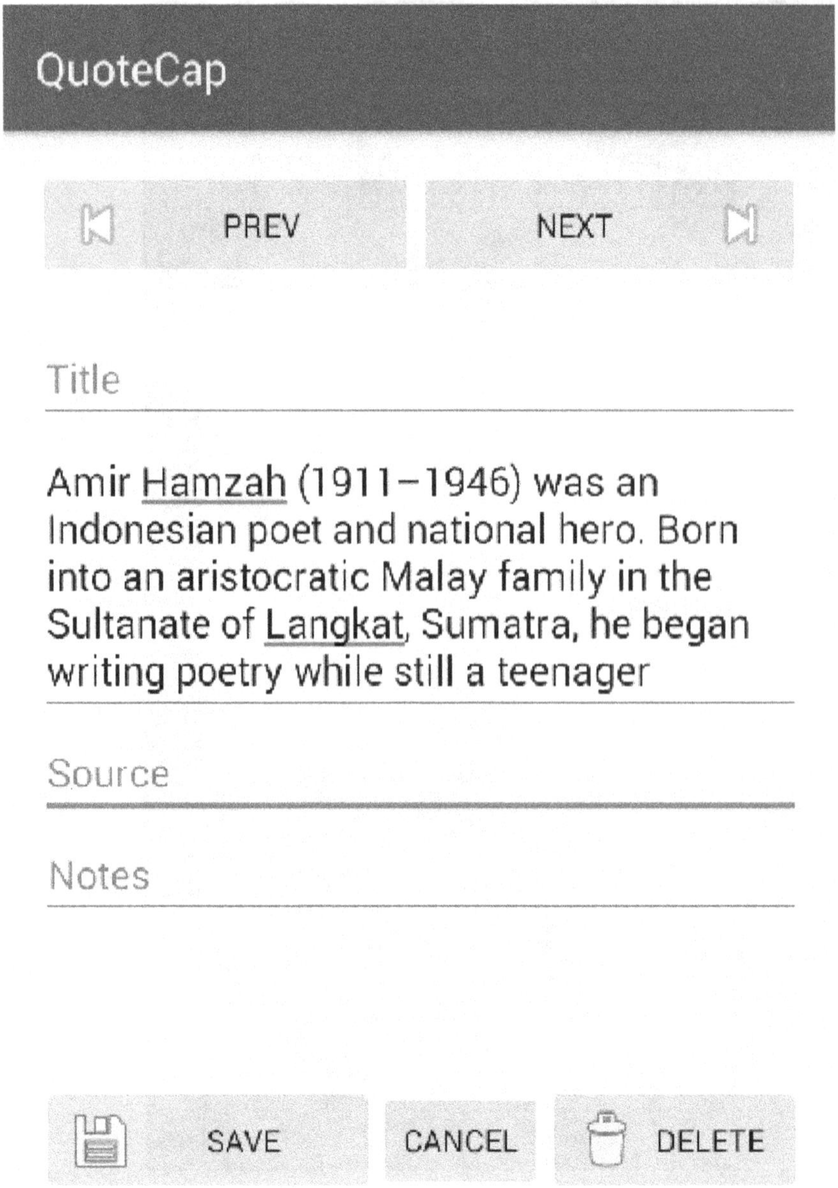
QuoteCap
PREV
NEXT
Title
Amir Hamzah (1911–1946) was an Indonesian poet and national hero. Born into an aristocratic Malay family in the Sultanate of Langkat, Sumatra, he began writing poetry while still a teenager
Source
Notes
SAVE
CANCEL
DELETE

Now, if we click the [Cancel] button at this point, the app will run the following code:

```
_cancelButton.setOnClickListener(new View.OnClickListener() {
```

```
@Override
public void onClick(View view) {
    Log.d("MainActivity", "CANCEL BUTTON");
    _binding.unbind();
    loadCurrentQuote();
    _binding.setQuote(_quote);

    }
});
```

The first thing we do is unbind the current object from the view because we are going to destroy the current object. Next, we call a method we wrote called loadCurrentQuote(). That method loads a quote from the database so we have something to display on the screen to the user.

In our case, we load the quote from the database with the largest _id value. This is an arbitrary decision. I figure that is the most recently added entry and so it is a good one to display to the user.

No Warning Dialog

In this case I have not added a warning dialog that you will lose the data that has just been copied in. You can implement that feature later if you like.

Here's a closer look at the code in the loadCurrentQuote() method.

```
private void loadCurrentQuote(){
    SQLiteDatabase db = _quoteDBHelper.getReadableDatabase();
    try
    {
        Cursor c = null;
        c = db.rawQuery("select * from quote where _id = (SELECT max(_id) FROM quote)", null);
        c.moveToLast();
        String text = c.getString(c.getColumnIndex("text"));
        Log.d("MainActivity", "text from query : " + text);
        _quote = new Quote(text);
        _quote.set_id(c.getInt(c.getColumnIndex("_id")));
        Log.d("MainActivity", "_id = : " + String.valueOf(_quote.get_id()));
        lastRecordId = _quote.get_id();
        _quote.set_source(c.getString(c.getColumnIndex("source")));
        _quote.set_title(c.getString(c.getColumnIndex("title")));
        _quote.set_note(c.getString(c.getColumnIndex(QuoteDatabaseContract.QuoteTableDef.COLUMN_NAME_NOTES)));
        c.close();
    }
    catch(Exception e)
    {
        _quote = new Quote();
        Log.d("MainActivity", e.getMessage());
    }
}
```

The first thing we need to do is get a readable database loaded up so we can call some methods on the database. Of course, we use our QuoteDatabaseHelper and call the getReadableDatabase() method since we just want to display (no writing at this point) the database record.

Next we set up a Cursor object that we can use to iterate through the records in the database.
To get the record we want (the one with the largest _id value) we call a helper method on the Sqlite database named rawQuery(). That method allows us to pass in a String representing a SQL statement which the database will run for us and return the resultset (matching rows).

More About the SQL Statement
This is a rather long SQL statement that we use because it actually contains a query and a subquery. In this case, the subquery (the Select statement further to the right) will be run first and then the main query will be run after that. The database will do this all as one operation for you.

Because the subquery is a normal valid query itself, you could run it on the command line against your database like the following:

```
adb shell sqlite3
data/data/us.raddev.quotecap/databases/quote.db 'select
max(_id) from quote' <ENTER>
```

My database currently has quite a few records in it from testing so my max _id is 112.

The max() is a built-in Sqlite SQL method that runs in the database.

You can see now via replacement that our original query would then look like the following:

```
select * from quote where _id = 112
```

That will return one record to us (the last one which was added to the database).

The next line uses the Cursor object to moveToLast() (since we know only one row was going to be returned we could've used moveToFirst() and there would be no difference) to read the record.

After that you see where we start getting the values from the record to instantiate quote object which contains the values from the row.

In the following code we use the Cursor's getString() method to get a string value that is stored in the text column. We store it in a local variable named text and then we use that text to construct our new Quote object.

```
String text = c.getString(c.getColumnIndex("text"));
```

```
Log.d("MainActivity", "text from query : " + text);
_quote = new Quote(text);
```

Next, we get the _id value out of the column using the Cursor again. Then
we set our newly instantiated Quote object's _id value to that same value.

```
_quote.set_id(c.getInt(c.getColumnIndex("_id")));
Log.d("MainActivity", "_id = : " + String.valueOf(_quote.get_id()));
lastRecordId = _quote.get_id();
```

Finally, we set the lastRecordId (since we've just queried for that value) to the
value we stored in the Quote oibject.

Then we initialize the rest of the Quote properties from the values in the row
using the Cursor.

```
_quote.set_source(c.getString(c.getColumnIndex("source")));
_quote.set_title(c.getString(c.getColumnIndex("title")));
_quote.set_note(c.getString(c.getColumnIndex(QuoteDatabaseContract.Qu
oteTableDef.COLUMN_NAME_NOTES)));
c.close();
```

Using The Original Constants We Defined
One thing to note here is that we passed in plain strings for the name of the
field we want to get the value from. However, in that last one where we get
the value that is in the note column I have used the constant that we created
earlier which represents the note field. It would really be best to use those
constant values because then you don't have to worry about misspelling a
field when you send in your new string since you know they are defined in
one place as constants.

Finally, we call close() on the Cursor to insure we close the connection to the
database.
When the method returns, remember that we called this method from our
[Cancel] button.

When the loadCurrentQuote method returns to the onClick method of the
Cancel button it will be at the highlighted line.
```
```

```
_cancelButton.setOnClickListener(new View.OnClickListener() {
    @Override
    public void onClick(View view) {
        Log.d("MainActivity", "CANCEL BUTTON");
        _binding.unbind();
        loadCurrentQuote();
        binding.setQuote( quote);

    }
});
```

Before that highlighted line runs, keep in mind that the binding has been removed. That means if we do not bind the newly instantiated and initialized _quote object then the View would not display the values of the object we just initialized. That's why we call _binding.setQuote(_quote) here.
When we do the UI updates and you will see the values from the record with the largest _id value.

The next and previous button both have some interesting code in them because of the way we have to keep track of the current record we are displaying.

Next Button Code

```
_nextButton.setOnClickListener(new View.OnClickListener() {
    @Override
    public void onClick(View view) {
        if ( quote != null){
            long currentId = _quote.get_id();
            if (currentId == lastRecordId){
                return;
            }
            else
            {
                DisplayRecord(String.valueOf(currentId),true);
            }
        }
    }
});
```

The first thing we do is make sure the current _quote object isn't null. If it isn't we set the get the _id value and store it in a variable for our use. We use it to compare the value to the lastRecordId.

Since this is the Next button and we are moving up through the records in the database if we are at the last item already then there is nothing further to do. If that is true then we simply return from the method. This is a short circuit to simply do nothing. We could make this code better by disabling the [Next] button so the user cannot click it again in an effort to indicate to the user she is at the end of the list.

If we are not at the end of the list then we call a method we wrote named DisplayRecord(). When we call it we pass in the currentId value and a boolean representing whether we are moving up through the list or down. In this case we pass true which means we are moving up.

Here's how the DisplayRecord() method works.

```
private void DisplayRecord(String id, boolean isUp){
    SQLiteDatabase db = _quoteDBHelper.getReadableDatabase();
    try
    {
        Cursor c = null;
        String directionSign = isUp ? ">" : "<";
        String query = "select * from quote where _ID " + directionSign + " " + id + ";";
        Log.d("MainActivity", query);
        c = db.rawQuery(query, null);
        if (isUp) {
            c.moveToFirst();
        }
        else
        {
            c.moveToLast();
        }
        String text = c.getString(c.getColumnIndex("text"));
        Log.d("MainActivity", "text from query : " + text);
        _binding.unbind();
        _quote = new Quote(text);
        _binding.setQuote(_quote);
        _quote.set_id(c.getInt(c.getColumnIndex("_id")));
        _quote.set_source(c.getString(c.getColumnIndex("source")));
        _quote.set_title(c.getString(c.getColumnIndex("title")));
        _quote.set_note(c.getString(c.getColumnIndex(QuoteDatabaseContract.QuoteTableDef.COLUMN_NAME_NOTES)));
        c.close();
    }
    catch(Exception e)
    {
        _quote = new Quote();
        Log.d("MainActivity", e.getMessage());
    }
}
```

This method is very similar to what we saw in the Quote.save() method so a lot of it will look familiar.

The DisplayRecord() method is called from both the [Next] button and the [Previous] button. This is a good reuse of code since the code result is so similar.

Howevever, you can see that the way we create the SQL query is interesting.

Ternary Operator
One of the first things I do is determine if we are moving up through the list or down. That determines whether or not we want a record with a higher or lower _id than what we have right now.

I use a ternary operator to set the directionSign (less than or greater than). The ternary operator is made up of a colon (:) and a question mark (?). It's nice for this type of one line if statements. It takes of form of :

```
Evaluation statement ? <1st value> : <2nd value>
```

That simply means we evaluate a statement to determine its boolean value and if it is true we return the first value and if it is false we return the second value.

In our case we check the isUp boolean variable. If it is true then we want our select statement to get an _id that is greater than the _id we are currently on and so our ternary statement returns a > (greater than sign). If isUp is false we return the second value which is a < (less than sign).

We then use that to construct our query string to the database by concatenating a few strings together:

```
"select * from quote where _ID " + directionSign + " " + id + ";";
```

So, if our directionSign is ">" and the id variable is 5 then the string would end up looking like:

```
select * from quote where _ID > 5
```

This retrieves all rows where the _ID is greater than 5 (our current _ID) so that we can make sure we get the next row (which may not necessarily be _ID = 6 since rows may have been deleted).

Once that is set up you can see that the rest of the code is the same as the Quote.save() method where we run a rawQuery() and then read the values out of the columns to initialize our _query object.

That's all there is too it. However, the challenge of keeping our current object in sync with the items in the database should be obvious. There are multiple rows in the database and we have to know where we are as we display them to the user so the user can move through the entire set of records.

Let's finish up our discussion of the QuoteCap application by discussing the main quote capturing and the workaround I had to create so that it would work.

Android Intent Bug & Workaround

The main thing we wanted to do in this app is allow the user to share text from another app.
Android provides a way to do this with an Android Intent which we have implemented according to the documentation on the Android Google Development web site.

The Problem
However, as I was testing the app on the emulator running API Level 15 I found that the text shared with QuoteCap worked the first time, but every time after that when I attempted to share text the text value sent in to QuoteCap was the same. That meant we didn't have a way to allow QuoteCap to keep running and easily add new quotes numerous times. That would've destroyed the purpose of the app so I had to find a workaround. I did create a workaround, but it took me a few days to get it to all working exactly as a user would expect.

Insuring We Always Get Shared Text
As I learned that the shared text was not updated I began to form a workaround. I tried various things to resolve the issue but none of them worked.
Finally I had to add a new Activity to receive the Intent. The reason I decided to add a new Activity is I discovered if I called finish() on the MainActivity (which ends up removing the Activity from memory -- completely destroying the Activity) then QuoteCap was stopped and the Intent Extras were reset each time and I could catch the new shared text every time.

However, that meant that if the user pop up a dialog box or switch the orientation of his phone or a received an incoming call then the app would be destroyed and possibly lose current unsaved data.

Workaround Explanation

My idea was to create a pass-through Activity which would accept the Intent Extras and then place the Extras in a Bundle which it then passed to my MainActivity. The pass-through Activity would then use startActivity to start the MainActivity which would guarantee that the pass-through Activity would go to the onPause() method. Then, in that onPause() method I would call the finish() which would destroy the pass-through Activity. The user would never see the pass-through activity and the problem would be solved because the pass-through Activity would be destroyed each time and receive new Intent Extras every time it was instantiated.

This works fairly well, but I learned to do this I also had to configure my pass-through Activity a bit differently in the AndroidManifest.xml.

```xml
<manifest xmlns:android="http://schemas.android.com/apk/res/android"
    package="us.raddev.quotecap">

    <application
        android:allowBackup="true"
        android:icon="@mipmap/ic_launcher"
        android:label="QuoteCap"
        android:supportsRtl="true"
        android:theme="@style/AppTheme">
        <activity android:name=".MainActivity" android:windowSoftInputMode="stateVisible|adjustPan">
            <intent-filter>
                <action android:name="android.intent.action.MAIN" />
                <category android:name="android.intent.category.LAUNCHER" />
            </intent-filter>
        </activity>
        <activity android:name="us.raddev.quotecap.QuoteCapGrabber" android:launchMode="singleInstance">
            <intent-filter>
                <action android:name="android.intent.action.SEND" />
                <category android:name="android.intent.category.DEFAULT" />
                <category android:name="android.intent.category.LAUNCHER" />
                <data android:mimeType="text/plain" />
            </intent-filter>
        </activity>
    </application>

</manifest>
```

You can see that I've added the pass-through Activity named QuoteCapGrabber. I've also added a launchMode attribute with a setting of singleInstance. That setting insures that there is only one of these Activities in memory ever. That helps insure that the system will destroy the Activity properly so that I always get the newly shared text.

After including this in the manfiest, it's a simple matter of adding the code in our QuoteCapGrabber.java.

Here's all the code from that class:

```
@Override protected void onCreate(Bundle savedInstanceState) {
    super.onCreate(savedInstanceState);
    //Get intent, action and MIME type
    setContentView(R.layout.grabber_main);
    Intent intent = getIntent();
    if (intent != null) {
        String action = intent.getAction();
        Log.d("MainActivity", "action: " + action);
        String type = intent.getType();
        Log.d("MainActivity", "type: " + type);
        Log.d("MainActivity", String.valueOf(intent.hasExtra(Intent.EXTRA_TEXT)));
        //Log.d("MainActivity", "clipdata : " + intent.get getClipData());

        if (Intent.ACTION_SEND.equals(action) && type != null) {
            if ("text/plain".equals(type)) {
                handleReceivedText(intent); // Handle text being sent
            }
        }
    }
}
@Override public void onPause(){
    super.onPause();
    Log.d("MainActivity", "finish()...");
    finish();
}

void handleReceivedText(Intent intent) {
    String sharedText = intent.getStringExtra(Intent.EXTRA_TEXT);
    if (sharedText != null) {
        Log.d("MainActivity", "sharedText : " + sharedText);
        Intent i = new Intent(getApplicationContext(),MainActivity.class);

        i.putExtra("SHAREDTEXT",sharedText);
        startActivity(i);
    }
}
```

You can see that when onCreate() fires we grab the Intent() and get the
Extras off of it to get the shared text.

We do that work in the handleReceiveText().
In handleReceiveText() when we get the text, we then create a new Intent
(our MainActivity) and then we use the putExtra() method to add the
sharedText we received onto the Intent Bundle.

Then we call startActivity passing in our Intent. When we do that, the new Intent will be displayed which will cause the QuoteCapGrabber Activity to go into pause mode. That will cause the overridden onPause method to be called.

Inside the onPause we call the Activity's finish() method which will destroy the QuoteCapGrabber object and remove it from memory. This guarantees us that the next time text is shared from an app that the shared text will come in properly. This took a lot of extra work and time to figure out, but it makes the app work as it should.

You've learned a lot with the the QuoteCap app. It's nice little app which can really help if you want to save text and quotes while you are reading on a device.

Now let's move on to our final app. This app will help you see how you can
1.   share data over an Internet connection
2.   Grab text (SMS) messages as they come into a device.
3.   A bit about multithreading and why you must not do a lot of work on your app's main thread.

We'll learn a lot more too as we write an app which will allow you to grab text messages as they come in and forward them to an account where you can pick them up via a web page and reply to them from the web page. Then, when you reply to the text message from the web page, the app will pick them up and send them from your registered device so that others who receive the text messages will get them from your phone even though you were able to type them on a web page.

I believe you'll find this app quite interesting. Let's go create it.

Chapter 10

TxtFwd : Building the App - Retrieve Your Text
Messages From Anywhere

Building our app which grabs text messages and forwards them to you so you
can edit them using a web page and keyboard will challenge our app building
skills from many angles.

There's a lot to do so let's talk about what we want our app to do and how we
might do it.

The Idea In A Nutshell
Here's the idea. I want to be able to start the app up and set a checkbox that
tells the app to grab each text message (SMS) that comes to my phone and
forward it to a location where I can read it from a web page and then reply
using my computer and that same web page. This will allow me to type text
messages I want to send using my normal computer keyboard without having
to purchase a separate bluetooth keyboard.

Of course, this app also allows us a way to investigate the various Android
APIs which allow us to do this work.

Grab A Text Message

The first thing I need to be able to do is grab a text message when it comes into my phone. Can you do that with the Android libraries? Fortunately it is quite easy to do and it's very similar to what we've seen using Intents.

Send a Text Message

We can also send an SMS message using the registered app that the user's phone already uses to send text messages. We just have to create an Intent and add the data we want to send.

###

Disclaimer

This application will use your phone's SMS service to send and receive text messages. Your normal charges will apply just as if you are sending and receiving the messages yourself. If you do not turn off the forwarding feature you may be sending and / or receiving an extra text message for everyone you send or receive and that could drive up your messaging costs. The author cannot be held responsible for any extra expense to you when using the app. Your use of the app indicates your understanding and acceptance of this disclaimer.

###

Where Do We Forward the Message?

The next thing to consider is where we can forward the text message. First of all, we certainly don't want our text messages to be exposed on the Internet no matter how benign they may be.

Also, how would you store those text messages so they may be displayed on a web page? How could all of this be secure?

There is a one word answer to that question: Firebase.

What's Firebase?

http://firebase.com

It's a highly-available, Internet, JSON (JavaScript Object Notation), NoSQL data storage which is easily accessible via HTTPS (Encrypted / Secure). Firebase provides a great, easy-to-use API which is accessible via Android apps and provides free developer accounts so you can get started for free.

What Does All That Mean?

This means we can create Java objects and serialize them to our own private (HTTPS secure) data store available via the Internet and the data is instantly available to other apps, web apps, and any other connected device or platform. Further, that means we can quickly and easily build an Android app which implements the Firebase database which allows us to forward text messages securely and store them in the Firebase database where they can be instantly retrieved via web page (or any other technology we build around it).

Security of Utmost Importance

I want to reiterate that all data sent to a Firebase data store using the Firebase APIs is encrypted via SSL (Secure Sockets Layer). This is the same encryption standard used when you purchase an item from an online retailer such as Amazon.com. This is important since we will be forwarding text messages over the Internet and it is interesting since there's no complicated configuration to be done when using Firebase. All we have to do is use the simple Firebase API to write our data to the remote storage and it is secure.

Here's the official quote from the Firebase site:

SSL by default

Every app is served over a secure connection, and we take care of provisioning the SSL cert for you.

There are a few parts to this app so I will break them down and show you a flow for each state in an attempt to communicate exactly how the app will work.

Entire Flow For Our App

Here are multiple flow diagrams to show how the entire process will work.

Private Data Store

First of all, there is the one-time configuration done in the app so user can identify himself and create a data store that is only accessible to him.

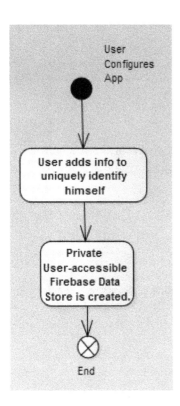

Configured and Ready To Run

After the user configures the app so that his private store is created in the Firebase database then he can turn on Text forwarding whenever he wants it activated.

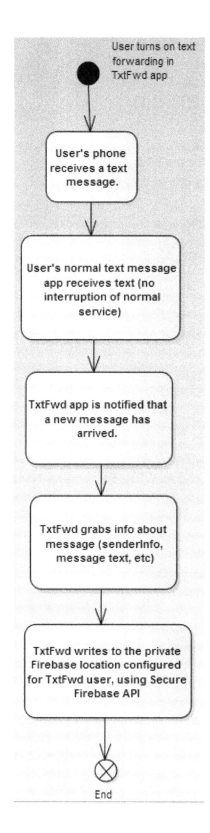

User turns on text forwarding in TxtFwd app

User's phone receives a text message.

User's normal text message app receives text (no interruption of normal service)

TxtFwd app is notified that a new message has arrived.

TxtFwd grabs info about message (senderInfo, message text, etc)

TxtFwd writes to the private Firebase location configured for TxtFwd user, using Secure Firebase API

End

TxtFwd Is Activated and Handling Messages

Now, as messages are received by the phone, they will be written to the private location so the user may read them using the web app.

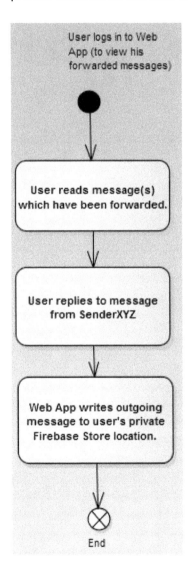

At this point, the user has viewed one or more messages and replied to a message. When the user replies using the web app then the message and details are written to an outbound location in the Firebase store.

TxtFwd Is Updated In Real-time About Outbound Messages

The app, running on the user's phone is instantly alerted that an outbound message is available.

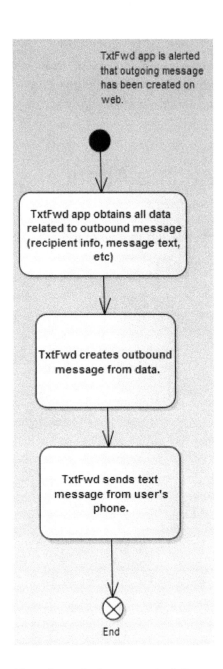

TxtFwd app is alerted that outgoing message has been created on web.

TxtFwd app obtains all data related to outbound message (recipient info, message text, etc)

TxtFwd creates outbound message from data.

TxtFwd sends text message from user's phone.

End

Knowing what you are building makes software development so much easier (and even possible). :)

Next Steps

Using those diagrams it is much easier to plan our app development. I know the app is going to need provide some sort of configuration Activity and it's going to need to save those values somewhere. I also know that I'm going to need to be able to :

1. Get Text message info
2. Write text message info to Firebase storage
3. Send a text message

Let's start by looking at how we grab an incoming text message.

Go ahead and start a new project, name it TxtFwd and choose the Blank Activity as your template for your MainActivity.

Add Permissions to Manifest

The first thing we will do is add a permission to our AndroidManifest.xml which allows us to receive text messages.

```
<uses-permission android:name="android.permission.RECEIVE_SMS" />
```

We have to do this so the user is warned when installing the app that it can read (RECEIVE_SMS) messages. A nefarious app could gather a lot of information by reading all the user's text messages so we have to give the app the explicit permission to be able to do so.

```xml
<?xml version="1.0" encoding="utf-8"?>
<manifest xmlns:android="http://schemas.android.com/apk/res/android"
    package="us.raddev.txtfwd">
    <uses-permission android:name="android.permission.RECEIVE_SMS" />
    <application
        android:allowBackup="true"
        android:icon="@mipmap/ic_launcher"
        android:label="TxtFwd"
        android:supportsRtl="true"
        android:theme="@style/AppTheme">
        <activity
            android:name=".MainActivity"
            android:label="TxtFwd"
            android:theme="@style/AppTheme.NoActionBar">
            <intent-filter>
                <action android:name="android.intent.action.MAIN" />

                <category android:name="android.intent.category.LAUNCHER" />
            </intent-filter>
        </activity>
    </application>

</manifest>
```

If we fail to add the permission to the manifest then the app will crash when it runs the SMS receiving functionality.

BroadcastReceiver : Override onReceive()

To implement the functionality of receiving the incoming text messages we simply create our own class which is derived from Android BroadcastReceiver class and override the onReceive() method. The onReceive() method of the BroadcastReceiver receives an Intent which will contain a Bundle we can get using the getExtras() method. That Bundle carries the information about each text message which is received. We just have to run a method on that data to convert it for our use. You'll see that in the code.

Let's go ahead and add a new class named MsgReceiver to our project and add it into our us.raddev.txtfwd package. Next go ahead and make sure MsgReceiver extends BroadcastReceiver and finally go ahead and implement the @Override of the onReceive() method.

Once you do all that, your class will look like the following:

```
AndroidManifest.xml ×    MsgReceiver.java ×    MainActivity.java ×

package us.raddev.txtfwd;

import android.content.BroadcastReceiver;
import android.content.Context;
import android.content.Intent;

public class MsgReceiver extends BroadcastReceiver {
    @Override
    public void onReceive(Context context, Intent intent) {

    }
}
```

Now we just need to implement the code for onReceive() which will get the information we want out of the text message.
Add the following code to the onReceive() method and when Studio attempts to help you add the imports make sure you add the android.telephony.SmsMessage.

```java
package us.raddev.txtfwd;

import android.content.BroadcastReceiver;
import android.content.Context;
import android.content.Intent;
import android.os.Build;
import android.os.Bundle;
import android.widget.Toast;

public class MsgReceiver
    @Override
    public void onReceiv

              Class to Import
          android.telephony.SmsMessage    ▶
          android.telephony.gsm.SmsMessage ▶

        SmsMessage message = null;
        if (Build.VERSION.SDK_INT >= 19) {
            SmsMessage[] msgs = Telephony.Sms.Intents.getMessagesFromIntent(intent);
            message = msgs[0];
        }
        else {
            Bundle bundle = intent.getExtras();
            Object pdus[] = (Object[]) bundle.get("pdus");
            message = SmsMessage.createFromPdu((byte[]) pdus[0]);
        }
        String body = message.getMessageBody();
        long when = message.getTimestampMillis();
        String from = message.getOriginatingAddress();

        Toast.makeText(context, from + " : " + body,
                Toast.LENGTH_LONG).show();
    }
}
```

Also you are going to see that we check the API Level in our code to
determine how we handle the SMS message. That's because we had to do
that a different way in APIs before Level 19 and we are supporting API Levels
all the way back to 15 (Android version 4.0.4 - Ice Cream Sandwich). This is
an arbitrary decision and we could just change our minimum API Level to 19
and forget about the old code if we wanted to.

You can easily see all the API Levels and their corresponding Android version names and code names at : https://source.android.com/source/build-numbers.html

Now we need to register our class as a SMS Receiver in our AndroidManifest.xml to insure it will receive the incoming SMS Messages. To do that you add the following XML inside your <application> tag:

```
<receiver android:name=".MsgReceiver">
    <intent-filter>
        <action
android:name="android.provider.Telephony.SMS_RECEIVED"/>
    </intent-filter>
</receiver>
```

The entire file now looks like:

```xml
<?xml version="1.0" encoding="utf-8"?>
<manifest xmlns:android="http://schemas.android.com/apk/res/android"
    package="us.raddev.txtfwd">
    <uses-permission android:name="android.permission.RECEIVE_SMS" />
    <application
        android:allowBackup="true"
        android:icon="@mipmap/ic_launcher"
        android:label="TxtFwd"
        android:supportsRtl="true"
        android:theme="@style/AppTheme">
        <activity
            android:name=".MainActivity"
            android:label="TxtFwd"
            android:theme="@style/AppTheme.NoActionBar">
            <intent-filter>
                <action android:name="android.intent.action.MAIN" />

                <category android:name="android.intent.category.LAUNCHER" />
            </intent-filter>
        </activity>
        <receiver android:name=".MsgReceiver">
            <intent-filter>
                <action android:name="android.provider.Telephony.SMS_RECEIVED"/>
            </intent-filter>
        </receiver>
    </application>

</manifest>
```

Let's build the app and deploy it and I'll show you how to test it on your emulator.
You can get the code at:
TxtFwd_v01.zip

Once you run the app, move back to Android Studio so we can start the Android Device Monitor (ADM).
You can get to the ADM from the menu bar at the top of Studio.

You can also get to it from the Tools menu:

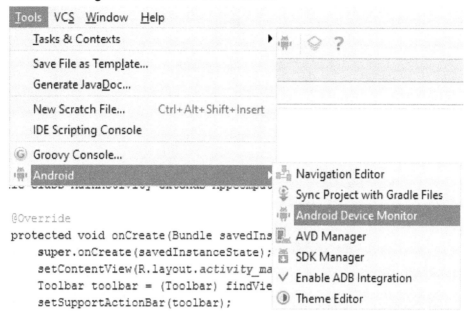

Once you start up the ADM it will look something like the following:

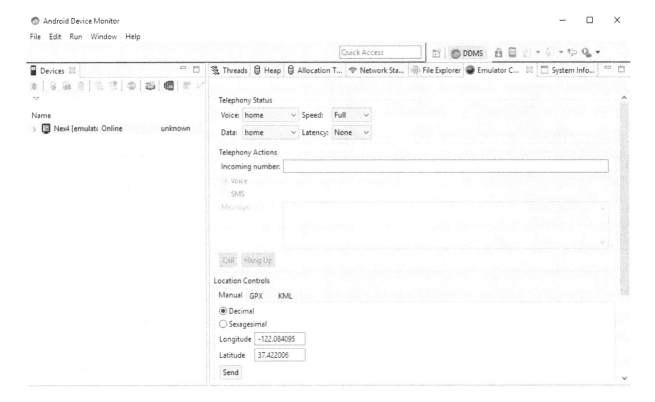

Take a close look at the menu buttons in the top right and you'll see that the DDMS tab is selected and you will also see that at the far left the current running emulator is chosen.

This is the DDMS (Dalvik Debug Monitor Server). This tool is somewhat poorly named because the Dalvik Virtual Machine is no longer used on the newer versions of Android (5.0 & up).

Sending A Text Message To Emulator
Right now we are interested in the main section on the right. That section will allow us to simulate sending a text message to our emulator.

Incoming Number
Using it is a bit odd, because you cannot do anything until you enter a number in the [incoming number] edit box. That is the number which will be reported to the app as the sender's number.

Go ahead and type a number like 5551234 in the edit box and then you will be able to choose the SMS radio button indicating that you want to send a text message. If you enter anything besides numbers in that edit box you will see that the radio buttons go back to disabled and you won't be able to send a text.

After you type a number in, select the SMS radio button and then the Message edit box will be enabled so you can type a message to send. Type a message in the edit box. Next, move your Android emulator so you can see it when you click the [Send] button.

I took a snapshot right after clicking the button and the toast message popped up in the TxtFwd app.

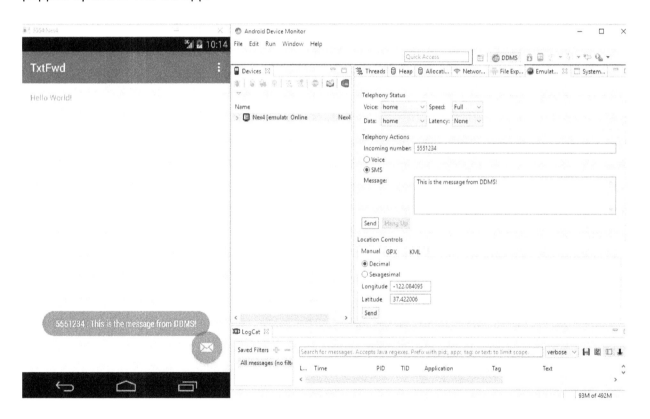

Create A Message Class

Now that we're all set up for receiving messages, let's create a better way to handle the text message info by wrapping it all up in a class. This will help is later when we write the data to the Firebase data storage anyways.

Designing Our Message Class

I want to add a property for each of the SMS values we grab:

1. originatingNumber (this is the number we will reply to)
2. Body (this is the actual message text)
3. receivedDateTime (a simple way to allow the user to know the age of the message)
4. isInbound (boolean which allows us to indicate if this is an inbound or outbound message)

Go ahead and add the new Message class to our main package and we'll add all of the properties above. Then you can generate the getters and setters for all of the properties.

Finally, you can add an constructor which takes all four values as parameters.

The Message class will look like the following:

```java
package us.raddev.txtfwd;

public class Message {

    public Message(String _originatingNumber, String _body, String _dateTimeCreated, boolean isInbound) {
        this._originatingNumber = _originatingNumber;
        this._body = _body;
        this._dateTimeCreated = _dateTimeCreated;
        this.isInbound = isInbound;
    }

    private String _originatingNumber;

    public String get_originatingNumber() {
        return _originatingNumber;
    }

    public void set_originatingNumber(String _originatingNumber) {
        this._originatingNumber = _originatingNumber;
    }

    public String get_body() {
        return _body;
    }

    public void set_body(String _body) {
        this._body = _body;
    }

    public String get_dateTimeCreated() {
        return _dateTimeCreated;
    }
}
```

Now we can open up the MsgReceiver class again and remove the toast message and add some Logging in its place. We'll now instantiate our new Message class in the onReceive() method.

The MsgReceiver code now looks like the following:

```java
public class MsgReceiver extends BroadcastReceiver {
    @Override
    public void onReceive(Context context, Intent intent) {

        SmsMessage message = null;
        if (Build.VERSION.SDK_INT >= 19) {
            Log.d("MainActivity", "I'm an NEWER API LEVEL : " + Build.VERSION.SDK_INT);
            SmsMessage[] msgs = Telephony.Sms.Intents.getMessagesFromIntent(intent);
            message = msgs[0];
        }
        else {
            Log.d("MainActivity", "I'm an older API LEVEL : " + Build.VERSION.SDK_INT);
            Bundle bundle = intent.getExtras();
            Object pdus[] = (Object[]) bundle.get("pdus");
            message = SmsMessage.createFromPdu((byte[]) pdus[0]);
        }

        String from = message.getOriginatingAddress();
        String body = message.getMessageBody();
        long receivedDate = message.getTimestampMillis();
        Date date = new Date(receivedDate);
        DateFormat formatter = new SimpleDateFormat("MM/dd/yyyy - HH:mm:ss");
        String formattedDate = formatter.format(date);

        Message msg = new Message(from, body, formattedDate, true);
        Log.d("MainActivity", "from : "+ from);
        Log.d("MainActivity", "body : " + body);
        Log.d("MainActivity", "receivedDate : " + formattedDate);

    }
}
```

I've cleaned up the code a bit and we haven't really talked about how this code does its work so let's take a closer look now.

The most important part of this code is how we receive the SMS message itself. As we said earlier, the Android APIs have changed a bit so that if the user is running API Level 19 or newer you can use the simpler method of pulling the message directly off of the incoming Intent with the call to getMessagesFromIntent(). This is slightly more direct way of getting the SMS info than the older version where you have to grab the extras Bundle off the Intent and then loading the "pdus" from the Bundle. PDU stands for Protocol Data Unit -- basically meaning a data type based upon a protocol (SMS being the protocol).

SmsMessage : Allows Us To Get Message Data
After you've retrieved the SmsMessage using either the new or old method then the code is the same. We simply grab the data that we are interested in using the built-in methods getTimeMillis() to get the Date-Time info the message was received. getOriginatingAddress() allows us to get the number we will use to reply and getMessageBody() allows us to retrieve the actual message which was sent.

Instantiate Our Message Class
After we obtain all the info related to the SMS message we go ahead and wrap it up in our user-defined type which we have named Message. This is a convenient way to keep the objects in our app separate but in a moment you will see that this also allows us to easily write our data to our Firebase storage location.

Firebase Account
To do the next work you should get your own Firebase account, but you don't have to, because the TxtFwd app will use the Firebase location that I've generated.

If you have a Google account it is extremely easy to sign up for Firebase. All you have to do is login using your Google account and Firebase will create an account for you and create an initial database. If you do that, it will look like the following when you first sign up.

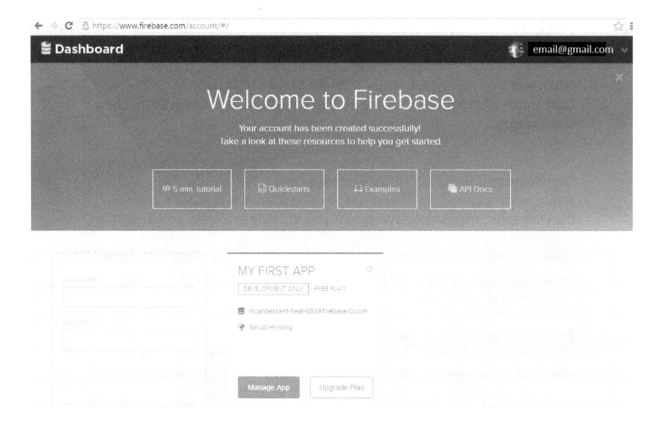

I'm going to go ahead and rename my default Firebase database to : TxtFwd
Now it has a better URL also:

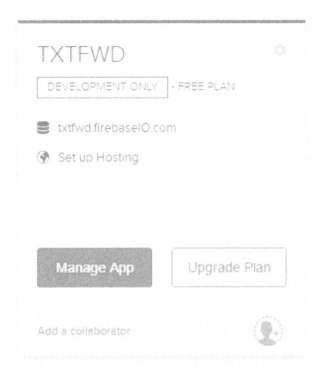

TXTFWD

DEVELOPMENT ONLY - FREE PLAN

txtfwd.firebaseIO.com

Set up Hosting

Manage App   Upgrade Plan

Add a collaborator

Now we need to add the Firebase SDK (which we get as a JAR file from the Firebase web site).
The information on how to do this work (slightly different) is at the official Firebase site at:
https://www.firebase.com/docs/android/quickstart.html

However, I found a bit simpler method to do this and I take you through it step by step as this chapter continues.

Firebase Android JAR
The Firebase SDK which is wrapped up in a JAR (Java ARchive) file for us.
As of this writing you can point your browser at:
https://cdn.firebase.com/java/firebase-client-android-2.5.1.jar
####################################

Note: As I went through this work I used version 2.5.1 of the SDK but it crashed every time I ran the project. Even though it was the latest version that is referenced on the quick-start page I had to get the older 2.5.0 version : https://cdn.firebase.com/java/firebase-client-android-2.5.0.jar
There's more about that problem at StackOverflow:
http://stackoverflow.com/questions/35522717/android-app-is-crashing-when-connecting-to-firebase
##

When you go through this there may be a newer version so check the quickstart page to be sure you have the latest.

This jar file extends the libraries which we are building our app on. If you examined the core Android libraries you'd find numerous jars where the functionality we find in packages is found. This jar file is provided by Firebase which provides this new package with functionality that allows us to do work specifically related to implementing Firebase.

Once you download that jar we need to reference it in our project.

Android Studio and Solution Explorer View
The default solution explorer view is based upon an Android project view so it hides some of the details you may not use often.
A basic Android project in the solution explorer looks like the following :

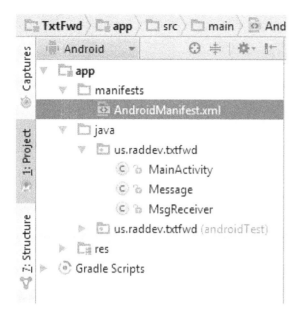

You can see the manifests, java folder and our base packages. You also see the res (resources) and the Gradle Scripts. All of those items are things you will often work with. I think InelliJ (developers of Android Studio) did a good job with this. However, to get to the place where we add our jar reference, we need to change the solution explorer view.

Changing the Solution Explorer View
To do that, we click that Android drop down menu (with the little green droid and the down arrow) at the top left of solution explorer. When we drop the list it will look like the following:

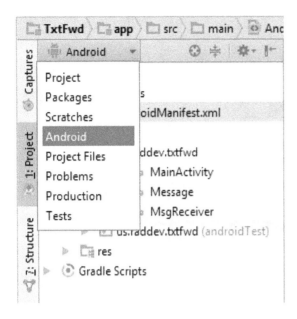

We want to choose the [Project] menu item which will reveal a bit more of the Project folder hierarchy to us.

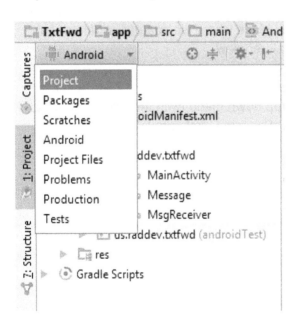

When you click the [Project] item, the solution explorer view will change.

The item we are interested in is the [libs] folder.

That is where we are going to add our new jar file so that it will be built into our solution and the Firebase API methods will become available to us for use.

Drag and Drop the Jar

To do this we can simply go to the location (using File Explorer) where you originally saved the jar file when you downloaded it and drag it and drop it. It'll look like the following:

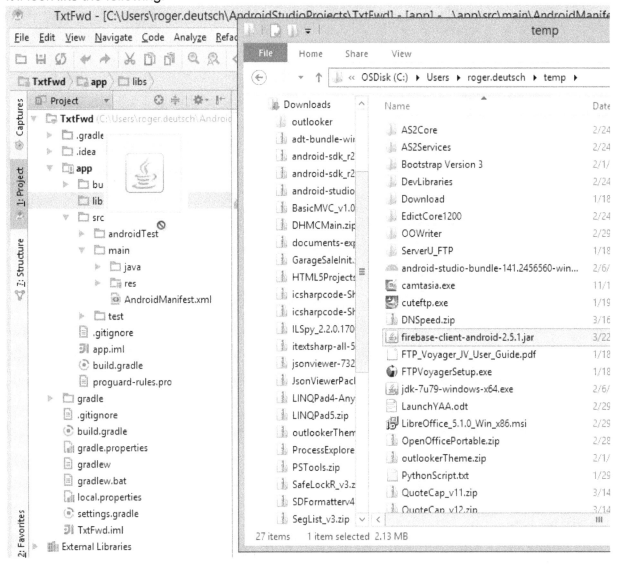

When you drop the file into the libs folder Android Studio will warn you about what you are doing and ask you to confirm the action.

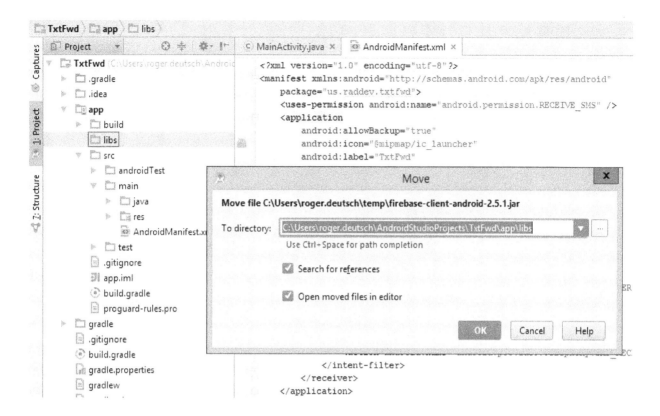

Click the [OK] button and Android Studio will warn you with the following (somewhat confusing dialog):

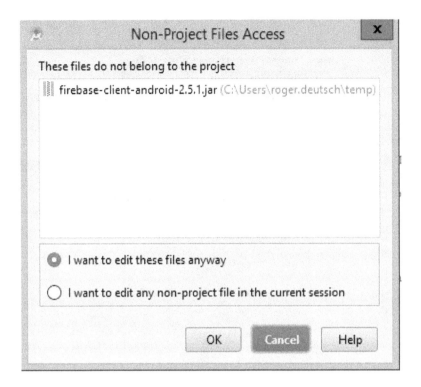

It's trying to tell you that you are changing your project. Make sure the [I want to edit these files anyway] radio button is selected and then click the [OK] button.

Now if you expand the [libs] folder you will see that the Firebase jar has been added.

Now, we need to explicitly add the library to Android Studio. Right-click on the jar file in solution explorer and then choose the [Add as library...] menu item.

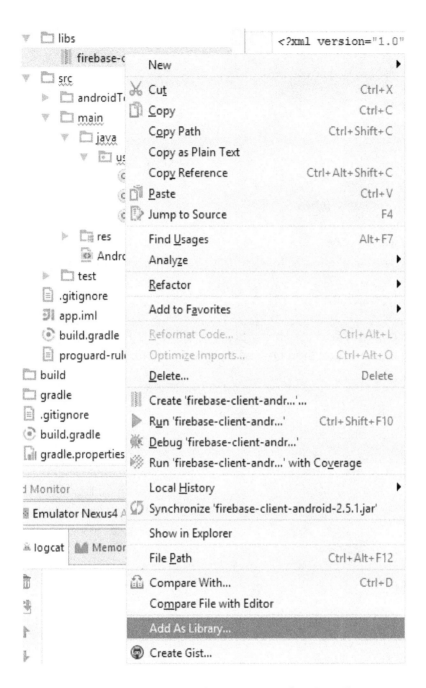

When you choose [Add As LIbrary...] then Studio will prompt you with a dialog.

You can click the [OK] button to add the library.

When you complete that step, some information is added to the Gradle build file automatically for you. If you were to look at that file you'd see it at the bottom:

```
dependencies {
    compile fileTree(dir: 'libs', include: ['*.jar'])
    testCompile 'junit:junit:4.12'
    compile 'com.android.support:appcompat-v7:23.1.1'
    compile 'com.android.support:design:23.1.1'
    compile files('libs/firebase-client-android-2.5.0.jar')
}
```

Adding the library added that last line.

We are still in Project view and the Android view is much cleaner so let's drop that original menu and choose Android again so we are back to our normal solution explorer view.

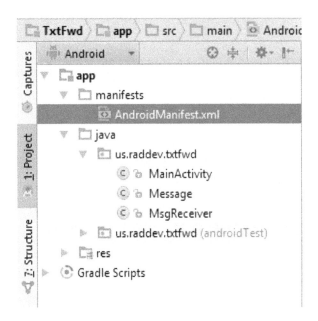

After I added that I went ahead and built the project again.
If it doesn't seem to build try cleaning the project and then building again.
Sometimes Studio and Gradle get out of sync.

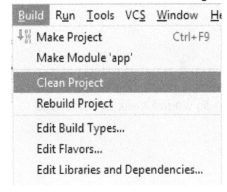

Then I built again and all the issues went away.

At this point we have the Firebase library added and ready to be referenced, but we are not using it yet. It is necessary to initialize Firebase before using it and we'll see how to do that. First we need to add a permission to our manifest though, because Firebase obviously saves our data at a remote location using the Internet as the transport. That means we have to add the Internet permission to our app.

Open up AndroidManifest.xml and add the following:

```xml
<uses-permission android:name="android.permission.INTERNET" />
```

Now, we have given two permissions to our app and our manifest looks like the following:

```
MainActivity.java ×    AndroidManifest.xml ×

<?xml version="1.0" encoding="utf-8"?>
<manifest xmlns:android="http://schemas.android.com/apk/res/android"
    package="us.raddev.txtfwd">
    <uses-permission android:name="android.permission.RECEIVE_SMS" />
    <uses-permission android:name="android.permission.INTERNET" />
    <application
        android:allowBackup="true"
        android:icon="@mipmap/ic_launcher"
        android:label="TxtFwd"
        android:supportsRtl="true"
        android:theme="@style/AppTheme">
        <activity
            android:name=".MainActivity"
            android:label="TxtFwd"
            android:theme="@style/AppTheme.NoActionBar">
            <intent-filter>
                <action android:name="android.intent.action.MAIN" />

                <category android:name="android.intent.category.LAUNCHER" />
            </intent-filter>
        </activity>
        <receiver android:name=".MsgReceiver">
            <intent-filter>
                <action android:name="android.provider.Telephony.SMS_RECEIVED"/>
            </intent-filter>
        </receiver>
    </application>

</manifest>
```

Initialize Firebase

To get the Firebase storage to work for us we have to call a one time initialization when our app starts. We can do that work in our MainActivity onCreate() since it starts when the app starts.

It's just one line of code to add and it looks like the following:

```
Firebase.setAndroidContext(this);
```

When you add that line, Studio will prompt you to add the Firebase import. The code in the MainAcitivty class will look like the following:

```
import android.view.MenuItem;

import com.firebase.client.Firebase;

public class MainActivity extends AppCompatActivity {

    @Override
    protected void onCreate(Bundle savedInstanceState) {
        super.onCreate(savedInstanceState);
        setContentView(R.layout.activity_main);
        Firebase.setAndroidContext(this);
        Toolbar toolbar = (Toolbar) findViewById(R.id.toolbar);
        setSupportActionBar(toolbar);

        FloatingActionButton fab = (FloatingActionButton) findViewById(R.id.fab);
        fab.setOnClickListener((view) -> {
                Snackbar.make(view, "Replace with your own action", Snackbar.LENGTH_LONG)
                        .setAction("Action", null).show();
        });
    }
```

Once you add that line, Firebase is ready to work for you. It's really very easy to use Firebase so lets add a few lines in the MsgReceiver class to write a record out to the Firebase store and then I'll give you the code you can build and test out.

First of all here's what the code that I'm adding looks like the in the MsgReceiver class.

```java
    public void onReceive(Context context, Intent intent) {

        Random rand = new Random();

        Long  userId = rand.nextLong() + 1;
        Firebase myFirebaseRef = new Firebase("https://txtfwd.firebaseio.com/demo/" +
                String.valueOf(userId) + "/");

        SmsMessage message = null;
        if (Build.VERSION.SDK_INT >= 19) {
            Log.d("MainActivity", "I'm an NEWER API LEVEL : " + Build.VERSION.SDK_INT);
            SmsMessage[] msgs = Telephony.Sms.Intents.getMessagesFromIntent(intent);
            message = msgs[0];
        }
        else {
            Log.d("MainActivity", "I'm an older API LEVEL : " + Build.VERSION.SDK_INT);
            Bundle bundle = intent.getExtras();
            Object pdus[] = (Object[]) bundle.get("pdus");
            message = SmsMessage.createFromPdu((byte[]) pdus[0]);
        }

        String from = message.getOriginatingAddress();
        String body = message.getMessageBody();
        long receivedDate = message.getTimestampMillis();
        Date date = new Date(receivedDate);
        DateFormat formatter = new SimpleDateFormat("MM/dd/yyyy - HH:mm:ss");
        String formattedDate = formatter.format(date);

        myFirebaseRef.child("dateTime").setValue(formattedDate);
        myFirebaseRef.child("body").setValue(body);

        Message msg = new Message(from, body, formattedDate, true);
        Log.d("MainActivity", "from : "+ from);
        Log.d("MainActivity", "body : " + body);
```

The lines which write to the Firebase storage are the two lines near the
bottom which I've highlighted. Before we look more closely at those let's take
a look at the first lines in the onRecieve() method.

The first thing I do is new up a Random object. The Random object allows
me to generate random values. In this case I am generating a random Long
value (8 byte value -- which is an extremely large number). I do this to
generate a fake userId each time the the app receives a message. This is
just for our testing purposes.

Create Firebase URL

Once I generate the fake userId I use it to create a Firebase URL which will point to the place where we will store our data.

In this case our Firebase URL will have a node named demo which will contain zero to many userId values. Each of the userId values will be a node which I use to write the dateTime and body (message text) to the storage.

This means that every time the application gets a new message it will generate a new fake userId and then add the dateTime and body (message text) values underneath.

Let's run the app and see what happens.

You can get the code up to this point at:
TxtFwd_v02.zip

If you build and run that code you will see there is no longer a toast message that appears, but instead the values are written to logcat.

You can see the from (I changed the number to 5551230) and the receivedDate where you can see that I am up after midnight writing this code and chapter of the book. :)

You can also see that I was running on an emulator that is running API Level 19 (Android 4.4) so it logs that I'm on the NEWER API LEVEL.

However, the code not only writes to the logcat, it also writes to the Firebase store. Here's what that looks like:

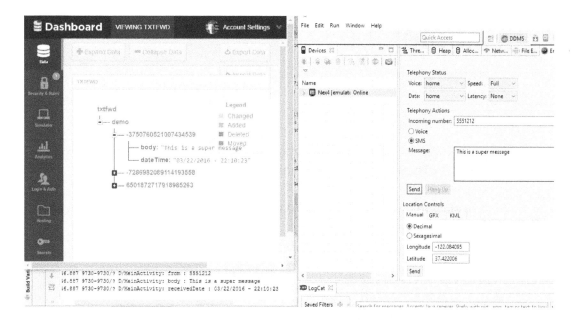

In this case I've stacked all the windows so you can see a few things.

1. On the far right I've sent a message (This is a super message) using the DDMS.

2. To the left you can see that the message was written at
   `txtfwd\demo\3750760521007434539\body`

3. You can also see at the bottom left that logcat also has the message written to it.

Now, any time the TxtFwd app is running on your device and you are connected to the Internet, your incoming text messages will be forwarded to this location.

Chapter 11
Continuing Work On TxtFwd

Obviously, the TxtFwd app was not complete as we left the last section of chapter 10. There are quite a few things to work on.

First of all, you have no way to view your forwarded messages from a web page.
Which obviously precludes you from replying to them also.

Ad Hoc Access and Security Challenge

The foremost thing about this app is that I want to allow you to try it out using my Firebase storage location if you'd like so you can get a feel for how it works.
However, that means your text message will be forwarded to my Firebase location (https://txtfwd.firebaseio.com). Even though the message is sent over a secure (SSL) channel, the message is plaintext after it arrives at Firebase.

DISCLAIMER: That means I would be able to read your forwarded text messages since the data is stored at my Firebase storage location.

The Easy Way To Solve This Problem

The easiest and most secure way to solve the problem is:
You should obtain your own free dev database at Firebase.com and then change the URL to your own in the MsgReceiver class and any other places where the Firebase URL is used in the TxtFwd app.

The Other Security Issue

The other issue is that I want to allow you to test the app before you go through all the work of learning all the code. I think if you see it working it will drive your interest and curiosity and I'm sure there will be a number of people who just want to see this thing work.

However, that means I need to be able to identify various users so I can allow them to see their own messages and only their own messages.

The Challenge of Identity Verification

Identifying a user is an entire project in itself, but we're trying to get to the core functionality of this app. There are at least a couple of ways to identify a user. One of the best ways is the Social Login (OAUTH) via Google+, Facebook or Twitter.

Using Social Login

This is one of the most secure ways to identify a user, however it can be one of the most difficult ways also. It's not necessarily just the difficulty of the work, but there is a lot to learn related to doing this. Using the social login we could force the user to login to the app (and web site) using her Twitter or Google+ account. That way you can tie the activity in the app to the Twitter or Google+ ID and only allow the authenticated user to retrieve the text messages and reply.

TxtFwd Is A Novelty App For Learning

However, TxtFwd is a novelty app to help you learn Android programming. Implementing the social login (OAUTH) is a lot of work for even just one social account like Twitter. There are a lot of things to do to incorporate the social login. I'm going to show you how to do that in my next book on advanced topics but for now it's just too much.

Alternate Identification Method

Fortunately Firebase provides a simple framework for implementing the identity work we need. It is the simplest way I can have the app and system identify the running user and connect her to the proper Firebase location so that is how we'll move forward in this section. However, please keep in mind that while Firebase's method is secure way to identify users the TxtFwd app is simply a tool for learning how you might implement this type of code.

Hardcoded Identity Values

Also, in an attempt to allow a user to easily try out the app I'm going to hardcode some values on the user's app on the device and use those values to help identify the user.   You will see all of the code along the way and know how it works but I wanted everything to be up front so you can decide if you want to use the app or not.

Incoming Number Filter

I will also show you how to set up a filter so you can run the app and only forward messages which come into your phone from a specific number. That way, not all of your messages are forwarded and you can try it on a limited basis if you want.

To create a very good number filter however, you really need to be able to easily grab the number you want from a list of numbers that you have already received a text from.

Capture Incoming Numbers

I'll add a feature to TxtFwd which allows you to turn on the capturing of incoming phone numbers. I'll display the items in a ListView and you'll be able to add them to a spinner (droplist) which will create a filter of numbers you want to forward.

More Sqlite

The best way I can think of to keep a list of numbers is to store them in a Sqlite database. Doing that will allow us to set a value and then query to determine if the incoming number is in the filter list or not and it will be very easy to do with a query to the database.

We saw a lot of the code that need to do that work when we created the QuoteCap application so I'll hit the high points here so you'll know what the database structure looks like.

Creating the Database

First, I added a Database Contract class to describe our table which I named capturedNumber. This table will be in a file named TxtFwd.db and will contain three fields:
1. **_id** - unique identity for the row
2. **contactNumber** - the incoming number
3. **isFilterOn** - an integer value which will represent a boolean true (1) or false (0) as an easy way to determine if this number has been added to the filter

```java
package us.raddev.txtfwd;

import android.provider.BaseColumns;

/**
 * Created by roger.deutsch on 4/4/2016.
 */
public class TxtFwdNumberDatabaseContract {
    private static final String TEXT_TYPE = " TEXT";
    private static final String INT_TYPE = " INT";
    private static final String COMMA_SEP = ",";
    public static final String SQL_CREATE_TXTFWD_NUMBER =
            "CREATE TABLE " + TxtFwdTableDef.TABLE_NAME + " (" +
                    TxtFwdTableDef._ID + " INTEGER PRIMARY KEY," +
                    TxtFwdTableDef.COLUMN_NAME_CONTACT_NUMBER + TEXT_TYPE + " UNIQUE, " +
                    TxtFwdTableDef.COLUMN_NAME_FILTER_ON + INT_TYPE +    " )";


    /* inner classes define tables */
    public static abstract class TxtFwdTableDef implements BaseColumns {
        public static final String TABLE_NAME = "capturedNumber";
        public static final String COLUMN_NAME_CONTACT_NUMBER = "contactNumber";
        public static final String COLUMN_NAME_FILTER_ON = "isFilterOn";
    }
}
```

You can see that I've also added a UNIQUE constraint on the contactNumber field. That way we will only add a number to the database one time (it will be unique) even if we receive more than one message from that number.

Here's a snapshot of some data (with fake numbers) from a query to the table:

Of course I also created a TxtFwdDatabaseHelper which will create the database the first time it is accessed. It's a very simple class which executes the SQL create database statement.

```
 */
public class TxtFwdDatabaseHelper extends SQLiteOpenHelper{
    public static final int DB_VERSION = 1;
    public static final String DB_NAME = "txtfwd.db";

    public TxtFwdDatabaseHelper(Context context) { super(context, DB_NAME,null, DB_VERSION); }

    @Override
    public void onCreate(SQLiteDatabase db) {
        Log.d("MainActivity", "creating DB...");
        db.execSQL(TxtFwdNumberDatabaseContract.SQL_CREATE_TXTFWD_NUMBER);
    }

    @Override
    public void onUpgrade(SQLiteDatabase db, int oldVersion, int newVersion) {

    }
}
```

Finally, of course there is a lot of work to get the GUI (Graphical User Interface) to display the data we have stored in the database and allow the user to configure the app for her use.

A look at the final app will help me explain the functionality of the app.

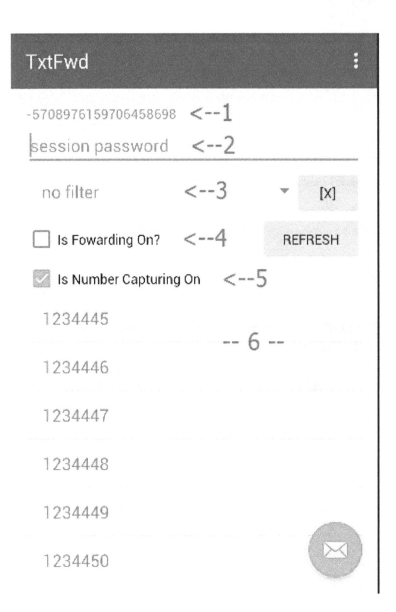

1. This is the globally unique ID that was generated to identify you and your messages. Keep in mind that this is just a randomly generated number.
2. Here you can see the hint text (session password). This allows the user to generate a session password which is then hashed and written to the Firebase storage location (over SSL so no one can

eavesdrop and grab the value). This allows the user to change the password as often or rarely as she wishes. Since the password is written and read in real-time (thanks to the Firebase API) the user can alter this value and other web sessions which could possibly be viewing her messages would (on other devices) would instantly be locked out. We'll talk more about how this works when we look at the web site that allows the user to view and reply to her forwarded messages.

3. This a spinner (droplist) which contains the list of numbers which are currently in the filter. Since the user has currently selected "no filter" it means that all messages that come into the phone would be forwarded. However, unless the next item we talk about (checkbox) is checked no messages are ever forwarded.

4. Is Forwarding On checkbox. This allows the user to turn off all forwarding with one tap. If this option is on and the "no filter" option is selected then all messages will be forwarded. However, if this option is checked and any item in the droplist is chosen then only the numbers which show up in the spinner list will be forwarded. Keep in mind that if forwarding is on, then even if the app is not running those messages will be forwarded. Uncheck this option if you don't want any messages forwarded. Don't just close the app to do that.

5. Is Number Capturing On checkbox. This checkbox allows you to turn number capturing on and off (checked or unchecked). Keep in mind that number capturing will occur even if the app is not running. That means if number capturing is on then every number that you receive a text from will be captured in the database.

6. This is a scrollable ListView of all the numbers that are captured in your database. If you touch one it can be added to your filter list (spinner from #3 above).

Here's a look at the spinner when it's opened for selection:

There are also a couple of buttons to allow the user to do some work.

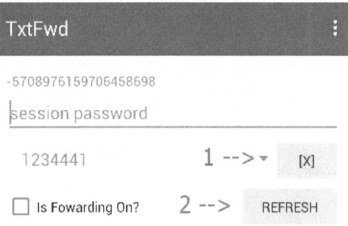

1. Allows the user to remove the item from the filter list. This only removes the item from the Spinner, but of course it leaves the value in the database.

2. The refresh button allows the user to refresh the ListView from the database to insure all captured numbers appear in the list. The read from the database and the initialization of the ListView only occurs when the app is started so if the user receives messages from new numbers while the app is running they wouldn't show up again until the next time you run. This alleviates that issue. There is a way around this but it can be a bit challenging and requires quite a bit more work since you have to take into account that numbers can be captured even when the app (and MainActivity) is not running.

First of all, let's take a look at the simple code that I use to iterate through the database to load the numbers into the ListView and Spinner when the app starts up.

You'll see that I create ArrayLists of the Message class so we can easily retrieve values we need to manage the display of data on screen.

You can see where this work is done in the MainActivity method initializeLists().

```java
    private void initializeLists() {
        TxtFwdDatabaseHelper dbh = new TxtFwdDatabaseHelper(this);

        Log.d("MainActivity", "querying database");
        SQLiteDatabase db = dbh.getReadableDatabase();

        try {
            Cursor c = null;
            String query = "select * from capturedNumber";
            Log.d("MainActivity", query);
            c = db.rawQuery(query, null);

            while (c.moveToNext()) {
                String contactNumber = c.getString(c.getColumnIndex("contactNumber"));
                int capturedNumberId = c.getInt(c.getColumnIndex("_id"));
                int isFilterOn = c.getInt(c.getColumnIndex("isFilterOn"));
                Log.d("MainActivity", "text from query : " + contactNumber);
                Message m = new Message(contactNumber, capturedNumberId);

                numberAdapter.add(m);
                if (isFilterOn == 1) {
                    adapter2.add(m);
                }
            }
            c.close();
            numberAdapter.notifyDataSetChanged();
            //adapter.notifyDataSetChanged();
        } catch (Exception e) {
            Log.d("MainActivity", e.getMessage());
        }
    }
```

This method (intializeLists()) is called from the onCreate() method when the app starts so that the ListView and Spinner are initialized with the appropriate values.

The first thing we do is new up a TxtFwdDatabaseHelper so we can get a readable database which will allow us to query the database.

```java
TxtFwdDatabaseHelper dbh = new TxtFwdDatabaseHelper(this);

Log.d("MainActivity", "querying database");
SQLiteDatabase db = dbh.getReadableDatabase();
```

The interesting code, however, is the code in the while loop. That is where we add new Messages (Message objects) to each adapter which is attached to the ListView and Spinner controls.

```
while (c.moveToNext()) {
    String contactNumber =
c.getString(c.getColumnIndex("contactNumber"));
    int capturedNumberId = c.getInt(c.getColumnIndex("_id"));
    int isFilterOn = c.getInt(c.getColumnIndex("isFilterOn"));
    Log.d("MainActivity", "text from query : " + contactNumber);
    Message m = new Message(contactNumber, capturedNumberId);

    numberAdapter.add(m);
    if (isFilterOn == 1) {
        adapter2.add(m);
    }
```

We are iterating through the records in the database, getting the contactNumber, _id and isFilterOn values. We then use these to new up Message objects. The Message object needs to be further developed but it allows us to attach an object (instead of a simple string) to the ListView and Spinner.

Why Attach An Object to A Control

The value of adding the object to the control comes later when the user clicks the item in the ListView or wants to delete the item from the Spinner.
When we write the code for the button which allows the user to remove the item from the Spinner, we also need to update the isFilterOn value to 0 in the database. However, to do that we have to know which row in the database to update. We can do this based upon the _id value.

However, you have to have stored that value somewhere. In our case, since we've attached the message object to the Spinner using the control, then we can easily get the Message object associated with the currently selected item in the Spinner. Then we can obtain the associated _id value and use it to update the value in the database.

Taking a look at the code in the deleteButton's onClick() is instructive about how this works.

C MainActivity.java ×   content_main.xml ×   C TxtFwdDatabaseHelper.java ×   Androi

```java
        deleteButton.setOnClickListener(new View.OnClickListener() {
            @Override
            public void onClick(View v) {
                Message item = (Message)spinner.getSelectedItem();
                String itemText = item.get_originatingNumber();
                if (itemText != "no filter")
                {
                    updateNumberFilter(item.get_capturedNumberId(), false);
                    spinnerAdapter.remove(item);
                    spinnerAdapter.notifyDataSetChanged();
                }
            }
        });
```

The first thing we do is get the currently selected Spinner item. When we do that using the Spinner control's getSelectedItem() method it will return the associated object. Since the control allows you to store a generic object you have to cast the object to the type that you know you originally stored. In our case that is the Message object. Now, because we set our Message object's _originatingNumber member to the value of the original number (and that is the value displayed in the Spinner) we can use it to simply insure we are not deleting the default item with the text "no filter".

Updating the Value In the Database

Once we insure that we are attempting to delete another item we call the updateNumberFilter() method with the item's capturedNumberId (_id) and send in a value (false) indicating that we want the isFilterOn to be set to 0 since this item will no longer be a part of the filter.

```java
private void updateNumberFilter(int capturedNumberId, boolean isActive) {
    Log.d("MainActivity", "capturedNumberId : " + capturedNumberId);
    TxtFwdDatabaseHelper dbh = new TxtFwdDatabaseHelper(this);

    Log.d("MainActivity", "Saving number to database...");
    SQLiteDatabase db = dbh.getWritableDatabase();

    ContentValues values = new ContentValues();

    values.put(TxtFwdNumberDatabaseContract.TxtFwdTableDef.COLUMN_NAME_FILTER_ON,
            isActive ? 1 : 0);
    long updatedRowId = db.update(
            TxtFwdNumberDatabaseContract.TxtFwdTableDef.TABLE_NAME,
            values,
            "_id = " + String.valueOf(capturedNumberId),
            null);
    Log.d("MainActivity", "updatedRowId : " + String.valueOf(updatedRowId));
}
```

This method sets up the objects we need so we can update the database. Then we call the db.update() method which will set the isFilterOn for the specific _id value to be 0. That means the item will no longer show up in the Spinner when the app initializes the controls.

Back in our deleteButton's onClick() method, we remove the item from the spinner by calling the remove() method with the object that we want removed. Finally, we make sure the adapter is updated so the control will reflect the removal we've just done.

Saving Session Password

Let's look a bit closer at saving our session password and what it does. Then after that we'll wrap this up with a look at how

I implemented the save from the application's settings menu simply because it was easy to get to that code.

When you type a password and click the [Save sesson pwd] item the application will do the following:
1. Hash the password
2. Convert hash to Base64 encoding -- this insures that every byte is converted to a displayable and easily transmittable character over the Internet.
3. Transmits the Base64 encoded hash over SSL (using Firebase API) to your Firebase storage location.

When you click that button the data written to the Firebase location will look the following:

```
txtfwd
  └── demo
       ⊞── -445264127371575680
       ⊟── -57089761597064586 98
            ⊟── Messages
                 ⊞── 1234444
                 ⊞── 1234445
                 ⊞── 1234446
                 ⊞── 1234447
                 ⊞── 1234448
                 ⊞── 1234449
                 ⊞── 1234450
                 ⊞── 1234451
            └── sessionPwd: "5wUkWPA33Gs2Y/DUVHALKhZrw2IyWj55mDk47lxsyf0="  ✕
```

You can see that the Base64 encoded hash is far longer than your original password. That's due to the 256-bit hash we created.

Since that value was transmitted over SSL there is no way anyone else can read that value, but even if they did it wouldn't matter because it is not your original password and since this is a one-way hash (cryptograph) no one else can crack it.

How Is Session Password Used?
I have to provide some means of security when you go the web site to retrieve your messages and this is one of the easiest ways. To retrieve the messages and reply you have to supply the web site with that same password. Since it is cryptographically hashed no one can read it.

Retrieving Messages Via the (Ugly) Web Site

This is all a prototype so it'll probably look better by the time you read this chapter. I'll clean it up on my site and you can generate your own web site to do the work.

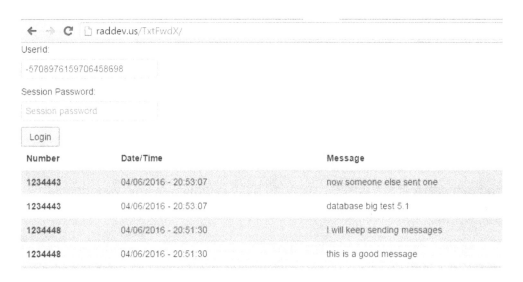

Web Sockets, Like Magic

Those messages were received in real-time. That means as your phone receives a message and forwards it you will see the message appear on your the web page with no refresh. WebSockets makes this magic happen and it is amazing to see your page updated with a new message without doing anything.

Using the Web Message Retriever
You have to know two things to use the Message Retriever / Responder:
1. Your unique user ID found at the top of the TxtFwd App
2. Your Session Password, which you set in your app as we saw earlier.

When you have those two items you can login and your messages will start appearing.

The web code uses the Firebase Web API to do the work of validating your password against the hash. It also retrieves the messages from your Firebase storage location each time one arrives.

That's it for the TxtFwd app. I'll make all the code available for download in the zip file available at my site at: http:/raddev.us/LYAA

Chapter 12
Quick Intro to Signing Up For Google Dev Account

It's finally time for us to sign up for a Google Developer account at the Google Play Developer Console.

You can sign up at:
https://play.google.com/apps/publish/signup/

When you go to that page you'll have to sign in using a Google account. Next, you should read the license agreement because you'll have to accept it to continue.

If you have done all that go ahead and [Continue to payment].

I form will popup so you can fill in your payment information.

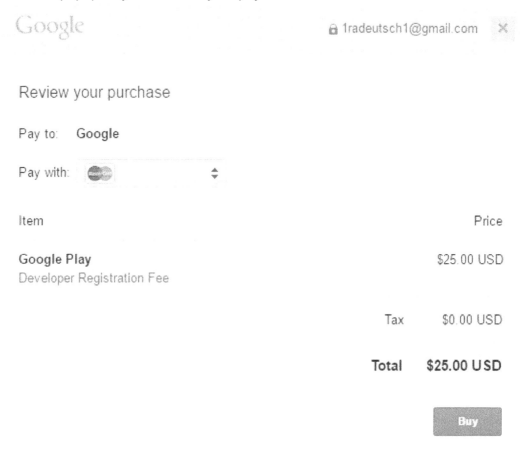

Click the [Buy] button if you'd like continue.

If you don't have a credit card associated with your Google account you will be prompted to enter details to set up a payment method.

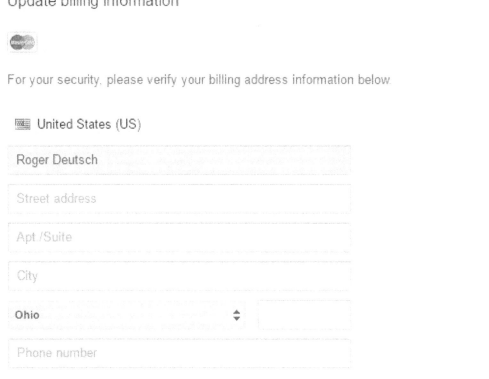

Fill out the form and click the [Buy] button.

When the transactions completes you'll see something like the following:

YOUR PAYMENT IS COMPLETE

You will receive a receipt by email.

Continue registration

Click the [Continue registration] button.

If everything went well you will be registered with your new Google Play account.

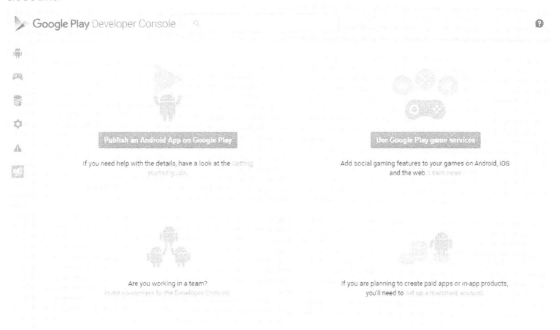

You are now ready to publish your app or set up a merchant account so you can get paid for your apps.

###############################

The End of This Book Is Not The End

We have come to the end, but there is more to this more to this book. If you've followed along for these 480 pages you have learned a lot about Android Studio and building real apps. However, this book is becoming overwhelmingly long. I am going to continue the completion of this app at my web site:

Http://raddev.us/LYAA

I will also be adding any fixes to this book there and I will add other supplementary materials. That is also where you can download all of the code for your use.

I've greatly enjoyed writing this book and I've learned a lot in the process myself. I hope you too have enjoyed it and learned much.

Keep on learning, keep on coding.

~Roger Deutsch 04/06/2016